THE PEKING GAZETTE IN LATE IMPERIAL CHINA

I0892887

The Peking Gazette in Late Imperial China

State News and Political Authority

EMILY MOKROS

UNIVERSITY OF WASHINGTON PRESS
Seattle

The Peking Gazette in Late Imperial China was made possible in part by grants from the Chiang Ching-kuo Foundation for International Scholarly Exchange and from the College of Arts and Sciences and the Department of History at the University of Kentucky.

Copyright © 2021 by the University of Washington Press

Composed in Minion, typeface designed by Robert Slimbach
Maps by Ben Pease, Pease Press Maps, www.peasepress.com

25 24 23 22 21 5 4 3 2 1

Printed and bound in the United States of America

All rights reserved. No part of this publication may be reproduced or transmitted in any form or by any means, electronic or mechanical, including photocopy, recording, or any information storage or retrieval system, without permission in writing from the publisher.

UNIVERSITY OF WASHINGTON PRESS
uwapress.uw.edu

LIBRARY OF CONGRESS CATALOGING-IN-PUBLICATION DATA
LC record available at https://lccn.loc.gov/2020047571
LC ebook record available at https://lccn.loc.gov/2020047572

ISBN 978-0-295-74878-8 (hardcover)
ISBN 978-0-295-74879-5 (paperback)
ISBN 978-0-295-74880-1 (ebook)

The paper used in this publication is acid free and meets the minimum requirements of American National Standard for Information Sciences—Permanence of Paper for Printed Library Materials, ANSI Z39.48–1984.∞

For my parents, Peggy and Hartmut

CONTENTS

ACKNOWLEDGMENTS

It is difficult to believe that I began this project nearly ten years ago. My initial motive for studying gazettes was to understand how spatially disparate subjects of the Qing empire came together to hold meaningful conversations about politics. Along the way, the project's direction has been shaped by my own conversations and relationships, both near and far. In an era when many of us are rethinking assumptions about media, the state, and political culture, there is much to learn from the story of the Qing gazette. I offer gratitude to everyone named here, and many who remain unnamed, for helping to make this book possible.

My deepest thanks go to Tobie Meyer-Fong and Bill Rowe for their rigorous yet patient cultivation of this project. Bill's questions have always found the heart of the matter and kept me thinking. Tobie is unbelievably generous with time, gentle encouragement, and incisive and bountiful advice. I have been extremely lucky to have such diligent and compassionate mentors. At Johns Hopkins University, I thank Yulia Frumer, Ho-Fung Hung, and Yumi Kim for their careful reading and incisive questions. Additionally, Marta Hanson, Erin Chung, Joel Andreas, Victoria Cass, Michael Kwass, Mary Ryan, and others offered questions, advice, and encouragement over the years. At Berkeley, where I had the pleasure of revising the manuscript, I offer gratitude to Wen-hsin Yeh, Nicolas Tackett, and You-tien Hsing for welcoming me into the fold and for offering substantial feedback and advice in the revision process.

For fellowships and grants that supported the research and writing of this project, I am obliged to the Johns Hopkins University, the Fulbright-IIE Program, the China Scholarship Council, Albion College, the China and Inner

Asia Council of the Association for Asian Studies, and the Harvard-Yenching Library. I was especially lucky that the Center for Chinese Studies at the University of California Berkeley offered me a postdoctoral fellowship in 2017–18. They also kindly funded a workshop on the dissertation-to-book process. Elinor Levine and Angel Ryono made sure that the year went seamlessly.

Everyone at the University of Washington Press has been patient, supportive, and efficient in the development and publishing process for this book, even in a time of unprecedented disruptions. I'm grateful to Lorri Hagman for steering this project through publication. Thanks also to Neecole Bostick, Beth Fuget, and Julie Van Pelt. Thanks to Richard Feit for copyediting and Cynthia Col for the index. The two anonymous readers for the press offered numerous trenchant comments and suggestions. I bear sole responsibility for remaining errors. I thank the editors of *Frontiers of History in China* for permission to draw on my article "Spies and Postmen: Communications Liaisons and the Evolution of the Qing Bureaucracy" for portions of chapter 1.

I benefitted immensely from the patient assistance and favors of expert staff at numerous libraries and archives. Thank you to the staff of the First Historical Archive in Beijing, the National Qing History Compilation Project, and the rare book collections at the National Library of China, Beijing University Library, and Nanjing Library. I am also indebted to the many libraries where I did research and writing, including the Taiwan National Palace Museum Library, the Bibliothèque nationale in Paris, the British National Archives, the British Library's Asian and African Reading Room, the School of Oriental and African Studies Archives at the University of London, the Library of Congress, the Center for Research Libraries in Chicago, the New York Public Library, the Gest Library at Princeton University, the Harvard-Yenching Library, and the Milton S. Eisenhower Libraries of Johns Hopkins University, the University of Michigan Asia Library, the Starr East Asian Library at the University of California Berkeley, and the University of Kentucky Libraries. Sara Chiesura and her colleagues at the British Library tirelessly accommodated my requests and curiosities. Martin Heijdra at Princeton University Library had materials digitized and offered substantial advice and encouragement. Xia Yixin at the National Palace Museum in Taiwan helped obtain last-minute illustrations and permissions. Special thanks to the Lieberthal-Rogel Center for Chinese Studies at the University of Michigan for allowing me to be a Center Associate with generous access to library resources.

Special thanks to Chuck Wooldridge for reading and commenting on an early draft, and Liang Luo for reading the final manuscript. I also thank Daniel Hausmann for close readings at many intervals along the way. Beatrice Bartlett has provided generous and honest mentorship on this project since its early stages. I owe special gratitude to Liu Wenpeng and his students for meals and outings in Beijing as well as unparalleled access and advice. Many other mentors and colleagues have offered feedback on portions of the manuscript. Among them, I thank Barbara Mittler, the late Rudolf Wagner, Sarah Schneewind, Lane Harris, Eugenio Menegon, Henrietta Harrison, Richard R. John, and Wen-hsin Yeh.

For sharing sources, advice, questions, and encouragement, I thank, among others, Ting Zhang, Susan Naquin, Pierre-Étienne Will, Luca Gabbiani, James Hevia, Elisabeth Kaske, Mark McNicholas, Kan Hongliu, Noël Golvers, Christopher Cullen, Matthew Sommer, John Carroll, Kai-wing Chow, Ondřej Klimes, Peter Ditmanson, Roger Thompson, He Bian, Yulian Wu, Jenny Huangfu Day, Rachel Silberstein, Maura Dykstra, Peter Thilly, Chelsea Wang, Devin Fitzgerald, Zhang Yichi, Wu Huiyi, Alexander Statman, Zhao Ying, Daniel Barish, Bingyu Zheng, Zhenzhen Lu, and Ma Zhao. While at Berkeley, I benefitted from the scholarly camaraderie of Brooks Jessup, Jonathan Tang, Linh Vu, Stacey Van Vleet, Tristan Brown, and Sixiang Wang. Special thanks to Tim Brook, Cynthia Brokaw, John Dardess, Sarah Schneewind, and Andrea Goldman for their comments on panels at the Association for Asian Studies meetings.

My colleagues and students have been supportive cheerleaders of my scholarship and teaching. Thank you to Yi-Li Wu for generously offering advice on the transition to assistant professor life. At the University of Kentucky, I owe deep gratitude to Karen Petrone, Akiko Takenaka, Phil Harling, and Abigail Firey. Thanks also to my friendly colleagues in History and Asian Studies, especially Vanessa Holden, Jeremy Popkin, Doug Slaymaker, Charlie Zhang, and Sihui (Echo) Ke. Shelley Zhou has been both a model student and a kind friend. The College of Arts and Sciences and to the Department of History offered crucial funding that supported the completion of this book.

Many graduate school pals have been fantastic companions along uneven paths. I benefitted from inspiring conversations, delightful meals, and companionship from my classmates Ting Zhang, Ke Ren, Ying Zhang, Jack Bandy, and Xiaoqian Ji. I am so happy to have developed close friendships with Lauren MacDonald, Ada Link, Will Brown, and Catherine Hinchliff. My Beijing roommates and friends, Zhou Wei, Hai Miao, Elizabeth Weber, and especially Liu Shanshan brightened many lonely days. Mélodie Kinet, Janet Moehring, and Kat Glass have always feted my achievements. I'm also grateful for the longstanding friendship of Rebecca Alderfer Rock, Dave Rock, Charles Greenberg, Rebecca Newhouse, David Yu, Cassie Gare, Michelle Chen, and Cindy Hong.

During the lifetime of this project, my family has grown in wonderful ways. The Carr, Mokros, Carleton, Clark, Hopper, and Jordan families all provided warm company. My siblings Arno, Alex, and Paul have each encouraged my work and provided levity over the years. My mother, Peggy, volunteers even-keeled support and cheerleading at a moment's notice. My father and stepmother, Hartmut and Hester, have always offered advice, encouragement, and comfort, and have stepped in to make life and work bearable in the last year. Joe's companionship and immense support has been constant, whether in the next room or across an ocean. Now, as Miles has joined our family, I could ask for no greater sources of love and motivation.

CHRONOLOGY OF MAJOR DYNASTIES AND QING REIGN PERIODS

QIN	221–206 BCE
HAN	206 BCE–220 CE
SUI	581–618
TANG	618–907
SONG	960–1279
NORTHERN SONG	960–1127
SOUTHERN SONG	1127–1279
YUAN	1271–1368
MING	1368–1644
QING	1636–1912
HONG TAIJI	1636–1643
SHUNZHI (SZ)	1644–1661
KANGXI (KX)	1662–1722
YONGZHENG (YZ)	1723–1735
QIANLONG (QL)	1736–1795
JIAQING (JQ)	1796–1820
DAOGUANG (DG)	1821–1850
XIANFENG (XF)	1851–1861
TONGZHI (TZ)	1862–1875
GUANGXU (GX)	1875–1908
XUANTONG (XT)	1908–1912

MAP FM.1. The Qing Empire, ca.1800

THE PEKING GAZETTE IN LATE IMPERIAL CHINA

Introduction

State, Publicity, and Political Culture in Late Imperial China

ONE LATE AUTUMN DAY IN 1862, WENG TONGHE (1830–1904), A young official in Beijing, the capital of the Qing empire, recorded a dream in his diary.[1] For more than a decade, a massive war had besieged the historically wealthy area surrounding his hometown of Changshu, keeping Weng away from home. In the dream, Weng found himself in his family's study, browsing his library. Before him appeared the ghostly form of the sixteenth-century connoisseur Xiang Yuanbian (1525–1590).[2] That Weng envisioned this meeting taking place among his books evokes the link between the men; Weng's family library held prized volumes once owned by Xiang.[3] Xiang explained that he had come to admire the fine books now housed in Weng's study, and the two discussed recent catastrophes that had caused the destruction of books in both the mortal realm and in the underworld. Many volumes, Xiang said, had been burnt so badly by the fires of war that in the underworld they appeared tattered and incomplete, as if damaged by water. In the afterlife, Xiang remained concerned about the current wars in China, and Weng wrote, "He also told me that he read the gazettes every day, as he had in the living realm. If unsettled events occurred on earth, they were also known in the underworld." The subject of discussion shifted, and Weng woke with a start.[4]

The gazettes (most commonly called *dibao*, *dichao*, or *jingbao* in Chinese) invoked in Weng Tonghe's dream belonged to a genre of official texts that granted access to state news for readers across the Qing empire, around the globe, and, if only in Weng's dream, into the underworld.[5] Published daily, these compact pamphlets reproduced edicts, listed imperial audiences, noted personnel transfers, and summarized memorials authored by capital and field bureaucrats. In Beijing, court officials selected documents for public release. From there, clerks recorded transcriptions, craftsmen laid print, local scribes made thousands of additional copies, and couriers delivered the gazettes throughout the realm.[6] In some senses, gazettes were a time-honored institution: precursors had been published by the court of the Song dynasty almost a thousand years prior. Late imperial scholars traced the lineage of state institutions involved in the publication of gazettes.[7] But in the nineteenth century, the reach of the Qing Gazette, called the Peking Gazette by foreigners, was unprecedented.[8] By 1862, readers of the London *Standard*, the Paris *Gazette de France*, the Shanghai *North-China Herald*, and the Hong Kong *China Mail*, among others, encountered translations from Chinese gazettes.[9] The Qing Gazette had entered global circulation.

This book begins with the seventeenth-century restoration of court gazettes as instruments of empire by the early Qing state and ends with their presumed disappearance in 1907, superseded by a new breed of government gazettes that drew on international models for public information. While the early Qing court resurrected gazettes to help restructure the bureaucracy and obtain the support of Chinese officials and elites, late Qing intellectuals and statesmen reconceived gazettes to be symbols of national legitimacy and tools of public instruction. As much as the sources permit, I offer a detailed chronology of policy, publishing, and reception, attentive to both continuities and changes in the political, administrative, and cultural role of gazettes.[10] Spatial and temporal frameworks are both essential to this story. The production, reception, and use of political news are situated in personal contexts of office and home, in local contexts of city and court, and in global contexts of empire. That personal, local, and global settings overlap serves as a reminder that "information" is both a tangible category—touched, inscribed, and read—and an abstract medium of exchange.

This book therefore deals with several key questions. What led the Qing state to expand the circulation of court gazettes during its reign in China? What did gazettes say to their readers about the nature and operations of the state, its politics and laws? How might reading and interactions around official news have shaped political culture during the Qing dynasty? From there, how and why did Chinese news come to occupy the attention of readers around the globe? Finally, why do gazettes matter for how we think about Qing China in the twenty-first century?

The Meanings of State News

By Xiang's time, and certainly in the era of Weng Tonghe, educated audiences acknowledged gazettes to be the most authoritative recurring source of political news of court and bureaucracy.[11] The many names employed to designate gazettes reveal the genre's historical and cultural significance. In its earliest sense, *dibao* referred to documentary intelligence collected by capital representatives. By the late Ming dynasty, the term *dibao* applied not only to court gazettes, but also to newsletters of a document-based format associated with capital politics.[12] Another common usage, *jingbao* (capital news), points to the genre's focus on metropolitan politics and origin in the communications pathways of the imperial capital.[13]

The common inclusion of references to scribal or print reproduction in the character *chao* (抄 or 鈔, used in the compounds *dichao, jingchao*, or *chaobao*, all variant names for gazettes) implies that political news derived from the process of excerpting and recopying state documents, rather than direct compositions by observers.[14] Layers of secrecy, criticism, and intrigue often accompanied the circulation of leaked and recopied documents and flavored the development of news culture in late imperial China. Gazettes drew authority from their origin in state documents, but they could be gathered and disseminated in both legal and illicit fashions. Some readers even made use of "unofficial gazettes" (*xiaobao* or *xiaochao*) compiled by private individuals that perhaps recounted unsanctioned intelligence or offered more critical perspectives.[15]

Other forms of communication outmatched state publications in their penetration of local society and relevance to ordinary people. Among non-elite and rural populations in China, oral networks predominated in news circulation through the early twentieth century.[16] Whether oral information qualified as rumor or as news was related to perceptions of trust and familiarity within social networks. Through letters with family and far-flung correspondents, merchants, literati, and scholar-officials made sense of political transitions. Still, even non-literates in nineteenth-century China demonstrated awareness that gazettes were the paramount source for official news.[17]

Gazettes in the Qing empire played a more significant political role than did state journals in other early modern news environments.[18] Not only did the Qing state devote considerable energy to supporting its official journal, but also scholar-officials throughout the late imperial period interpreted reading gazettes as a requisite practice for informed participation in the political community. In Mughal India, whereas princely states compiled court diaries, oral communication networks prevailed in local society.[19] In early modern Europe, written news proliferated amid commercial, intellectual, and political transitions in distinct regional and national contexts. Two genres that emerged in Europe but were not prominent in Chinese history are merchant newsletters and politically oriented publications that antagonized rivals and treated foreign as well as domestic news.[20] In Europe, savvy audiences claimed to scorn state publications, which often struggled in competition with private outlets. In China, some readers used *xiaobao* and other non-official publications and correspondence to poke holes in state-produced accounts. However, no informed reader would neglect to consult the state news.

Inside the Chinese Gazette

No original copies of gazettes survive from the age of Xiang Yuanbian, but Qing dynasty gazettes are found in libraries around the world. The majority of surviving copies date to the nineteenth century. Few if any verified originals have been found from earlier than the eighteenth century.[21] A substantial proportion of extant editions are found in foreign, particularly European, collections, testifying to longstanding interest in collecting Chinese state news.[22] In China, by contrast, gazettes were ephemeral texts, not collectibles, leading to their rarity in archives and library collections. Although an internet resale market for gazettes has heated up in the present era, they were used as wall coverings and wrapping paper through the mid-twentieth century.[23] Gazettes survive in a variety of formats and appearances: handwritten and printed, squat squarish booklets and slim yellow-covered pamphlets, both pristine and marked with marginalia. These distinctions evince the variety of publishing formats employed within the commercial gazette trade, as well as the differing ways that readers handled their gazette copies. A glimpse inside one nineteenth-century gazette helps us envision the experience of reading state news in Weng Tonghe's day (figures I.1a, b, and c).

Beijing residents like Weng purchased gazettes in roughly printed pamphlets with yellow covers, stamped with the title *Capital Gazette* (Jingbao) and the name of a publisher such as Hecheng Baofang, an outlet in Beijing. Though no price was affixed to the booklet, gazettes could be purchased individually for about ten copper coins, delivered by monthly subscription, or even rented and returned. Inside, the first page included the date of the edition and a brief

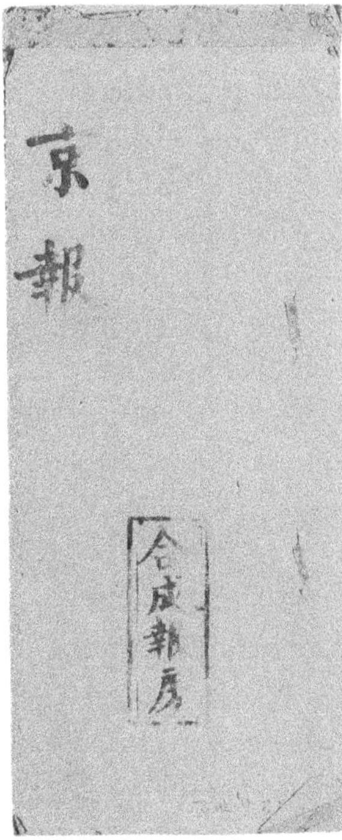

a

b

FIGURE I.1. (a) Cover, (b) contents, and (c) interior of a Beijing gazette, dated September 30, 1864 (TZ 03/08/30). Courtesy of the East Asian Library and the Gest Collection, Princeton University Library.

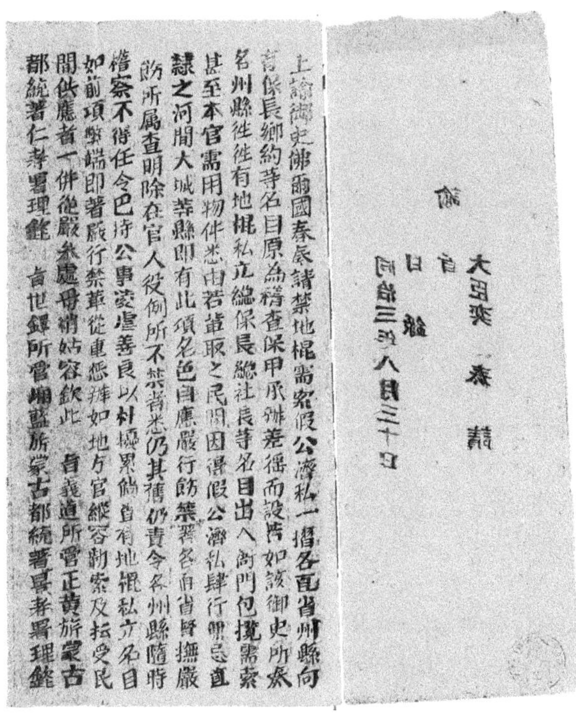

c

table of contents. Like many imperial publications that gave precedence to the emperor's words, gazettes listed the emperor's latest edicts and rescripts (*yuzhi*) as the first item, followed by memorials listed by author and type. The table of contents of the copy pictured here, dated September 30, 1864 (thirtieth day, eighth month, third year of the Tongzhi reign), lists a single memorial authored by Yikuang, Prince Qing (1838–1917). On the next page the entries began, packed into wobbly columns suggestive of the movable-type process used in late nineteenth-century gazette publishing. In total, this issue numbered nine pages, although these pages were of unequal length—in order to include the full text of some lengthier items, publishers commonly folded wider sheets of thin paper into the uniform-width pamphlets.

The main contents of gazettes encapsulated communications between court and official. The first edict urged greater oversight of "local toughs" who pretended to act on behalf of local administrators but in fact served their own interests. It was followed by two brief notices regarding military appointments. Next came an edict concerning funding to plant trees on routes to the imperial tombs in the suburbs of Beijing.[24] The first memorial followed, authored by Yikuang together with the imperial clansman Zai Dai and the elite Manchu official Wenjun. This report concerned the recent and embarrassing desecration of the tomb of a consort of the long-dead Kangxi emperor.[25] A second and final memorial, also authored by Yikuang and the two others in their capacity as guardians of the Eastern Tombs, returned to the matter of the trees.

These items do not correspond to business transacted on a specific day as did the court diaries (*qijuzhu*), nor do they relate directly to the entries written for the historical annals known as the *Veritable Records* (Shilu). Clerks abridged government communications into gazette entries similarly to the ways they shortened memorials for inclusion in the *Veritable Records*. However, these two records were compiled for different purposes. Whereas the *Veritable Records* treated an entire reign period, gazettes were produced in real time. Some gazettes, compiled for specific audiences, focused on items pertaining to individual provinces or agendas. Most Beijing gazettes prioritized ongoing matters of consequence to the larger bureaucracy or the court's current concerns. Thus, the imperial edict concerning "local toughs" contained instructions directed to "all provincial governors" and "all district magistrates." The two memorials likely prompted the emperor's comments on the repair of the imperial tombs; whereas the edict was promulgated on

September 28 (two days prior to the gazette's publication), the memorials had been presented several days prior.

Gazettes privileged the emperor's words but also included treatises by statesmen. Importantly, memorials were published only after an imperial response had been released—the court did not permit gazettes to reveal items still under consideration. Not all gazettes were organized around a single topic; most varied in contents. The gazette issue profiled here focused on the imperial tombs, excluding an edict found in the *Veritable Records* for the same date regarding the then-current Nian Rebellion, or one that responded to a troubling accusation of disloyalty among field officials. The exclusion of these two items may have resulted from their relevance to ongoing military campaigns. The decision to keep certain military discussions out of circulation had been made in the preceding decade out of concerns about weakened information security. Indeed, the Qing state administered gazettes according to an evolving set of agendas. As a result, any single gazette issue is a snapshot of state news as it was read at a given moment in the history of the dynasty.

State News and Its Audiences

Prior to the advent of the mass press in China, state news was one of the most important genres of information exchanged on a regular basis by members of the bureaucracy and their families, employees, and acquaintances. State-sponsored gazettes were the main vehicle by which such news was conveyed from the state to readers. Only relative elites had the means to purchase gazettes and the political awareness to make gazettes meaningful and comprehend their terse documentary language. However, gazettes were widely known in late imperial society. Over the course of the Qing dynasty, this limited audience grew larger, and by the nineteenth century, readers with fairly casual interests and cursory understandings of statecraft and politics began to peruse gazettes.

If we imagine Weng Tonghe and Xiang Yuanbian continuing their conversation, these two men might realize that not only did they read fairly different texts, they belonged to distinct reading communities. For his part, Xiang presumably drew upon handwritten copies of court news that circulated in the late Ming dynasty. Although no original editions of Ming gazettes have survived to the present day, archival records and reader's notes indicate that official editions relayed capital news with a special orientation toward regional officials.[26] Unofficial editions were said to offer more ideologically motivated perspectives on the state, especially in moments of crisis when state publishing lapsed. Though not an official himself, Xiang, whose brothers held high office, possessed the social connections to read gazettes with an insider's eye. Xiang and other men of his position embedded notes on their gazette readings in correspondence, jottings, and essays that manifest close ties between elite readers and the personages mentioned in the official dispatches.[27] Characteristic of the intense moral politics of the era, written and spoken conversations involving gazettes centered on the words and deeds of the men featured within them.[28]

Social and economic transitions between the sixteenth and the nineteenth centuries underlay the evolution of Chinese official news and its readership and the political culture in which this readership participated.[29] Printing and publishing blossomed from the late Ming dynasty onward. Most importantly, the declining cost of labor and the increasing availability of component resources transformed printing from a slow and strictly controlled enterprise to a dynamic set of speedy, highly mobile, and cost-efficient practices.[30] For most of its history and across most of the empire, gazette publishing was a commercial trade, a point not well understood in past scholarship.[31] Material evidence—consideration of the paper, wood, wax, and ink that made up gazettes—helps trace the changing features of gazettes in connection with different points of production. The flexibility of movable-type printing techniques allowed gazette publishing to occur not only in traditional centers of publishing activity, but also to feature prominently in each of the empire's administrative centers. Demographic expansion from the seventeenth century onward ensured that labor costs remained low. Thriving urban centers supplied copyists and couriers. As a result, state news remained inexpensive throughout the late imperial period.[32]

Most important for the rise of official news as a subject of elite, public, and global attention were the policies of the imperial state. Qing rulers deliberately paid more attention to the court gazettes than had their dynastic predecessors in the Ming. As Manchu rulers engaged in bureaucratic governance in China, they understood that state documents bolstered political authority. As a result, the Qing state adopted a policy of releasing bureaucratic documents in various genres. Proclamations, gazettes, and compilations all consisted of direct excerpts from the imperial communications system. Limited demonstrations of transparency showcased the state's perceived need to buttress bureaucratic accountability, legitimacy, and discipline. In addition, these items became essential tools for governance and sources for commentary on current affairs and administration. The rules of the documentary communications system also prohibited access to items still under discussion. These policies showcased the state's conception of a limited forum for political discussion. Legitimate members of the forum were officials in the bureaucratic community who held the right to submit memorials to the throne. At most times, non-officials were barred from commenting on affairs of state via official media. At the same time, the longstanding practice of releasing documents for open circulation supported elite readership of court news and over time augmented this audience.

Throughout the late imperial era, readers associated with the bureaucracy constituted the most significant readership of state documents. Weng Tonghe, the son of an official who later achieved considerable political stature in his own right, read gazettes from a comparatively expert position. He, like other members of the scholar-official class, possessed the linguistic and cultural skills to parse the language of official treatises. Weng and his counterparts dissected gazettes with a specialist's eye. Through reading, they understood current agendas in the bureaucracy and recognized the names of contemporaries who moved in and out of favor. With time, a sense of familiarity with politics and administration could be garnered—for this reason, the famed eighteenth-century official Chen Hongmou (1696–1771) urged that all academies that were training prospective officials adopt subscriptions to the imperial record.[33]

News of the Qing state circulated to a large and diverse audience during Weng Tonghe's lifetime. New readers included those with limited claims to social power and cultural capital. In the nineteenth century, growing numbers pursued connections with the state, either by climbing the ladder of civil examinations that promised access to an official position, or by working for the state in a subordinate and auxiliary role.[34] The imperial state sold credentials throughout most of the dynasty and expanded this program in the nineteenth century.[35] The enlarging population of eligible officeholders and non-officials affiliated with state enterprises—what might together be called a "bureaucratic public" as compared to the more limited "bureaucratic community"—flocked to read the empire's official journal. Unlike studious intellectuals or experienced officials, newcomers often prioritized career advancement or even simple entertainment as they paged through gazettes. Evoking the extended reach of state news, a poem titled "Reading the Gazette" (Kan jingbao) pilloried a hypothetical capital resident who, despite being illiterate, purchased a gazette subscription. He was therefore forced to beg his friends to read the gazettes aloud to him.[36] This putative reader saw gazettes as markers of social status but possessed no means to comprehend the records of personnel transfers, proposals for militia formations, or discussions of criminal cases contained in the gazettes.

Another growing audience hailed from outside the empire. Even as a young official, Weng Tonghe likely knew that some of China's foreign residents read gazettes and even translated these materials for Western-language newspapers published in China and in Europe. From the seventeenth century onward, Western visitors to China sought out gazettes as information sources for deciphering court agendas. This was not particularly difficult, due to the state's tacit willingness to supply official news to foreign audiences. Within the empire, any willing buyer could purchase the gazette. As missionaries, diplomats, and adventurers publicized their Asian activities, the so-called Peking Gazette grew in fame. In fact, both the enthusiastic renderings of Chinese politics by eighteenth-century Enlightenment thinkers and the more condescending analyses of nineteenth century "sinological" readers were influenced by sources that came directly from the Qing state. Gazettes thus supplied the raw information for starkly divergent perspectives on the politics of the Chinese empire.

Inventing the Qing Gazette

Weng Tonghe read state news in a format shaped by the distinctive agendas and experience of the Qing dynasty. Beginning in the early seventeenth century, when Manchu leaders organized a conquest force to overtake the armies of the Ming dynasty, the Qing state employed public texts to pursue authority and legitimacy.[37] In famous incidents, Qing emperors used publicity to silence critics and clarify their agendas.[38] The formation of laws, policies, and procedures relating to political information lay at the heart of the state-building process, particularly with respect to relations between the court and bureaucracy. Over time, these came to constitute a coherent "information policy." From the mid-eighteenth century onward, the court, with input from bureaucratic officials, required defined procedures for information control in and around the palace. At the same time, it permitted diffuse models for publishing and distributing political information across the empire. The Qing court supervised the gazette with attention to governing a diverse empire, balancing trust with Chinese literati elites, and improving the moral efficacy of the bureaucracy. Finally, gazette publishing allowed the state to pursue these policy goals with a relatively small administrative footprint and low cost.

Language and Empire

In marking gazettes—Chinese-language publications necessarily centered on the imperial court in Beijing—as signature institutions of the Qing state, this book adopts a different focus from a recent and distinctive generation of scholarship that emphasizes ethnicity, identity, and Inner Asian connections as defining features of Qing rulership and administration.[39] Court gazettes were never published in Manchu or non-Chinese languages, nor were they as energetically distributed to the borders of the Qing state as they were disseminated within China proper. Indeed, distance and differing administrative priorities made the documents customarily excerpted in gazettes less relevant for field administrators in outlying regions, especially frontier areas added by military conquest.

Chinese officials and Manchu emperors alike saw releasing official texts as offering a solution to the cultural divides between court, bureaucracy, and cultural elites that challenged the state enterprise in the early years of the dynasty.[40] As early as the seventeenth century, Manchu and Mongol bureaucrats encountered and understood the use and utility of these documents.[41] Emperors and regents prioritized the circulation of official documents and news as a component of the monumental task of pacifying and governing China. The early Qing court therefore gradually restored bureaucratic control over the gazette distribution network that had received only limited oversight during the Ming dynasty.

The court's focus on China proper and on Han Chinese officials in overseeing gazette publishing does not imply the sinicization of the Qing enterprise, but rather the characteristic adaption of distinct institutions for constituent parts of the empire.[42] The early Qing court's consolidation of power involved recruiting Chinese literati to participate in the state bureaucracy. To do so, they needed to assure the Chinese elite that the Qing could manage administrative matters that had notably lapsed in the late Ming dynasty. Restoring the court gazette thus constituted an important part of the Qing agenda for its Chinese territory and population.

Secrecy and Curated Transparency

Scholars of the Qing state generally accept that imperial communications shaped imperial power. In the twentieth century, the discovery of thousands of memorials held in the Qing palace archives exposed the seventeenth- and eighteenth-century formation of an expansive system for the exchange of confidential correspondence between the throne and bureaucratic officials.[43] Foundational studies and those that followed took secret memorials (*mizou*) as the defining institution of the Qing "information order"—the set of communications pathways by which social intelligence was gathered, organized, and disseminated by the Qing state.[44] This scholarship demonstrated that the revamped communications system enabled strong-willed emperors to consolidate their power vis-à-vis the bureaucracy. At the same time, because communications pathways centered on the throne, state functions suffered when relatively weak monarchs reigned.[45]

With its emphasis on secrecy, scholarship on Qing communications has neglected the central state's investment in *curated transparency*: the regular selection of state documents for circulation to the wider bureaucracy. While by no means a complete view of state business, the scope of such information release was extensive enough to give the impression that at least some systems (particularly examinations and personnel administration) were committed to transparency.[46] The volume of public documents (including often lengthy routine memorials called *tiben*) matched or even exceeded that of classified communications.[47] Curated transparency therefore played just as essential a role as secret networks in guaranteeing the long-term durability of the Qing bureaucracy.[48] Whereas many studies of the Qing state take individual institutions or genres of official communications as their starting point, by the middle of the eighteenth century, the Qing gazette comprised documents originating in both open and confidential communications networks. By studying gazettes—as by reading gazettes—we encounter a more encompassing view of Qing communications.

The Qing court made no assertion that its public texts were comprehensive portraits of state activities, nor did it suggest that their dissemination would facilitate popular empowerment. At moments in dynastic history, the state's claim to curated transparency became fragile. For instance, the rise of secret memorials initially destabilized this project. A preponderance of "information scandals" in the late seventeenth and early eighteenth centuries attests to the close intersections between communications and power and the state's limited ability to control the exchange and use of official information. Although relatively unknown, an essential task of the early Grand Council was restoring the dissemination of certain high-level policy memorials via gazettes. Moreover, the Qing court, especially in the eighteenth century, directed large-scale censorial activities to restrain literati activism, particularly ethnically based criticisms of the Manchu ruling house. The state sponsored some modes of scholarship and proscribed others in order to limit literati agendas.[49] Finally, problems such as foreign interference and the political mobilization of the press in the late nineteenth century weakened the court's commitment to transparency.

By contrast, the court imposed fewer constraints on the everyday exchange of information about the empire's personnel, laws, and policies. They described court rituals and printed moralizing imperial edicts but also reproduced details relating to frontier wars, unruly officials, and natural disasters across the empire. Foreign readers wondered at the state's willingness to reveal the ugly side of the bureaucratic state and the emperor's apparent openness to criticism from various levels of the bureaucracy. These impressions were only partially accurate. Gazettes publicized matters deemed essential for bureaucratic functionality, often routine or mundane, and although not all published items were flattering, nor did gazettes publicize overt battles against imperial authority. In addition, foreign military intervention and exposure to new concepts of the press compelled the Qing state to redefine its political goals and management of gazette publishing. In response to the growing foreign readership of gazettes in the nineteenth century, the state explicitly blocked discussion of military defense from publication. Later experiments with a new-style "official press" foreshadowed the more restrictive information regimes of twentieth-century China.

Bureaucratic Goals and the Pursuit of Documentary Authority

Qing rulers incorporated both punitive and symbolic modes of regulating the bureaucracy. The complex task of maintaining discipline among officials and their subordinates invited some to devise rules, punishments, and rewards, whereas others focused on the moral and patriarchal role of the superior official or monarch. Balancing these administrative styles represented a long-standing concern of dynastic states in China and of the Qing state in particular, as shown in the historical scholarship of Thomas Metzger, Madeline Zelin, Philip Kuhn, and Pierre-Étienne Will, among others. For scholars like Metzger, laws, regulations, and internal social pressure sufficed to maintain the integrity of the system; others, like Kuhn, see a state whose internal characteristics hinged closely upon the personage of the monarch.[50]

As seen through the lens of gazettes, official projects to use documents to expand dynastic legitimacy, discipline the bureaucracy, and improve the flow of state information jointly advanced the Qing state's *documentary authority*.[51] The state constructed rules concerning documents (such as their redaction, filing, release to or restriction from public view) with an eye toward protecting and enhancing its perceived authority. Though not unique in its use of documents to pursue political goals, the Qing state aligned measures of control with measures of publicity. Thus, as we shall see, the eighteenth-century court not only engineered new classified communication channels for high-level conversations, it also developed mechanisms for those policy discussions to eventually make their way to the bureaucratic community through gazette publication.[52]

Public documents did more than highlight the imperial will. They also reminded bureaucratic officials of the many rules and regulations that might be enforced to control malfeasance. In this way, curated transparency offered an institutional solution to the problem of bureaucratic discipline. In particular, the court used open communications to publicize complex matters fraught with possibilities for malfeasance, particularly the civil examinations, the personnel administration, and the distribution of tax remissions and disaster relief. Once made public, a notice of demotion or censure could not be easily ignored.[53] Imperial announcements told the populace of the impartial proceedings of examinations, relief decisions, personnel recommendations, and other matters involving favor and merit. This strategy used the expansive potential public audience for political news as a counterweight to force bureaucratic elites to collect taxes in proper fashion, to serve in office as instructed, and to enact justice without preference.

Curated transparency presented the state as the court wished it portrayed, thereby flattening the messy realities of government work. Imperial agendas influenced how readers understood the operations of the bureaucracy. For instance, the rule that documents required imperial sanction before release for wider examination supported the authority of the monarch by obscuring matters still under consideration.[54] Gazettes also promoted the structures of provincial administration devised under Qing rule. Gazettes ensured that informed readers knew the names and agendas of the high officials that headed each province because the memorials of provincial governors and governors general were so frequently published.[55] District officials, who lacked the right to directly memorialize the throne, might appear as subjects in personnel memorials but not as authors. And when gazettes published the remonstrances of censors and the deliberative reports offered by metropolitan agencies, readers saw the court working in consultation with the bureaucracy.[56]

Gazettes and the Outsourced State

In elucidating the pervasive circulation of state texts, this study suggests not imperial overreach, but rather that the Qing state relied on characteristic principles of decentralization or even "outsourcing" in disseminating political information. In terms of interpersonal relationships, skilled and manual labor, and material and ecological resources, the activities of the Qing bureaucracy constituted a complex circuitry of exchange, an information economy in its own right. The enterprise of publishing official documents, gazettes, and proclamations reached far beyond the imperial palace. Remarkably, although the activities of local, provincial, and central levels of administration shaped and fueled the imperial information economy, the Qing court and its agents ceded operations to the commercial realm.

The state's consistent willingness to accept limited control of the information trade marks a point of connection to emerging scholarship on the Qing state's entrepreneurial activism. Loath to manage the expensive and chaotic task of periodical publishing under state auspices, agents for both the central state and provincial governments outsourced publishing and distribution to commercial actors. Scholars have begun to render in clearer details the work of intermediates in local administration and justice.[57] Just as magistrates relied on local assistants and personal allies, officials of the imperial bureaucracy likewise depended on vast numbers of unnamed individuals to carry out scribal, clerical, and transport duties. Metropolitan clerks hired auxiliary copyists, governors hired capital liaisons, and examination superintendents contracted temporary assistants. In Beijing, among the largest cities in the world, established relationships between clerks, messengers, go-betweens, and scribes allowed visitors to purchase troves of information about the state and its laws, personnel, and territory.

The public's ability to censure officials on the basis of openly available evidence offered a disciplinary shortcut for a central state committed to a small footprint. An entry in the seventeenth-century diary of Yao Tinglin (1628–after 1697) evinces this strategy. From his vantage on a small farm outside Shanghai, Yao described how local officials were forcing residents to pay illegal surcharges on land taxes. Although residents spoke out against the practice, they saw little recourse against official abuse. One day, a messenger arrived bearing a gazette, which reported that the local magistrate had been removed from his post and sentenced for corruption. The people cheered and brought the notice to the provincial judge, urging him to proceed to the local *yamen* (administrative offices) and retrieve the bad magistrate's seal of office.[58] In this anecdote, the timely arrival of an official notice not only represented a vector of news from the capital, but also provided the means for the people to exact justice from a detested and corrupt administrator. In other words, the release of bureaucratic information to the public supported the enforcement of order and discipline within the bureaucracy and vis-à-vis local society.

◆ ◆ ◆

The many stories that can be told with and about gazettes reflect the Qing state's longstanding involvement with shaping its public image. The Qing state had followed imperial antecedents in sponsoring court publishing, but it outstripped these forerunners in articulating political goals of publicity and embracing commercial publishing to disseminate official texts. Such a longstanding commitment to curated publicity speaks to the importance of political communications—conducted in public—to the formation of imperial authority. These activities of political legitimation proceeded in the same era in which states around the globe grappled with—and were even toppled by—the political consequences of print. State censors in other contexts became notorious symbols of autocratic and unjustified rule. In China, the Qing state managed to retain and defend its hold on political communications, despite the fact that print publishing was both well-known and widely accessible.[59] The Qing state employed limited publicity to satisfy the interests of its literati elite, control the bureaucracy, and support its ideological agendas.

The Qing state's public image was not mere propaganda. If modern propaganda is a technique to inspire mass mobilization by presenting a single, top-down interpretation of events, then early modern publicity entailed a more complex mixture of political and administrative goals. Authorized state news in the Qing dynasty acknowledged the presence of dissent, hardship, crime, malfeasance, and, most importantly, debate. In the decades that succeeded the fall of the dynasty, Chinese governments sought to infuse state agendas more directly into public life. In the twentieth century, the mass public would become a population to be shaped, controlled, and mobilized. Mass political engagement paved the way for more drastic state interventions. And in the twenty-first century, media platforms offer further opportunities for state- and corporate-led manipulation of citizens and consumers. While the story of the Qing gazette warns against conflating promises of transparency with public empowerment, it nonetheless illustrates that a multivocal political culture filled the pages and hid between the lines of this much-maligned court mouthpiece.

CHAPTER 1

The Qing Information Order

IN THE FIRST CENTURY OF QING RULE IN CHINA, THE COURT, MEMbers of the metropolitan bureaucracy, and provincial officials all participated in defining practices for the processing and circulation of imperial documents. Court and bureaucratic actors invoked both practical and ideological concerns in negotiating the reach and articulating the pathways of the Qing information order, a process that was largely completed by 1760. The information policies enacted by the early Qing state successfully extended the range and perceived legitimacy of state communications. Whereas the clout of state publicity had withered in the late Ming dynasty, official readers now widely considered court gazettes to be desirable and authoritative information sources made reputable by court sanction.

From the perspective of state power, information policies facilitated central oversight of the empire, its peoples, and its officials. For this reason, establishing communications procedures was seen as just as important as repairing roads and staffing the bureaucracy. Certain priorities guided the construction of Qing information policy. First, it was essential to restore the loyalty and functionality of the territorial bureaucracy. For the bureaucracy to function, the state needed to instill safeguards to improve morale and accountability. Second, official documents needed to garner acceptance as representing the authority of the imperial state. In this regard, state actors sought to ensure that imperial documents were applied uniformly across time and space—what we might call *information symmetry*—and that documents could be checked for authenticity, even outside of the capital. With these necessities in mind, early Qing state actors evaluated the policies of the last dynasty and struck forth with new models for political communications.

To help solve these problems of imperial governance, the Qing state restored instruments of publicity, particularly the court gazette, that had been employed by earlier dynasties but which had lapsed prior to the Qing conquest. The court and members of the capital bureaucracy shared the notion that curated transparency—the widespread circulation of selected imperial documents—could improve the administrative efficiency and moral coherence of the bureaucracy. From the perspective of the court, releasing documents that revealed the workings of state offices helped ensure that government personnel conducted themselves properly. From the perspective of the bureaucracy, open communications practices balanced the political agendas of the state and limited the autocratic impulses of the throne. Administrative goals influenced how both sets of policymakers developed rules for the processing of official documents, their redaction and publication, and the distribution of gazettes and other types of imperial publicity.

Gazettes and Politics before the Qing

Even before the Qing conquest, official communications lay at the center of political life in imperial China. States in China—as in other imperial contexts—used communications to express authority across diverse territories. Laws, edicts, and imperial decisions all needed to be communicated to the empire's population by way of its governing bureaucracy. In order to retain authority over bureaucratic officials, Chinese states devised means of periodically evaluating field administrators and channels by which positive and negative reports could be communicated to the center. Meanwhile, distant officials, from governors to envoys, needed ways to receive and authenticate central communications. Geopolitical transitions, from the westward extension of the Tang dynasty to the cataclysmic loss of North China during the Song dynasty, necessitated new techniques for the circulation and control of imperial documents. From the Tang dynasty onward, field officials understood gazettes to be repositories of administrative information collected in the capital. However, the imperial center did not always monopolize control of gazette production. Over the longue durée of imperial history, central authorities possessed varying degrees of control over the production and dissemination of gazettes, as well as the overall information order.

From their famously cosmopolitan capital city of Chang'an, the rulers of the Tang dynasty constructed a vast empire that reached deep into Central Asia. In order to manage this territory, the central state ceded regional control to a number of military powerholders. Regional powers posted representatives in the capital, who served as intelligence officers for their commanders in institutions called the Capital Liaisons Offices (Jinzou Yuan). Capital liaisons curated dispatches for their regional commanders. Supplied with information about capital politics, these regional powers grew in strength to challenge the authority of the central state.[1]

The dissolution of central power in the Tang dynasty provided a powerful warning to the early emperors of the Song dynasty, with ramifications for central information policies. The Song court took the Capital Liaisons Office and refashioned it into a Memorials Office.[2] The Memorials Office presented documents to the court that had been authored by territorial officials and distributed court documents to personnel and offices throughout the bureaucracy. No longer staffed by territorial appointees, the Memorials Office now symbolized the centralization of political communications under court control.[3] Cognizant of the consequences of uneven administrative knowledge among different levels of the territorial bureaucracy, the central state began to circulate occasional court documents and eventually regular dispatches to field officials. These dispatches became known as *court reports* (*dibao*), a term that emphasized the central origin of the disseminated reports. In content, they roughly matched their later counterparts, with lists of personnel movements and court audiences, transcriptions of imperial edicts, and excerpts from policy memorials. The Song state may well have been motivated to publish gazettes by the growing enthusiasm of period intellectuals and officials for political information. In circulating documents on its own terms, the court sought to head off the political elite's tendency to seek information through illicit means, such as by purchasing leaked documents.[4]

As compared with the Song dynasty, liaisons and publishers of the Ming dynasty compiled and distributed official gazettes through a decentralized process with limited bureaucratic supervision. These practices followed larger trends in the organization of the Ming state. Following the Ming founder's efforts to strip down government activities, the early Ming state devolved responsibility for maintaining courier routes and postal stations to local society.[5] In parallel, while palace institutions guarded the passage of official memorials within the palace, once a memorial had been rescripted and approved, the document lay open to bureaucratic scrutiny. Both gazette scribes based in the capital and "communication liaisons" (*titang guan*) who served regional civil and military administrators could copy out memorials bearing imperial rescripts at will, and relay copied documents to customers and patrons. In the secondary capital of Nanjing, government offices received gazettes via special couriers from Beijing.[6] The Ming court and metropolitan offices ensured that certain informational genres, such as examination results, were published regularly and continually. But for the most part, the court allowed officials to solicit information on the basis of their own interests and postings.[7]

Especially during and after the reign of the Wanli emperor (1572–1620), when many bureaucratic functions were crippled by imperial inaction and bureaucratic gridlock, some liaisons, publishers, and private individuals began to circulate court dispatches to a wider audience.[8] The participation of unofficial distributors in the gazette trade had profound implications for Ming subjects' understanding of state affairs. Ming contemporaries used the terms *dichao*, *xiaobao*, and *xiaochao* to refer to unofficial and privately published papers that reported on court news.[9] Most unofficial compilers were evidently based in the capital, but some assembled editions in other urban centers.[10] The persistent delays that marked the central state's reduced capacity to process and publish documents highlighted for readers the relative efficacy of private news networks, as well as the implicit value of an editor unconstrained by state regulations.

Indeed, many readers, even if they held office, encountered gazettes in a private capacity while seeking news. Readers' notes, writings, and communications involving gazettes illustrate that elite and official audiences engaged deeply with official communications as news sources.[11] Late Ming readers clearly designated some items as originating from unofficial sources and commented on flaws within the official systems for publishing and distributing gazettes. For instance, in the early seventeenth century, one official speculated that Jesuit missionaries had paid local publishers to insert memorials in the Nanjing edition of the court gazette in order to promote the false impression that the Wanli emperor had reviewed their submissions.[12] In the chaotic last decade of Ming rule, concerned readers reached for both state-managed and privately curated sources, using unofficial copies as enticing first notices and employing official editions to confirm rumors and hearsay.[13]

Although it is not clear whether blocked routes, stalled government offices, or lapsed print shops are to blame, the circulation of official gazettes certainly broke down in the last years of the Ming dynasty. Qing forces evidently sought out spies and other contacts who could secure access to internal documents of the Ming state, including its gazettes. However, in the last years of the conflict, the Qing leadership stopped pursuing documents purported to originate from the Ming court. The Manchu imperial regent Dorgon (1612–1650) later called the intelligence value of the Ming gazette "laughable" because the court could not control whether the contents were modified after gazettes were released from the capital.[14] That unofficial sources prevailed over state publications spoke to the substantial loss of imperial control over information.

News and Documentary Authority in the Conquest Period

In the summer and autumn of 1644, news of military contests and political upheaval came suddenly to the people of China. In his autobiography, the Shanghai native Yao Tinglin described a holiday banquet interrupted by an acquaintance carrying a privately authored news sheet (*xiaobao*) that told of the suicide of the Chongzhen emperor and the siege of Beijing. After this initial report, more rumors flooded Shanghai, including tales of the cooperation of the general Wu Sangui (1612–1678) in helping Qing troops to pass through the Great Wall.[15] The scholar-poet Qian Chengzhi (1612–1693) reported the arrival of a visitor to a garden residence in Suzhou where he had been shut away from the world reading and writing poetry. The visitor reported that official communications channels had been interrupted for the past month and speculated that the capital had fallen. Just a few days later, Qian and his colleagues learned of the death of the Ming emperor and began planning to nominate a relative to form a court-in-exile.[16]

For these recipients, each incoming snippet of news about conquest and military pursuit felt like a sudden onslaught. Their reactions illustrate the experience of living within a disorderly information environment. The fall of the Ming state exacerbated shared experiences of uncertainty, but the official communications system had also been deteriorating for years. Delays and uncertainty about the authorship of documents and the authority of information drew suspicion to texts claiming official status. In such a time, people turned to unauthorized sources, but these were dependent on personal connections, traveled at an uneven pace, and provided inconsistent information.[17] In Yao Tinglin's account, the abrupt entrance of a newcomer bearing news of conquest evoked the fast-paced exchange of information by refugees and runners. However, not only did the news arrive in Shanghai as a surprise more than forty days after the event had transpired, but also, according to Yao's recollection, the report misdated the suicide by several weeks.[18]

Even the officials dispatched to administer conquered territories relied on incomplete and often contradictory intelligence relayed by travelers and refugees. Late in the summer of 1644, Wang Aoyong (d. 1644), charged with the pacification of the Shandong peninsula, reported intelligence that a Ming remnant had been installed as emperor in Nanjing. Wang told the court that he obtained this important news from a lowly attendant who had recently journeyed to his home district near Nanjing.[19] Wang relayed this to another Qing official on the road south from Beijing. The colleague's own record of the conversation recalled Wang's frown as he added that propaganda attributed to the Southern Ming court had been found as far north as Jining in central Shandong.[20] If even these Chinese officials serving the ascendant Qing dynasty relied on personal sources to learn about affairs in the south, then likely no official forms of intelligence yet moved from south to north, or at least not as quickly as hearsay.

Just a year later, government couriers brought official notices of Qing military victories from Beijing to field postings throughout North China on a regular basis. The efficient dispersal of these communications in the spring and summer of 1645 contrasted with the unruly situation a year prior. The recipients of these notices, many former Ming officials, recognized the significance of such quick transport and catalogued transit times in their responses to the capital. When Qing forces took Nanjing, a military courier took about ten days to reach the court in Beijing, which published the victory announcement seven days later. This announcement reached Tianjin in four days, Jinan in fifteen days, and distant Ningxia in seventy-seven days.[21] Thanks to the state's immediate efforts to shore up communications routes, capital dispatches could reliably reach a growing proportion of provincial posts under Qing control. The dates mentioned in the responses to victory announcements illustrate the relative rapidity with which official communications moved through pacified territory, in contrast to the slowness of transit through frontier territory.

The ascendant Qing court issued many dispatches, victory notices, and court gazettes, each of which marked initial steps in the more expansive endeavor of defining political power under a new dynasty. These documents described occasions of deep significance—the beheading of a false prince, the order that all Chinese males shave their foreheads and adopt the queue, and countless military victories.[22] Victory notices, like all proclamations disseminated by the court to the conquered territories, were snippets of wartime propaganda and elements of the political process of conquest. Meant to hearten allies and frighten foes, they alerted readers of the military successes of Qing armies and reminded them of the vast territorial and dynastic ambitions of their new rulers. At the same time, they summarized the recent and expected triumphs of the Qing military. As the populace gained access to imperial texts, they became assured of the stability of the new regime and the authority of state-authored news. Posted field officials took special notice. Especially for holdovers from the Ming dynasty, the resumption of authorized imperial notices assured the legitimacy of the new regime.

By autumn 1645, announcements arrived reliably enough that Chinese officials cited court announcements as bearing more authority than local rumor or hearsay. On the way to far-off Gansu, censor Wei Guan (d. 1668) wrote to the court to verify reports of the death of rebel leader Li Zicheng. Wei explained in his memorial that his travels prevented him from receiving the gazettes (*dibao*) delivered by government couriers to provincial posts.[23] Wei's confident expectation that a file of court documents awaited him at his destination reflected his understanding that the Qing state had already restored its communications functionality. Serving officials no doubt continued to utilize private resources in soliciting news about the state and empire in formation. Within state communications channels, however, they increasingly referred only to official genres.

These pieces of correspondence exchanged between field officials and the palace make clear that the Qing immediately resuscitated the court gazette upon assuming power in Beijing.[24] Frustratingly, there seem to be no material remnants of the gazettes produced in the first years after conquest, nor do official archives shed light on the specific process of renewing this production. Readers' notes tell us more about the meanings assigned to state communications in this era than their appearance or institutional contexts. When Qing officials stopped citing private sources and made consistent reference to centrally curated gazettes, they demonstrated the emerging consensus that state communications were widely available, trustworthy, and bore out the political authority achieved by the new dynasty. As for the process of deliberation that led to this resuscitation of imperial publicity, although surviving archival materials from the early Qing period are fragmented, they evince substantive official discussions concerning the intersections of information and governance.

The Transformation of the Information Order

Among imperial institutions, the Censorate (Duchayuan) hosted some of the most significant conversations about the ideological underpinnings of the imperial communications order in the late seventeenth century. In the Chinese bureaucratic system, members of the Censorate held far-reaching responsibilities of supervising "all personnel and operations of the entire governmental mechanism."[25] This task, combined with the desire to convince Manchus to work credibly with Chinese counterparts, predisposed censors to make arguments about the uses of secrecy and transparency within bureaucratic communications. At the same time, imperial anxiety about information security grew in stride with the intensifying pace and quantity of bureaucratic correspondence. Both sets of interests influenced the development of routines and institutions for the release of bureaucratic documents and correspondence. The resulting documentary practices enshrined, in limited form, ideals of transparency and information symmetry.

Communications and Control of the Bureaucracy

Communications, according to the Chinese officials who advised the early Shunzhi court, represented the circulating lifeblood of the imperial state. Thus the censor Luo Guoshi (*jinshi* 1637) described the courier relay and postal routes that brought documents and personnel between territorial posts as the "blood and veins" of the empire, while his counterpart Zhao Kaixin (d. 1663) elucidated that if the bureaucracy itself might be considered a body, then this body's veins carried words for blood.[26] These court advisors understood that managing bureaucratic communications was about more than record-keeping—to distribute access to the throne through written and especially confidential correspondence was to maintain the balance of power.

The most crucial issues were balancing power between Manchu and Han officials and implementing a coherent internal communications and archival system that could accommodate the multilingual bureaucracy. It was in these terms that the outspoken Zhao Kaixin defended the importance of the communications institutions of the preceding dynasty. Zhao defined imperial communications as consecrating the bond between rulers and officials: "In governing the realm, if it is said to be essential for the ruler [*jun*] and people to be as one unified body, then this must certainly originate from the ruler and his ministers acting as one unified body. And circulation, in this body, rather than veins, is instead the 'road of words' [*yanlu*]." Zhao thus defined the bureaucracy as a body of officials, but also a body of words. In more specific terms, his argument sought to preserve the candid role of the censor and reasoned that the responsible monarch should treat opinions presented by officials on an equal basis regardless of ethnic background, subjecting all opinions to discussion.[27] More generally, his invocation of the "road of words" as an ideal represented the central importance of communications for the bureaucracy to fulfill its political functions. The term *yanlu* referred to the toleration of candid criticism, from censors under ordinary conditions and from an expanded retinue of memorialists under special circumstances declared by the emperor. In this statement, he alluded to the political breakdown of the previous dynasty. In Zhao's day, it was widely accepted that stark factionalism and successive emperors' inability to work with the bureaucracy had destroyed the Ming state from the inside. He therefore suggested that the effective monarch needed to find regular opportunities to convene the members of his advising bureaucracy and to balance and curtail the influence of different parties and agendas.

If selfish interests motivated the pursuit of political information, then the ideal of bureaucratic transparency could motivate a critique of central surveillance. Word spread in the 1640s that imperial regent Dorgon had appointed Manchu personnel to perform surveillance in the capital and to infiltrate provincial offices. One Chinese censor, Zhang Guoxian (*jinshi* 1646) took offense at the revelation that these palace inspectors opened incoming and outgoing messages and reminded the throne that surveillance forces, such as the eunuch secret police of the late Ming dynasty, often tended to overstep their legitimate roles and victimize those they surveilled.[28]

Zhang Guoxian then offered a defense of transparency within the transformed multiethnic bureaucracy. He wrote, "Now, Manchu and Han have come together in moral vigor, and any initiative shall be perceived together by all in the capital and in the provinces [*zhongwai jianjian*]."[29] With this metaphor of distant officials perceiving new agendas in the capital, Zhang suggested that the renewed political community could operate on a more open basis if it were freed from mutual suspicion. Such enmity had been bred by ethnic divisions, but it was also inherited from the moral politics that plagued the late Ming bureaucracy. Common awareness of the conversations unfolding within the bureaucracy would not only improve the integrity of the community, but also reduce the necessity of surveillance from above. Chinese censors like Zhang urged the court to adopt procedures that ensured fair standards of confidentiality and openness; if the memorialist desired his message to be delivered in confidence, this should be respected, but officials also expected the bulk of bureaucratic communications to be accessible, with confidential communications reserved for sensitive duties of remonstrance.

The Manchu court, for its part, used related arguments to impugn censors' susceptibility to personal interests, which led them to present spurious or interest-driven accusations with little objective basis. Both Dorgon as regent and the Shunzhi emperor, once enthroned, denounced censors' predilection to impeach rivals on spurious grounds. Too often, Dorgon complained, censors followed personal motivations and compiled accusations on the basis of "hearsay" (*fengwen*).[30] He instructed Chinese censors to submit compelling evidence to accompany their claims. These instructions thus required a more comprehensive presentation of the grounds for impeachment. In this way, fuller details of the case would be presented, not merely to the court, but also to gazette readers should the impeachment go through and the memorial be released for review.

Contrary to the regent's wishes, however, the pursuit of evidence could also endanger the security and procedures of the court communications system. In this bureaucratic system in formation, advance or unsanctioned access to documents could spell important advantage. Officials in the Transmissions Office (Tongzheng Si), the initial clearinghouse where incoming communications were checked for form and adherence to procedure, complained in late 1645 about the leaking into public circulation of "reference summaries" (*jietie*), short documents intended to remain in the custody of clerical offices while memorials were under deliberation. Access to these items alerted interested parties as to matters under consideration, even those intended never to be made public. In response, an imperial edict affirmed the ban on illicit circulation—but also promised amnesty to previous offenders, suggesting that the leaks were quite extensive in scale.[31]

Incidents like these convinced the court that for political communications to support bureaucratic order, the central state needed to formalize standards for the compilation and release of information. The primary rule became that of imperial review. No document could be released to public scrutiny before it had been considered by the emperor. This rule reprised a principle of privileging the imperial voice already in effect during earlier dynasties.[32] The renewed emphasis signaled that the Qing court—unlike its lapsed predecessor—would enforce prohibitions on leaking details and documents from the court. Besides consolidating the power of the throne, as emphasized in earlier scholarship, the insistence on waiting for documents to pass before the emperor's eyes also involved a practical concern for the coherence and consistency of information.[33] If proposals could be disseminated before receiving approval, who would know if they should be applied? If accusations could be read before obtaining judgment, who would decide if punishments should be executed?

Censors, as well as the court itself, made arguments supporting imperial review for the sake of effective administration. One, Feng Pu (1609–1691), referred to the jarring sense of confusion that resulted when different parties received divergent versions of an official text. This issue, according to Feng, had already become a problem for the bureaucracy in the early 1650s. In the cases that Feng highlighted, although palace secretarial offices had released reviewed copies (*hongben*) of received memorials, the emperor and his advisors altered their decisions on these memorials subsequent to the documents' publication. Such careless actions wreaked havoc for bureaucratic order. The court needed to be consistent, Feng urged, so that the authority of imperial commands might remain intact.[34] In this case, the court's prevarications, rather than the predilection of bureaucratic officials to spy, was to blame for inconsistencies. When administrative concerns were taken into consideration, both censor and court therefore recommended a more limited form of transparency.

Palace Institutions

In the second half of the seventeenth century, the court, together with members of the Censorate, designated procedures for the review, redaction, and release of documents for wider circulation. These procedures created interlocking systems of record-keeping in the Six Sections (Liu Ke) and the Grand Secretariat (Neige) to safeguard against the improper release of information. The institutions and rules that the early Qing courts employed to organize incoming and outgoing communications originated from Ming precedents but strengthened both the court's control of documents in circulation and its commitment to publicity. Adapting Ming offices and practices to suit standing practices in the Manchu conquest organization and the prerogatives of dynastic rule in China could be a complex task. For instance, although the Grand Secretariat traditionally served as a communications clearinghouse, it had become a sprawling institution during the Ming dynasty, at times adversarial to the monarch. For this reason, the early Qing emperors were slow to revive the Grand Secretariat, and it had a checkered history before the Kangxi emperor's assumption of personal rule in 1670. As a result, regulations for the exchange, proofreading, and approval of documents were initially informal.[35]

Procedures began to formalize in the 1660s. Technically, any official communication that was not designated as secret could be made available for consultation and copying in the Grand Secretariat. Only rescripted communications could be released. After memorials authored by individual officials or representing various institutions received imperial rescripts, scribes reviewed them and recopied the annotated memorials for circulation.[36] They processed documents sequentially, subsequent to a nominal delay meant to ensure, as Feng Pu had urged, that only finalized decisions be released.[37] For this reason, edicts often moved through the clearing process in advance of the memorials to which they responded, a circumstance that observers of gazettes would remark on throughout the dynasty.[38]

The documents that officials, clerks, and gazette scribes obtained from palace offices bore marks of authentication and could be traced to document registers and archives. Two sub-offices of the Grand Secretariat, the Chinese and Manchu Registries (Man Han Piaoqian), redacted most texts for the sake of brevity, with appointments and dismissals condensed down to a single line item. Several layers of recordkeeping kept track of the documents destined for external release. The Secretariat Registries maintained itemized records of "documents for release" (*ling xia hao bu*) to track the processed items.[39] A 1658 edict named supervisors (*zhushi*) in the Six Sections to compile a "register of circulated documents" (*fachao ji ce*) corresponding to the secretariat records. In the Six Sections, a long-standing secretarial body for document management within the palace and capital bureaucracy, clerks matched lists of documents designated for release with corresponding document summaries.[40]

Supervising secretaries (*jishizhong*) at the head of the Six Sections took on primary responsibility for oversight of gazette processing. Though they held low-ranking positions, supervising secretaries had important responsibilities and often moved into the Censorate after successful terms.[41] The supervising secretaries noted the provenance of documents as they moved through the palace's bureaucratic circuitry and later sanctioned their final release.[42] In addition, they periodically reviewed outgoing materials in order to ensure felicity to authorized material. Accordingly, in 1660, Sun Guangsi (1624–1709), a longtime supervising secretary who was instrumental in the organization of the clerical system, deemed the inspection of documents marked for inclusion in court gazettes to be one of the nine guiding tasks of the supervising secretary. Sun specified that materials exiting the palace for printing and distribution must be complete and error free. Whereas gazette copyists had previously entered the Six Sections to transcribe material, Sun preferred to have Six Sections personnel make copies, then deliver transcripts to messengers for gazette publishers and the capital-based liaisons charged with distribution to provincial offices.[43]

Taken together, these procedures made up a centralized process for the authorization, compilation, and release of bureaucratic documents. Safeguards in the system preserved the secrecy of confidential documents and prevented all items from exposure until they had completed the deliberative process. For the court, this centralization represented a triumph over the less coordinated procedures inherited from the Ming dynasty. Still, while the new regulations made it easy to account for the movement of documents, they were silent on the specific topics included or excluded from publication in gazettes. Commentary by gazette readers provides important clues as to their contents.

The Purview of the Gazette

For the most part, clerks and secretaries involved in the redaction of documents for publication in gazettes selected and edited texts based on convention rather than explicit regulation. The standard topics included in court gazettes appears to have been common knowledge among both officials and members of the literati elite.[44] The seventeenth-century intellectual Wang Fuzhi (1619–1692), for example, denoted "ordinary appointments and removals, demotions and transfers, opinions and accusations, recommendations, items of procedure, criminal and grain administrations, and labor service" as topics authorized for coverage in the court gazette. These allowable categories encompassed the bulk of the routine work of the central bureaucracy, with an emphasis on personnel matters. Wang, like officials of his era, distinguished between public matters and those that should remain confidential for administrative purposes. Classified matters included two main areas of concern: secret criminal investigations and major military campaigns, where espionage was an inherent risk.[45]

As brief daily publications, gazettes could not treat the affairs of the bureaucracy in toto. Instead, some priorities overruled other administrative concerns in determining the contents of gazettes. Bureaucratic discipline was an area of special interest. As early Qing officials elucidated, publicizing notices of the reward of meritorious individuals and punishment of the corrupt could help improve official behavior by example. Despite their claims to moral integrity, officials abused their positions for personal gain. Circulating notices of awards and punishments increased shared awareness of the risks of such behavior. Since malfeasance involved subverting the greater good to private interests, advocates premised, why not reverse this formula and use public information to weaken enticement to private gain? In 1658, the censor Ren Kepu (d. 1703) responded to the Shunzhi emperor's call for proposals on eliminating abuses in government in these terms:

> Imposing a punishment after an abuse is committed is not as good as preventing that abuse from the start. Since the Bureau of Civil Appointments [Wenxuan Si] of the Board of Appointments [Libu] has established procedures for advancement and promotion, why not go ahead and post in front of the Board of Appointments offices, an ordered list of names, salaries, commendations, and demerits, so that all might see and hear? Itemized descriptions of administrative hearings should likewise be as a rule promulgated, so that people do not misunderstand or distort their importance. As for official appointments, we can use the board dispatches [*kechao*]. In the past, the circulation of such records totally reversed the trend of abusive behavior.[46]

Ren's proposal invoked the power of categorized information to make government officials more accountable for their actions. Most radically, he imagined the threshold of the Board of Appointments' offices in Beijing as a signboard of official records for perusal by passersby. In more practical terms, he suggested that official discipline could be improved by expanding public knowledge. Simply put, board dispatches describing recent appointments, awards, and sanctions would be published and distributed in the court gazettes. Ren suggested that this method had been successfully implemented in past eras. This proposal accorded with the common understanding that humans were by nature responsive to both positive and negative exemplars, to both punishment and reward.[47]

Ren Kepu further suggested that state publicity could support the internal order of the wider bureaucracy prior to the formal publication of administrative regulations. If the primary failing of the individual was the pursuit of personal gain, then the primary failing of the bureaucratic system was that selfish preferences continued to infect the ostensibly neutral processes of grading the civil examinations and awarding appointments. According to this official, such abuses persisted despite the fact that the Board of Appointments had defined standards for the designation of promotions and official careers in general. Could it be that common abuses reflected insufficient understanding of these regulations? Ren articulated these points more than two decades before the dynasty published its first full-scale compilation of administrative regulations in the Kangxi-era *Collected Statutes* (Da Qing huidian, 1690). His remarks suggested that publicizing administrative standards encouraged officials and would-be officials to behave with integrity when they participated in complex bureaucratic activities such as the examinations and appointments. Even in the absence of large-scale compilations of law and regulation, the state could support the bureaucratic order by communicating its norms and standards on a more piecemeal basis. Such policies not only prevented systemic transgression, but also supported the moral standing of the state.[48]

Other seventeenth-century directives demonstrate the use of publicity to mitigate problems of information asymmetry between capital and periphery. These problems could occur spontaneously in the course of sending time-sensitive directives across vast distances or conducting investigations that involved several different provinces or administrative units. Other times, however, local officials might purposefully obfuscate information received from the capital. The Board of Appointments deliberated on these problems in the 1660s. It was accepted wisdom among officials that a service record clear of cases of fiscal management or local banditry would improve one's chances of promotion to a better post. As a result, officials picked up the habit of hiding any such matters until receiving a notice of promotion, upon which they rushed to conclude the investigations. The board, working on the understanding that either a gazette or an individual promotion notice could reach any distance within the limits of the empire within two months, thus recommended that officials be required to clearly designate *when* such incidents had cropped up. The central authorities would then use this two-month limit as a marker for determining whether deliberate obfuscation had occurred.[49] Therefore, by publishing personnel records, the state attempted to reduce individual officials' tendency to hide local problems in service of their own advantage.

Intentional manipulation of the imperial communications system for personal gain seems to have been rife among field officials of the late seventeenth century, when the state information order was not yet well defined. Cases of fraud and deception among administrators made publicity venues like the court gazette particularly important. In his discussion of secretarial work, Sun Guangsi pointed out, "Often, there are items like newly established matters and precedents or decided cases, which the conniving underlings of provincial offices obstruct and do not circulate. But, when enumerated in the court gazette, the local [official] finally learns [of the matter]." A lifetime capital official, Sun felt that any alteration at all to the contents of the gazettes or change to its distribution could be attributed to administrative abuse at some point in the bureaucratic system, most often at the provincial level.[50] In other words, the court gazette was such an integral institution for preventing malfeasance that even the tiniest errors could be hints at conspiracy to obscure information.

Ren Kepu and Sun Guangsi both addressed the priorities and goals of court publicity from the perspective of administrative rationale, not classical inspiration. Their arguments did not summon classical tropes relating to the exchange of communication between the people and the ruler, as would late-nineteenth century advocates for press reform.[51] This divergence highlights that the tangible goal to optimize the bureaucracy's operations—not the more expansive desire to properly align ruler and subject—guided institutional developments in the seventeenth and eighteenth centuries. Official commentary focused on improving the bureaucracy's functions, and the Qing state followed this agenda. In particular, the publication of personnel details, including explicit descriptions of individual achievements and crimes, was meant to simultaneously shore up the moral standards of the bureaucracy and improve the coherence of information received by officials stationed across the empire. How these officials would receive gazettes, meanwhile, was left to the individual provinces.

From the Capital to the Provinces

The distribution of gazettes to individual field administrators relied on a system of communications liaisons (*titang guan*) centered on Beijing and the provincial capitals. Like the gazettes themselves, the communications liaisons had institutional roots in earlier eras, but their operations diverged during the Qing dynasty.[52] The position of capital liaison (*zhujing titang*) was reinstated in 1647 following the proposal of governor Zhang Cunren (d. 1652), a former Ming military commander.[53] Liaisons, appointed by governors, were charged with ensuring that capital communications reached provincial administrators. In addition to gazettes, items in their charge included seals of office, imperial gifts, and other formal notices. Whereas capital liaisons resided in Beijing and organized the distribution to provincial capitals, provincial liaisons (*zhusheng titang*) based in each locale oversaw the delivery of materials to subordinate officials and compiled a corresponding provincial gazette that reported the meetings and other affairs of the provincial governor.

Both metropolitan agencies and provincial officials were involved in directing the operations of the capital liaisons. Initially, the provinces did the bulk of supervision, but by the mid-eighteenth century, in response to a series of incidents involving capital liaisons working covertly for their superiors, the Yongzheng and Qianlong emperors moved to place the position under central bureaucratic supervision. These reforms designated the liaisons under the jurisdiction of the Board of War (Bingbu). Candidates for the position of capital liaison could be nominated by governors so long as they possessed a provincial or national-level military degree. Capital liaisons, most of whom were Han, served three-year terms, then often transitioned into mid-level positions in the Green Standard Army.

Liaison practices influenced forms of commercial participation in the official gazette trade through the end of the dynasty. Allowing liaisons to coordinate with the commercial realm in filling the supply of gazettes fulfilled the state's desire to minimize expenditures and administrative burden. While liaisons were made responsible for ensuring that gazettes reached the provinces, they were not commonly involved in the production process. With the exception of an experimental project in the Qianlong and Jiaqing reigns that placed the sixteen capital liaisons jointly in charge of gazette publishing in Beijing, the liaisons coordinated with commercial publishers to compile and print gazettes for provincial use. After arranging for the publisher to have access to the required content, liaisons purchased gazettes and sent them on to their province by courier. These arrangements contributed to the growing commercial market for gazettes. Moreover, they introduced openings for interruptions and mistakes in the flow of official materials from the capital to the provinces. These invited consternation, especially when they intersected with major court initiatives, such as the development of the palace memorial system.

The Imperial Information Order in the Eighteenth Century

If the policies constructed in the seventeenth century heralded the court's commitment to limited measures of transparency, by later in the Kangxi emperor's reign, the monarch had become convinced of the expanded need for secrecy. In the 1690s, the Kangxi emperor initiated a palace memorial system (*zouzhe zhidu*) that involved direct and unmediated exchanges of documents between territorial officials and the throne. The use of palace memorials expanded the surveillance power of the throne and sidestepped the traditional advisory role of outer court institutions. It consolidated imperial control of communications, particularly high-level discussions pertaining to the military and other sensitive topics.[54]

The system matured under the Yongzheng and Qianlong emperors, who resolved to manage these classified communications together with a group of trusted councilors. First, the Yongzheng emperor turned to a series of informal advisory councils to deliberate upon the confidential dispatches, laying the groundwork for "ministerial administration."[55] His successor, the Qianlong emperor, created a formal successor to these groups, the Grand Council (Junjichu), which as a circuit board for imperial communications became the most important political institution at court for the remainder of the dynasty.[56] From an optimistic perspective, the confidential confines of the Grand Council enabled flexible decision-making and debate; from a pessimistic view, this group soon became a cabal of imperial relatives, career bureaucrats, and divided perspectives.[57]

Within a few decades, these confidential institutions would be well integrated in the broader information order. Along with the creation of the Grand

Council came the implementation of new recordkeeping systems that distinguished secret from ordinary documents and made clear which documents were retained within the Grand Council and which had been released to the wider bureaucracy. Especially important, as more and more officials submitted palace memorials, would be defining a route for the release of secret memorials to the wider bureaucratic community. The recordkeeping and reference materials of eighteenth-century palace institutions thus highlight the mechanisms by which secret documents were incorporated into the larger information order. These records indicate that although some were closed off in classified archives, a substantial portion of secret communications could be read after a delay in gazettes and other published venues.

Incorporating Palace Memorials

Territorial officials responded to the initiation of the palace memorial network and the establishment of the Grand Council by sending a larger proportion of their communications to the throne in the form of palace memorials. Routine memorials (*tiben*), lengthy reports composed of standardized summaries of field reports from local jurisdictions, still accounted for the bulk of documents handled by the metropolitan bureaucracy. In palace memorials, field officials presented compact overviews of ongoing and more urgent concerns, such as criminal investigations, the status of transport and defense infrastructure, disaster relief initiatives, and other policy initiatives.[58]

As more provincial officials enclosed their most important correspondence in palace memorials, it became necessary to find a more direct route for publicizing this expansive communications genre. Around 1737, the Grand Council implemented regulations that allowed palace memorials to be directly routed to the Grand Secretariat and then relayed to the wider bureaucracy.[59] These regulations made it possible to publish excerpts from palace memorials in court gazettes, the purview of which had previously been limited to routine memorials. The effects of this transition can be seen in the pages of court gazettes and in transcribed records by readers.[60] From the mid-eighteenth century onward, the majority of communications presented in court gazettes were copied by readers as memorials (*zou*), rather than routine communications (*ti*). In this way, the formation of the Grand Council expanded readers' access to substantive policy discussion, which had been curtailed by the initial implementation of the palace memorial system.

The Grand Council maintained records of the documents that were processed and released for wider review. In *Register of Documents as They Come to Hand* (Suishou dengji), Grand Council clerks listed memorials by date and author and included brief notations as to the memorial's disposition after imperial review. These records are extant between the early Qianlong era and the end of the dynasty.[61] Only a minority of memorial communications, usually confidential reports pertaining to military affairs, were returned to the memorialist by personal courier. The remainder were either retained in Grand Council archives or made available to metropolitan institutions—either a specific body, such as administrative board, or, as designated by the notation "transfer" (*jiao*) in document registers, to the Grand Secretariat for open review.[62] In the early Qianlong reign, items designated as not to be transferred were explicitly labeled "do not copy" (*bu chao*) in registers, but in later years, it was more common to simply leave the bottom of the page blank. In contrast to the secret communications that received priority handling, "do not copy" documents were matters of marginal interest to the wider bureaucracy. The information-dense appendices of crop prices, rainfall, and other tables that governors appended to periodic memorials were never disclosed, nor were congratulatory memorials submitted on the occasion of military victory or an imperial birthday, or gratitude memorials sent in upon receipt of an appointment or honor.

While *Register of Documents as They Come to Hand* provided a concise record of memorials received by the Grand Council, a series of registers called *Outgoing Archive* (Wai ji dang) maintained by the Grand Secretariat described in more substantive detail the memorials submitted by field officials that did not move through confidential channels.[63] Like the Grand Council records, these registers were organized in chronological fashion and listed memorials by author in the order received. However, the individual entries in the Grand Secretariat volumes are far lengthier. These transcriptions of the contents and responses to memorials served as backup copies of the transferred memorials rather than as an index of communications. Another indicator of the archive's function is the immense size of the monthly volumes. Most measure over one foot tall and nearly a foot wide (38 cm tall by 29.5 cm wide).[64] Such large proportions could indicate that these registers were made available to multiple clerks for copying or that individual pages were posted for copying prior to binding in the monthly register. Given the length of most document transcriptions in *Outgoing Archive*, it is clear that a second stage of abridgment took place in preparing memorials for publication in the relatively concise gazettes. This process likely took place in the Six Sections, but records and regulations have not survived.

In the archives of the outer court, Manchu- and Chinese-language versions of *Registers of Silken Words* (Si lun bu) accounted for the items read and annotated by the emperor and released to the bureaucracy.[65] This register had also been kept by the Grand Secretariat during the Ming dynasty. Gazette scribes and communications liaisons (or their subordinates) may have headed to the registry offices to consult this register in selecting documents for copying. Compilers also drew on *Registers* in composing the imperial court diaries (*qijuzhu*).[66] In contrast to the Grand Council records, *Registers of Silken Words* indexed communications by the imperial response granted to them, not by the author of the initial memorial. In addition, this register included documents originating from the routine communications system.[67] As is the case for all existing registers, the contents of the *Registers of Silken Words* are more comprehensive than the items selected for publication in the gazettes. The register for the ninth year of the Kangxi reign, for example, listed more than ten thousand items, an average of about twenty-eight documents per day.

Faced with the demands of translating Chinese bureaucratic language for bilingual registers and channels of communication, Manchu clerks turned to administrative glossaries for clarification. The best known of these glossaries was *Administrative Terms of the Six Boards* (Liubu chengyu), evidently first released in 1742.[68] The glossary described the gazettes emanating from the center and those distributed by capital liaisons (*dibao* and *tangbao*, respectively) as "reports" (*boolara bithe* in Manchu) and distinguished these official editions from gazette copies (*dichao*), termed "clear copies" (*doolama araha* in Manchu).[69] These translations were identical to Manchu terms included in Shen Qiliang's *Complete Book of the Great Qing* (Da Qing quanshu), the earliest identified editions of which were published in 1683 (figure 1.1).[70] Shen's dictionary ordered the terms by their place in the Manchu syllabary, whereas the administrative glossaries organized terminology according to administrative use, therefore making reference to gazettes in sections concerning the Board of Appointments and the Board of War. These translations continued to be employed in administrative parlance through the nineteenth century.[71]

The development of the Grand Council and the gradual process of establishing procedures for handling incoming and outgoing documents resulted

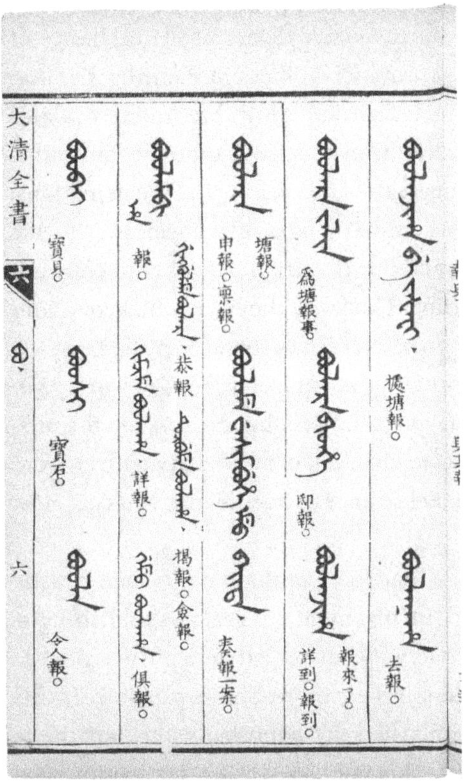

FIGURE 1.1. Manchu terminology for gazettes in *Complete Book of the Great Qing* (Da Qing quanshu, 1683). Courtesy of Staatsbibliothek zu Berlin.

in the expansion of the clerical personnel that staffed metropolitan offices. In addition, clerks, capital liaisons, and other government personnel established more complex connections to the commercial realm. Board officials in the eighteenth century submitted repeated requests to hire new clerks. Clerks themselves often hired messengers, scribes, and other assistants on the side, paying these subordinates out of their own stipends. Both Manchu and Chinese personnel factored into the growing secretarial workforce.[72] By 1760, the court, at the impetus of metropolitan officials, would act to clarify the relationship between the central state, communications liaisons, and commercial vendors in the realm of gazette publishing. In so doing, it condemned the unprincipled behavior of commercial publishers and distributors while simultaneously upholding the public function of court gazettes.

Commercial Interactions and the Gongshen Tang Experiment

In 1756, the imperial censor Yang Kaiding (b. 1707) penned a report to the throne concerning the aftermath of a bungled enterprise. Yang's report resulted from his investigation into certain unreasonable delays in the exchange of official texts between the capital and provincial offices in Baoding, the seat of Zhili. As capital communications liaison for Zhili, Mu Yaonian (dates unknown) was charged with the distribution of various types of communications to provincial officials, including seals of office, imperial proclamations, regular correspondence, and gazettes summarizing capital business. Mu, like many other liaisons of his day, contracted with a local publisher to copy out the gazettes for distribution to Baoding. However, the liaison had gone into debt with his designated publisher, who had refused to hand over the expected gazettes until he was paid up, culminating in the delay. What's worse, Mu had attempted to take up the missing work himself, but he bungled the process. Officials of the Six Sections detected his lack of familiarity with current procedures for the authentication and clearance of documents. Mu's gazettes were a total failure.

The censor's resulting argument—that the Qianlong court take drastic measures to eliminate commercial involvement in gazette publishing—emphasized the importance of state publicity but denied the legitimacy of the commercial relationships that made government publicity possible. In his review of the case, Yang Kaiding lambasted the publisher's unsympathetic decision to cut off the supply of news. This publisher, like other commercial agents contracted for state business, "knew no scruples." In the censor's telling, the publisher's pursuit of profit had caused him to disregard the gravity of his duties. By insisting that the debt be repaid, the publisher had debased the functionality and even the integrity of the government communications system.[73]

Yang Kaiding judged the gazette trade to have fallen victim to selfish commercial interests. He wrote, "Transcripts of our dynasty's official matters, meant to be disseminated far and wide, have instead become documents hoarded and bid upon in the marketplace."[74] Some years earlier, the Yongzheng emperor, wary of state overextension, had rejected a bid to place gazette publishing under direct government control.[75] Qianlong, by contrast, was more amenable to proposals for increased surveillance. In fact, prior to Yang's revelations, the Qianlong court had already implemented an intermediate arrangement that instructed each capital liaison to personally supervise the copying of palace documents at a location proximate to the Six Sections. Section clerks recorded the names of hired copyists in order to improve accountability in cases of mistakes.[76] Still, problems from leaks to delays recurred, and memorialists in a chorus pled with the court to punish the "gazette publishers who bought copy and the clerks who sold copy" (*mai chao zhi baofang, mai chao zhi shuban*) for preying on state business.[77]

At the impetus of scandalized officials like Yang Kaiding, by 1760 the Qianlong court had shuttered the city's gazette publishers and ordered capital communications liaisons to directly publish gazettes. Their publishing house, the Gongshen Tang, operated for about sixty years, although new commercial gazette imprints began to emerge in the later part of its tenure.[78] The establishment of the Gongshen Tang compelled capital liaisons for the various provinces to work together to supervise the process of gazette publishing. Capital liaisons used funds remitted by provincial governments to cover the expenses of hiring, materials, and equipment.[79] The institution's name thus referred to its common funding and commitment to improved vigilance against errors and delays in the publishing process. The Gongshen Tang experiment, as well as being an attempt to eliminate malfeasance by commercial producers, represented a power struggle between the court and provincial officials over access to information.[80]

Though relatively short lived, the state concern did inhibit the flow of illicit information from capital intermediaries to provincial and capital powerholders. Gazette publishing still operated on the basis of personal relationships, but these were less subject to abuse. In 1820, the hired manager of the Gongshen Tang reported that stamped scribal documents for printing were delivered daily by a clerk named Zhang, after which the liaisons were charged with delivery to the provinces.[81] The new publishing house had at least in part been intended to improve the discipline of capital liaisons, who had previously moonlighted as personal spies for provincial officials. However, despite their guaranteed funding under the Gongshen Tang system, capital liaisons neglected their duties and siphoned funds to other purposes.[82] Accounting for debts owed between different liaisons resulted in confusion and dispute. By the mid-nineteenth century, the state publisher had lapsed, allowing commercial publishers to resume direct interaction with palace offices to obtain gazette materials.

◆ ◆ ◆

From the Shunzhi emperor in the conquest period through the Qianlong emperor in the mid-eighteenth century, early Qing rulers allowed the window of public documents to open wider. They claimed a commitment to fairness and transparency in their words, and they sponsored institutions and policies that ensured wide access to imperial documents. Publicity continued to be a central pillar of Qing information policy even as rulers consolidated power through secret communications and used censorship to crack down on perceived dissent. Although secret communications systems are among the best known institutional innovations of the Qing dynasty, in fact whenever new instruments for secret communications were introduced, measures to publicize subsets of this correspondence soon followed. Indeed, each new documentary conduit and institution developed during the Qing involved considerations that weighed the relative political value of secrecy and transparency. In implementing procedures that both improved confidentiality in the communications process and offered access to recorded decisions, the Qing state pursued documentary authority.

The result was an information order that granted substantial visibility of the imperial state, its officials, and its procedures. After taking control in 1644, the Qing court began to publish gazettes and other public documentation for official use. By the mid-eighteenth century, the Qing state had stabilized a system for producing, regulating, and disseminating public documents in the form of gazettes that had devolved to the private sphere in the preceding dynasty. However, in reasserting control, the central state did not dominate all aspects of the gazette trade. Instead, it worked together with commercial agents and provincial institutions. This decentralized structure—like the use of publicity to replace direct supervision—reduced the burden of the central state but encompassed certain security risks. In the next chapter, we see how the uses of secrecy intersected and conflicted with policies of publicity during the formative period of the Qing information order.

CHAPTER 2

Challenges to the Information Order

THE QING INFORMATION ORDER, REALIZED BY THE MIDPOINT OF the eighteenth century, comprised a tripartite model of political communications that coordinated the activities and work of four layers of political actors: the emperor and his closest advisors, the larger metropolitan bureaucracy, the provincial administrations, and local officials. The most closely guarded communications, including military reports and palace memorials, passed exclusively between memorialists and the inner court. Next, administrative information, inscribed in routine memorials (*tiben*) and other highly standardized modes of correspondence, was circulated between the locale, province, and central bureaucracy. Finally, open media, including gazettes and proclamations (*gaoshi*), were made available to the full bureaucracy and even the wider public. These three communications genres were not mutually exclusive; both routine and palace memorials could be excerpted and republished in gazettes and proclamations.

Emergent practices of secrecy and publicity shaped the strategies that historical actors employed to secure political information. Successive administrations grappled with palace spies, document leaks, and rumor mongering. To a certain extent, the pursuit of political intelligence was a routine component of capital life. However, cases of document theft and misuse proliferated at specific moments in the construction of the information order, particularly during the emergence of the palace memorial network and the Grand Council in the late seventeenth and early eighteenth centuries. These incidents suggest that the uncertainty generated by unfamiliar communications practices, especially those relating to state secrecy, motivated the illicit pursuit of documents and information.

During these moments, the imperial court condemned and investigated in public view "information scandals" involving the misuse of state documents, elevating the spectacle around incidents that might otherwise elicit little notice. Consistent with its use of publicity to encourage bureaucratic accountability and moral governance, the Qing court exposed information scandals to dissuade future outbreaks of covert intelligence gathering. Evidentiary traces of scandals gleaned from the archival record attest to the political prerogatives of the historical actors involved as compilers, informants, and suspects. As historian Philip Kuhn wrote about the Qing bureaucracy and its documentary record, "Every document generated by an 'event' . . . must be read both as description of an outer reality and as reflection of the political needs of its author."[1] References to unverified "copies" (*xiaochao*) implied unsanctioned materials to be uniformly unreliable; references to "fake reports" (*jiabao*) and "forged memorials" (*weigao*) suggested documents to be purposeful and malicious fakes. Yet copies, forgeries, and fakes all obtained audiences and commanded attention (and financial interest) from political elites and ordinary audiences alike. In examining information scandals, it is important to remember that the received archival record prioritizes the agendas and predilections of the ruling emperor and obscures relationships and motivations less relevant to the imperial psyche.[2]

The Shifting Boundaries of Secrecy

In the seventeenth and early eighteenth centuries—a crucial era for the negotiation of interests between court and bureaucracy—political actors followed a variety of strategies to obtain information against the wishes of the imperial court. The task of finding trustworthy political information involved different practices when one was stationed in a southern city, a frontier garrison, or in the capital city. For all, information stemming from the court and palace garnered intense interest. As a result, the corridors of palace offices became arenas where clerks and informants contended to obtain the latest and most valuable documents for distant administrators and local audiences.

The Kangxi and Yongzheng emperors, each in his own way, frequently expressed preoccupation with ensuring that the state bureaucracy remained trustworthy and condemned the surreptitious pursuit of palace information. Both traced information scandals of various types to originate in failures of trust and loyalty. The most explosive and punitive responses resulted from intelligence leaks surrounding events that have emerged as crucial touchpoints in scholarship on the mid-Qing period: frontier campaigns, succession crises, and outbreaks of dissent from Chinese subjects. In other cases, when infractions were clearly unintentional or resulted from administrative ambiguities, the court responded with lenience.

The Emperor's Intelligence Networks

For some field administrators and palace officials, the Kangxi emperor's exchange of "secret" memorials with privileged correspondents disrupted expectations of standard operating practice. Beginning from their initiation in the 1690s, Kangxi's secret correspondence networks soon became an open secret in the bureaucracy. It was well known that his correspondents were primarily Manchu officials, especially those stationed in the capital city and southeast China, and that their exchanges focused on matters that benefitted from a dose of secrecy—back-biting reports on corrupt officials, intelligence reports on restive communities and incipient rebellions, and other sensitive topics. The emperor used these confidential networks to police loyalty and employed secret memorials to solicit intelligence.[3] At the same time, Kangxi used information as a reward for loyal subordinates. In both cases, the exchange of secret memorials advertised the existence of trust between the emperor and certain privileged officials.

In the summer of 1715, the Kangxi emperor dispatched couriers bearing detailed accounts of the defense of imperial posts in East Turkestan, penned by the emperor himself, to a few key correspondents. Earlier that summer, the emperor had been shocked to hear from garrison commanders in Hami that the formidable Junghar Mongols, led by their embittered leader Tsewang Rabdan (r. 1697–1727), had pierced Qing fortifications and attacked the military outpost. Eighteen years prior, he had led a victorious but grueling campaign to eradicate the territorial claims of the semi-nomadic Junghars by eliminating Galdan, their erstwhile leader and Tsewang Rabdan's uncle.[4] The 1715 attack convinced Kangxi that his empire was not secure, and he resolved to expand military strength in the region.[5] In the imperial mind, the danger lay not just on the frontier, but also in the talk of Qing weakness that might emerge in response, particularly among southern Chinese detractors.

For Kangxi, personal communications networks appeared to be an important tool for navigating the potential complexities of a renewed military campaign against the Junghars. Kangxi chose two trusted Manchu officials, Hešeo (d. 1719) and Mamboo (1673–1725), to receive curated reports of the planned response.[6] He reminded these officials that the inevitable rumors that swirled around war could not be trusted. To Hešeo he wrote, "You are a Manchu, and I fear you might believe the heedless rumors that the Han disseminate, so I have copied out a summary of the real circumstances for your information."[7] To Mamboo he wrote, "Fujian is far away, and fake reports (*jiabao*) of the various provinces are extremely numerous."[8] In this correspondence, Kangxi suggested that the source of doubt lay not at the frontier or capital, but with the Chinese populace of the south who would distort imperial policy for malicious reasons.

Kangxi's messages to the two Manchu officials drew attention to the uncertainty of local rumor in southern China even as he implied that written reports from the front were both trustworthy and freely available. Kangxi instructed the two officials to secretly forward to the palace any unsanctioned reports, specifically those that presumed to quote the emperor's intentions. He affirmed the accuracy of the frontier reports which he had personally excerpted. Even though the emperor had embedded his war reports in the endorsements to private greeting memorials (*qing'an zhe*), he instructed the two men to inform other officials of their details.[9] Not only Mamboo and Hešeo, but all of the officials in the south could plausibly trust this information derived from confidential written reports.[10]

Field officials in other regions were not so lucky as to receive personal dispatches from the emperor, and relied on official and unofficial news sources and conversations with their own networks to learn about the campaign. The shocking news of a Mongol siege on an imperial garrison prompted the aged governor of southwestern Guizhou, Liu Yinshu (1637–1723), to send his own memorial to the court. He urged Kangxi to delay what he understood to be an imminent military expedition to the front. Although Liu had found no reference to such plans in the court-authorized gazettes, he had learned about the prospective campaign from other, unnamed sources, and he made the risky calculation to trust these descriptions. The court response was swift and negative. Court advisors described Liu's missive as uninformed and careless. Kangxi lambasted the governor in an edict: "Liu Yinshu believed rumors and [unauthorized] gazettes and heedlessly submitted a memorial on defining borders. He should really drop this business. . . . Since Liu has not yet declined into old age, let him ride a military horse to the front, and observe matters to his heart's content. Only then should he submit such advice."[11] The emperor's response mocked Liu for his gullibility and inability to discern fact from fiction.[12] It grouped unofficial news sources together with popular talk as not worthy of credible belief. The situation resulted, however, not merely from the Guizhou official's credulity, but from the systematic ways in which the secret memorial system granted information to some and denied it to others. Officials on the outs with the monarch thus struggled to vet intelligence sources.

Moreover, even officials with guaranteed access to confidential communications found it advantageous to assemble multiple avenues of intelligence. Mamboo, Kangxi's trusted correspondent in Fujian, faced challenges similar to Liu Yinshu in authenticating local reports about the western frontier. Four years after Kangxi sent him exclusive dispatches from Hami, Mamboo revealed to the emperor that the Fujian capital communications liaison had sent bad information from the capital at that time. Mamboo argued that Kangxi's gift of confidential dispatches had intimidated this underling and convinced him to send only materials authorized by the palace bureaucracy's Six Sections (Keya), rather than unverified reports like those which Liu Yinshu had unfortunately trusted.[13] However, as it later came to light, Mamboo also commanded an extensive network of informants in the capital. His spies had penetrated the palace, reading the secret messages that the emperor exchanged before the documents were returned to their recipients.[14] Thus, while Mamboo cited the emperor's trust as the key element supporting his awareness of imperial news and confidence in ridding his region of false rumors, covert sources played an equally important role.

The open secret of confidential correspondence networks gave rise to political tensions and openings for intrigue in the territories and in the closer palace community. Individual memorialists knew that their counterparts in neighboring regions also exchanged messages via privileged channels. Meanwhile, officials left out of the network struggled to make sense of prevailing rumors about court politics and frontier exploits. The Hami crisis revealed flaws in Kangxi's strategy of managing political loyalties through correspondence networks. The system presumed personal allegiance and trust to accompany the exchange of secret messages. But distance challenged these assumptions, as each side gambled against the other. The emperor's use of information as a reward for demonstrated loyalty and service foreshadowed the factional divides that would emerge after his death. The covert exchange of courtroom information concerning matters both routine and extraordinary—including the troubled issue of an heir for the emperor—exposed major faults in the information order of the late Kangxi era.

Courtroom Spies

Liu Yinshu, the ill-fated governor who was fooled by faulty information, had reason to believe that rumors and documents purported to have been leaked from the palace might reflect real conditions. Indeed, by the last years of his reign, the Kangxi emperor was no stranger to the pervasive dangers of spies in the courtroom and in palace halls. The enmity between Kangxi's sons, in particular the chief contenders for the imperial throne, nurtured factional alliances that flourished in the late Kangxi reign and persisted through the early eighteenth century. Court advisors suggested to the emperor that these conspiracies were behind the persistent leak of unauthorized news reports and documents out of the palace.

In the last two decades of his reign, Kangxi watched with dismay as his chosen heir declined into insanity. The emperor's secret correspondence when away from the capital focused on tracking the activities and misdeeds of the heir apparent. By 1708, it became necessary to confine the former crown prince and to determine a new heir. However, the meeting convened between palace advisors failed to determine a viable option. Almost immediately, the story of the meeting and its participants spread throughout the capital's rumor networks.[15]

Since official gazettes recorded only communications sanctioned for release by the court, news of the secret meeting obviously drew on unauthorized intelligence. Suggestions that princely factions might have prompted spies to fuel the exchange of stories emerged in the meeting's aftermath. Had a prince, or perhaps one of the meeting participants, granted access to a spy? Kuixu (1675–1717), an elite Manchu official and a prominent participant in the meeting, perhaps sought to distract from these intrigues by labeling the spies as ordinary copyists soliciting public attention: "Those who transcribe official reports [*baowen*], besides copying the daily summaries of board business [*kechao*], are in the habit of gathering intelligence [*tanting*] into accounts called 'short reports' [*xiaobao*], and sending them all about. In the worst cases, they willfully fabricate tales meant to shock readers and listeners. [We should] strictly forbid this practice, so that all meddlesome and dishonest men will be fearful."[16] Kuixu depicted the unauthorized journey of the meeting's details out of the palace as the consequence of habitual connections between news-writers and palace clerks. With his reference to intentional distortions meant to "shock" readers, the official implied that the reports were circulated as entertaining stories for uninformed audiences.

Behind this dismissive appearance, Kuixu's use of the term *short reports* to describe the unlicensed publications in fact offered a more pointed reference to the political power of news in Chinese history.[17] In the Song dynasty, short reports had become game pieces in political contests that pitted literati factions against one another.[18] Literati and official readers exchanged court news according to their own interpretive priorities, and conversations about these dispatches became the grounds for political action.[19] In more recent memory, the proliferation of short reports, anonymous broadsides, and polemical accusations had also characterized the divisive politics of the late Ming dynasty. After the establishment of the Qing state, both monarchs and officials often brought up the disorderly politics of the previous dynasty's decline as a negative example of the dangers of unrestrained bureaucratic infighting.[20] Kuixu's warning thus hinted at the return of an age of factional politics. With his implication that false news could mislead popular audiences, the official suggested that factional politics could provide the seeds for wider social disorder. By extension, the circulation of uncontrolled political news challenged court authority.

The Multilingual Court

Kuixu's logic proved persuasive, and his proposed ban on unauthorized copying was entered in the dynasty's administrative statutes.[21] Prosecutions, however, were few. Still, other defining characteristics of the Kangxi courtroom created openings for security lapses that could incite the leaks palace officials feared. The emperor made policy and conducted advisory meetings in conversations conducted in multiple languages. In addition, he often issued oral edicts (*kouyu*) that carried the force of law comparable to pronunciations enforced in writing. These activities led to confusion—what pronunciations held force, and which were ephemeral comments?

One day in 1717, the link between courtroom ambiguities and leaked documents became clear. A group of Hanlin officials relaxed outside the Court Diaries Office (Qijuzhu Guan) discussing recent imperial distributions of tax relief funds. One Chen Zhang asked his colleague Zhao Xiongzhao (1663–1721) if he recalled when an imperial edict had been proclaimed on a recent relief request. Zhao had personal connections to the matter because his father was the powerful head of the Board of Revenue (Hubu), and although he felt unable to remember precisely, he felt certain that the matter had transpired.[22] Because they suspected the matter to have been discussed in Manchu, the pair summoned an unnamed translation clerk (*bitieshi*) to locate evidence in the archives of the Court Diaries Office. The clerk entered the archives and found "amongst the waste-paper" records, a note about Kangxi's conversations on the matter. He wrote down the corresponding date and emerged to hand the item to his interlocutors. Satisfied, the Hanlin officials took the record as proof and later tore it into pieces and threw it away.[23]

In fact, the emperor had issued no such ruling. Although Kangxi had considered a request for tax relief by the governor Hešeo, he had rejected the request upon suspicion of Hešeo's motives. Kangxi issued no edict, and the matter was not publicized. The emperor was outraged to find out that the officials had sent a clerk to copy items out of the archives to satisfy their own personal curiosities.[24] Furthermore, the capital officials' mistaking oral conversations as documentary facts suggested that they lacked understanding of the principles behind administrative procedures. If they haphazardly drew conclusions from courtroom transcripts without considering whether such decisions had been finalized, the officials could sow wider confusion about the court's policies and agendas. The mishandling of palace documents challenged even routine matters of administration.

Secrecy and Power in the Yongzheng Reign

In 1723, Kangxi's fourth son won the contest for the throne and began to rule as the Yongzheng emperor. Kangxi's will had been revealed only on his deathbed, and some whispered that a covert ally had altered the text in order to award the throne to the would-be Yongzheng emperor. The new emperor thus assumed power in a fraught and suspicious political climate. He remained critically attentive to the activities of his brothers—his onetime rivals for the throne—and the ways that their behavior could be construed to undermine his reputation and authority. At the same time, the Yongzheng emperor and his allies turned their attention to sources of weakness and insecurity inherited from the ruling practices of his father's court. In this, Yongzheng targeted weak points of the Kangxi emperor's courtroom conduct and his overuse of the secret memorial system. These points of emphasis facilitated his sustained critique of his father's misplaced trust in the correspondence contained in palace memorials and advanced his dogged investigation of perceived enemies and potential conspiracies organized by factional groups.

As Yongzheng set up his court, a memorial authored by the Manchu censor Yentai (d. 1738) urged the new monarch to guard against information leaks stemming from his courtroom. He proclaimed that the publishing of unauthorized news challenged "the ability of all under heaven to discern truth from falsehood [*nan bian zhenwei*]."[25] More than a rehearsal of Kuixu's earlier condemnation of palace leaks, Yentai's accusations illustrate how allies of the new emperor campaigned to secure the court environment and root out political enemies. Yentai's memorial, which combined condemnation of inherited practices with praise of the new monarch, is characteristic of bureaucratic responses to customary calls for critique issued at the beginning of each reign period. Yentai, a Manchu bannerman, had risen through the bureaucracy from a clerical position in the Grand Secretariat over a thirty-year career and had in fact retired a decade earlier. During Yentai's retirement, the future emperor reportedly traveled to the northeast and met Yentai and his son. When Yongzheng assumed the throne, he recalled Yentai and named him to high posts in the Grand Secretariat, the Board of Works, and subsequently the Censorate.[26]

Yentai's report argued that the informal court environment and highly personalized political practices of the late Kangxi emperor embodied serious security risks. He highlighted Kangxi's conduct of multilingual meetings and issuance of courtroom lectures and edicts as particularly disruptive. The prevalence of orality in the court had enabled all sorts of individuals to skulk around and even transcribe conversations under guise of preserving archival records, court diaries, and gazettes. Many of these agents did not restrict themselves to sanctioned materials, but rather recorded "every move and word" of the emperor. According to Yentai, not only had unsanctioned records of court activity remained the subject of conversation, they were sold under the provocative name of "evening notes" (*wantie*) and circulated widely.

The sale of unauthorized reports also portended underhanded political action. Their circulation, Yentai argued, distorted faraway officials' perception of the activities of the court. Rumors of immoral conduct by the monarch could stir up movements to critique or even plot against the throne. In addition, the availability of intrusive reports emboldened corrupt officials to fabricate notices that they had been favored with gifts from the emperor and bribe capital liaisons and gazette publishers to record these in gazettes.[27]

Such concerns remained salient beyond Yongzheng's reign. About fifteen years later, another official reminded the court that trumped-up notices of gifts could be used for the pursuit of personal advantage. As a result, no political information could be considered neutral. By soliciting the publication of evidence of gifts and tribute bequeathed between emperor and official as representations of imperial favor, an official pursued selfish fame and perhaps even more sinister motives. Since these records were generally not released by the court, they could only be obtained and published through "inquiries on the sly."[28] In these appeals for confidentiality, personal motives that overrode court and state objectives appeared the foremost threat.

In the second year of his reign, Yongzheng responded to the prompting of Yentai and other associates by rebuking past misuses of the secret memorial system. The details of the edict suggest that the new emperor almost immediately ordered an investigation into spying and communications practices in his father's palace. Yongzheng summoned the example of Mamboo, the Manchu official in Fujian whom Kangxi had so trusted, as well as another prominent Manchu governor. Both were guilty of recruiting underlings to spy on secret communications in the palace. These revelations cast Mamboo's past correspondence in a new light. Had Mamboo invalidated the capital liaison's reports through legitimate or underhanded means? For Yongzheng, these crimes illustrated the danger of a monarch's overreliance on personal trust.[29] The authority of communications relied on shared trust. In principle, trust enabled participants in a confidential exchange to speak of each and every matter, leaving nothing out. Yet the use of secret communications in no way guaranteed mutual trust. The accusations against Mamboo thus proved his essential lack of mutual trust. Yongzheng condemned the spying—but more so the system that enabled and shielded it: "These abuses originate in the officials' inability to trust themselves, and their resultant inability to trust their emperor. If their intentions are thus, then what use are secret memorials?"[30]

While Yongzheng perceived that ordinary mistakes and even structural problems could generate problems in the documentary communications system, he was far more predisposed to suggest political motives as underlying factors. Kangxi had understood personal ties supported by secret communications to support the monarch's power. Yongzheng believed the opposite, especially concerning personal ties among officials and other interested parties. In his essay "On Factions" (Yuzhi pengdang lun, 1725), the emperor reiterated and expanded on themes introduced in his edict of the preceding year. The essay dismissed interest-based groupings as totally unacceptable and contrary to the goals of an effective state.[31]

The legacy of personal relationships in mediating imperial communications took a toll in governance. Secret memorials, which had appeared to solve the problem of confidential communications across vast and uncertain territory, also introduced new complexity. Between emperor and official, as well as between provincial and capital correspondents, the very secrecy of these communications made it difficult to assess their truth. Although the emperor could balance the suspicions of his territorial officials against each other, he could not account for their proclivity to use other networks, whether bureaucratic or personal, to advance their own interests. Especially in times of war and intrigue, the monarch could not rely on distant correspondents, but required intimate consultation with close advisors in secure settings to guide the imperial helm.

Leaks, Rumors, and Factions

In the early Yongzheng reign, rumors proliferated concerning the emperor's conduct—one featured variant portrayed the ordinarily austere emperor hosting drunken after-hours antics with favored officials. Emperor and courtier alike connected these persistent social rumors to probable lapses in palace security. Informants claimed that rumors originated from leaks, forged documents, and unauthorized gazettes and used these incidents to argue that the recent preventative measures had been ineffective. They indicated that the low-status clerks and scribes who risked their positions by copying unsanctioned documents, smuggling items out of the palace, and recording secret conversations worked at the command of more powerful masters. Reports of document leaks consistently suggested that factional action lay behind the intrusions of information networks.[32]

The fact that Yongzheng and his subordinates closely controlled the documentary record is both well established and makes it difficult to separate fact from imperial agenda.[33] Officials' willingness to blame factional alliances for information leaks may reveal more about the emperor's concerns than the real contexts in which political information changed hands. Yongzheng's obsession with conspiratorial groups of bureaucrats and imperial clansmen as sources of political enmity steered court interpretations of the reasons behind spying and leaks. Still, whether or not factional interests were the chief motives behind leaks and the dissemination of rumors, the problem of factions compelled the Yongzheng emperor to devote remarkable attention to minor document leaks and trivial talk.

For instance, Yongzheng repeatedly lashed out at rumors concerning his use of alcohol and his conduct with favored associates. He was particularly galled when such tales made their way into unauthorized but widely read records of court news. In the fourth year of the Yongzheng reign, an unofficial gazette edition recorded that the emperor drank and caroused in the imperial summer palace with favored officials. After describing his alibi in a public edict (Yongzheng had treated his ministers to a "meager and humble" meal), the emperor determined that the source of the story in the gazette should be located "in order to dissuade the formation of evil cliques." Once the two publishers were executed, the emperor swiftly accused three of his brothers and political enemies of organizing a factional conspiracy to plant the story.[34]

Two years later, in 1728, in raising the issue of a letter filled with accusations against the emperor that had been delivered to his post, the provincial official Yue Zhongqi (1686–1754) speculated that constant public attention could transform any mundane statement in the authorized gazette into salacious rumor. For example, according to Yue, gossips and travelers had distorted the intended meaning of a recent memorial by official Lu Zhenyang that mentioned the emperor's sparing use of alcohol after the missive was published in the court gazette. On the streets, innocuous statements had been transformed into the rumor that the emperor imbibed so frequently that he could no longer hold his liquor.[35]

Yue Zhongqi's cautious reminder of the natural occurrence of rumor targeted the emperor's penchant for addressing rumors with dramatic public pronouncements. The official's admonition did not succeed in restraining the emperor. In one of the most striking moves of his reign, Yongzheng went so far as to publish a lengthy question-and-answer tract that acknowledged and countered the claims of a dissident scholar against the legitimacy of the Manchu claim to the throne. The emperor ordered this text, *Great Righteousness Awakening from Delusion* (Dayi juemi lu), distributed to every official and government post in the empire.[36] Yongzheng's acknowledgment of controversial and even salacious cases in public edicts and published collections reflected his awareness of the utility of publicity as a political tool directed toward an audience of Chinese elites.

In the prefaces that he authored for a variety of imperial publications, the Yongzheng emperor emphasized his desire to present his perspective directly, without the potential interference of intermediaries. While Kangxi before him and Qianlong after oversaw more expansive publishing projects that were meant to solicit the talents of the scholar class, Yongzheng's compilations highlighted the monarch's personal agendas and interests.[37] In this vein, the emperor sponsored publications as varied as topical collections on Buddhism, orthodox conduct, and Banner affairs, a compilation of rescripted memorials from field officials, and the massive collection of public edicts, *Edicts to the Grand Secretariat* (Shangyu neige).[38] The memorial compilations in particular supported the emperor's promotion of accountability and uniformity in bureaucratic governance. In his introduction to *Edicts to the Grand Secretariat*, Yongzheng wrote that an official compilation thus avoided the problem of disparate editions circulating in the different provinces, a result of the unreliability of the clerks and scribes that transcribed them.[39] In other words, centralized control and transparency eliminated the risk of distortion. Controlled transparency unified imperial policy.

Although the publicity afforded to his remarks made the cases famous, it did not always succeed in clearing the emperor's name. The tale of the two executed news publishers later became a go-to example of the characteristics of an Oriental despot for European audiences after Jesuit missionaries referred to the story in their correspondence.[40] Rather than neutralizing the rumors, publicity made these scandals notorious. The notoriety of information scandals nurtured the assumption among Europeans that the exchange and manipulation of even the most commonplace of news concerning the Qing court and its activities originated from the highest levels of political intrigue.

Anxiety about factional connections more than concern for the mere existence of informal and unauthorized news networks motivated Yongzheng's scrutiny of information scandals during his reign. Further illustrating this is a case brought to the emperor's attention by the Sichuan governor Hiyande (d. 1740) in 1727. Hiyande reported that Cheng Rusi, a former administrator in custody for corruption, had hung himself with a pair of pants in jail two days prior to his scheduled execution.[41] Cheng Rusi's case involved shocking revelations of violence and greed, but it is important to note that he was one of the many political casualties of the extended investigation led by Yue Zhongqi into the clique associated with former imperial favorite Nian Gengyao (d. 1725). Thus, the case was a political priority by association. Yongzheng demanded an inquiry and suggested that Cheng Rusi's collaborators and informants must be apprehended.

Once the possibility of factional action seemed improbable, the emperor's enthusiasm for the investigation waned. When Hiyande suggested institutional reforms to improve administrative certainty across distances, the emperor responded with apathy. In his report on the case's investigation, Governor Hiyande premised that the condemned man had obtained the notice of his sentence from an unofficial gazette copy (*jingbao zhi xiaochao*) and decided to end his life on his own terms. Since gazettes and their unofficial copies circulated widely, it would be impossible to find the source of the information. Moreover, these details were not fabricated or erroneous but simply leaked in advance of the official execution notice.

The emperor accepted the hypothesis and wrote in the margin of Hiyande's memorial, "I hadn't thought of gazettes."[42] Turning to Hiyande's suggestion for the total abolition of court gazettes in consequence of the case, Yongzheng abruptly dismissed this proposal and the matter was concluded. After all, unauthorized news in this case had merely provided advance notice of a legal certainty and had not facilitated subversive activities or undermined state power. Although the suicide of Cheng Rusi would seem to illustrate the need for substantial reform, the case left the monarch's attention because in the absence of factional intrigue, it seemed trivial, not scandalous.

The Rise of the Grand Council

Preoccupation with issues of trust directed the Yongzheng emperor's oversight of cases involving government communications. The emperor often turned to publicity in response to perceived betrayals, forcing members of the bureaucratic community to acknowledge his agendas. At the same time, Yongzheng steered the highest levels of the Qing state away from openness and toward secrecy. In a set of pioneering moves, Yongzheng curtailed the power of bureaucratic institutions, in particular the Grand Secretariat and the Censorate, by limiting their purview of state communications. Next, a series of elite councils (the forerunners to the Grand Council) supplanted these outer court institutions in advising the emperor. As we shall see, these momentous shifts in power and institutional arrangements at court generated disturbances. The rise of the Grand Council, whose activities were not well known to outsiders, destabilized relationships between the capital and members of the bureaucratic community who saw themselves as further curtailed from essential, top-level discussions. As details of information scandals in the Yongzheng and early Qianlong reigns reveal, the price of political information went sky-high in this era of institutional change.

Factions, Trust, and the Grand Council

Yongzheng's distaste for the factional politics that he perceived as inveterate in larger and mixed bureaucratic institutions informed his implementation of administrative reforms involving the state communications system. These reforms defined clearer boundaries between court offices and between the inner court and the outer bureaucracy. The emperor rejected large audiences and met with advisors behind closed doors. Consolidating the Six Sections within the Censorate reduced the power of censors by increasing their administrative workload.[43] When a legal commission convened by the emperor compiled a schedule of punishments for administrative crimes involving the misuse of political information, it made supervising officials responsible for the crimes of their subordinates. This choice reflected the monarch's belief that political powerholders influenced the information trade. Drafted amid his prosecution of several frontier campaigns, the laws also reflected increased concern for crimes with connections to war and espionage.[44] Especially in the second half of his reign, military concerns influenced the composition of the courtroom. Most importantly, the Yongzheng emperor convoked successive informal councils to deal with pressing issues of the day, including ongoing frontier campaigns and financial overhauls of the imperial bureaucracy.

Yongzheng granted expanded access and power to trusted councilors in exchange for the stability that confidential advisory boards promised. His turn to "monarchical-conciliar administration" resulted in important reconfigurations to the palace memorial system.[45] The emperor allowed key members of his councils to collaborate in deliberating upon and drafting responses to secret memorials. Responses to secret memorials authored by these councils became known as "court letters" (*tingji*).[46] Where the Kangxi emperor had promised complete secrecy to his palace memorialists, these revisions converted the palace memorial network into a secure, top-level communications system. Participation in the palace memorial system no longer entailed the promise of utmost confidence between memorialist and emperor.

A series of remarkable institutional transitions took place in the months following the death of the Yongzheng emperor in October 1735. According to precedent and expectations, an appointed transition council began to assist the new emperor, Qianlong, with his monarchical duties. However, by comparison both with earlier transition periods and with the Yongzheng emperor's preference for flexible appointments, the council and its membership became permanent components of inner court administration. Empowering the group, the Qianlong emperor appointed an expanded staff and widened the jurisdiction of the council. The throne continued to deny the existence of a fixed ministerial council through the first fourteen years of the Qianlong reign, but the Grand Council operated beginning during the Yongzheng-Qianlong succession.[47] From then onward, the members of the Council would continue to enjoy expansive access to the monarch and oversight over incoming and outgoing communications.

Grand Council Document Leaks

The emergence of the Grand Council attracted notice from the outer court and field bureaucracy. Prior to the spread of informed knowledge about the council's activities, its procedures were the subject of interest and confusion. Not only had the Grand Council developed a new documentary genre in the court letter, but it also controlled its own separate archives and employed distinctive documentary procedures. As a result, items originating from the Grand Council were initially not available in court gazettes. In a series of cases exposed in the first decade or so of the Qianlong reign (and thus the early years of the Grand Council's existence as a formal institution), clerks and other subordinates earned large sums of money for illegally extracting documents from the Grand Council and other bureaucratic institutions. The investigations had a perfunctory air in comparison with the politically charged exposés of the Yongzheng era. Earlier, these enterprises might have been viewed as dangerous plots. Qianlong, however, responded to the incidents not with personal scrutiny, but by implementing bureaucratic solutions to expand access to central documents and mitigate the wider bureaucracy's poor understanding of new institutions.

The establishment of the Grand Council disrupted expectations for the relay of information and documents between capital subordinates and provincial officials for a lengthy period of time. In the spring of 1746, a capital liaison named Yu Zhuo wrote to the Guangxi provincial governor with some exciting news. Yu explained that he and other provincial agents had recently struggled to procure documents because the Grand Council guarded its materials so strictly. Yet governors across the empire were eager for news of the council's dealings. Yu had found a contact, a clerk (*gongshi*) for the Grand Council, who provided access to documents for a steep fee. Yu was allowed to copy only the general sense rather than the particulars of these "most important" documents. The liaison evidently expected that his superior would be pleased with this new channel of secret intelligence and provide the cash for this expensive deal. The governor, fearing scrutiny, instead decided to turn Yu in.[48]

Personal relationships and monetary exchanges smoothed the process of smuggling out court documents for interested parties. In a subsequent investigation of Yu Zhuo and his accomplices, the capital police found a chain of associations from Yu Zhuo to the Grand Secretariat clerk Qian Wu, who worked as a messenger between the Grand Council and the Grand Secretariat. Many of the intermediaries in this plot were Zhejiang natives, and according to their confessions, they relied on native-place ties to secure documents for Yu Zhuo and other capital liaisons, each taking a fee along the way. Chen Yaowen, a clerk implicated in the plot, reported in his confession that in a two-month period, the group obtained "forty to fifty" items. The majority (about thirty) of these items had been intended for eventual release to the outer bureaucracy, as they had been marked "for copy" (*ying fachao*). The clerks selected documents in an undiscriminating fashion and did not seek out details related to a particular political agenda.[49]

Investigators deliberated appropriate punishments for involved parties according to the relative priority of the documents they had stolen. Most important in sizing up an individual's offense was the location of the purloined document in the deliberative process at the point when it was removed from the palace. Yu Zhuo's case was considered to be particularly problematic because his accomplices leaked Grand Council documents not yet presented to the emperor. By contrast, in another case investigated in the same year, all the involved documents, such as file copies of memorials already returned to provincial officials (*lufu zouzhe*), document summaries (*lüejie*), and finalized edicts, had already been reviewed by the emperor. Even though these materials were not intended for release to the outer bureaucracy, leaking these documents was considered less serious than exposing unpresented documents.[50] Investigators moreover paid attention to whether Grand Council documents were "ordinary" (*xunchang*), a formal designation applied by the Qianlong-era Grand Council to non-military files.[51] Thus, whereas Yu Zhuo was stripped of his degree status and sent away in disgrace, the clerks who smuggled already-presented and "ordinary" documents were merely removed from their positions, and their supervisors received minor stipendiary fines.[52]

The substantial sums exchanged for documents speaks to the perceived value of documents associated with the Grand Council. A decade earlier, a document smuggling ring had directed dozens of unreleased documents to ten distinct clients. In total, the clients paid their several informants and messengers more than fifty taels per month, with one capital liaison alone paying twelve taels monthly.[53] Now, Yu Zhuo's expenses spurred him to contact the provincial governor for assistance, and indeed he paid his sources somewhat more than twenty taels per month. The clerks who obtained pre-reviewed documents earned between one and three taels per delivery.[54] Just as the trade in "ordinary" documents troubled investigators less than that in confidential materials, these documents were worth less. For instance, a 1741 investigation revealed that a Grand Secretariat clerk earned 500 cash (*wen*) per month for information and occasional documents, a paltry sum in comparison to the fees paid for Grand Council materials.[55]

Smoothing the Flow of Documents

In the archival record of the mid-Qianlong reign and thereafter, leaks of central information became relatively rare. New institutional measures allowed central documents to be legally published in court gazettes and thus slowed the illicit flow of documents out of metropolitan offices. Regulations adopted by 1737 created a sanctioned procedure by which palace memorials could be redirected from the Grand Council to the Grand Secretariat and therefore relayed to the outer bureaucracy.[56] In its early years, this procedure may have generated confusion, thus resulting in the spate of leak cases in the first decade after 1737. But growing familiarity with new procedures—as well as the happy recognition that more documents were being publicized—eased the demand for central documents.[57]

The court enacted a final administrative measure concerning the release of central information for gazettes in 1748. By precedent, most documents could be released for publication in gazettes five days after they received imperial approval and were sent to the relevant administrative board. This measure, initiated by Guangdong governor Yue Jun (1704–1753), suggested that some cases, particularly criminal cases of murder or brigandage, required a longer buffer of ten days. In this way, the state could ensure consistent handling of these delicate matters.[58]

Even more than the procedural changes it effected, Yue Jun's memorial is worth considering for its invocation of principles of transparency, secrecy, and information symmetry. His use of these concepts illustrates wider acceptance of these governing principles of the Qing information order by the mid-eighteenth century. He began by explaining that the imperial state's use of publicity supported the functioning of a well-ordered bureaucracy. The practice of publishing gazettes, he wrote in a memorial, "was originally meant to illuminate [*zhao*] the numerous achievements and all of the splendors of sagely rule." In Yue's formulation, a gazette reader would perceive the everyday triumphs as well as the overarching agendas of the imperial state. He continued, "Following the standard practices for the entire realm, in important criminal cases, one considers the seriousness of the case in determining its handling. All aspects of [these cases] are distinctly well suited for demonstrating proper usage of the law. This has real benefits for personnel administration [*lizhi*]." By studying complex cases in other districts, officials could take instruction as to how best to administer matters in their own domains.

However, Yue pointed out, more often than not, gazettes detailing the handling of important cases made their way out of the palace sooner than expected, and perhaps sooner than these matters had been concluded. "When the gazettes are sent out first," he wrote, "there is no guarantee that secrets are not divulged [*buchi jishi bumi*]," employing a classical allusion to make his point. Even in minor cases, to casually publish imperial emanations did not show proper respect to the throne. For this reason, he suggested extending the document delay for such important matters. Furthermore, Yue argued, provincial offices receiving gazettes should keep a closer watch over state news and not allow it to filter haphazardly into the public realm. The court approved the suggested document delay but did not respond to this warning that widespread interest in court news in fact challenged the state's administrative capacity.[59]

Court News beyond the Palace

Interest in court news could take many different forms. It was one thing to indulge in gossip about the emperor's behavior and quite another to hire clerks to smuggle documents out of the palace. Still, both practices existed within a continuum of strategies undertaken by Qing subjects to learn about the imperial court and its activities. One early eighteenth-century Chinese official described the outward circulation of news from Beijing in the following terms:

> The capital city is the central hub for the spokes of the four directions. Here, any tale, any story, can easily travel and spread. All the people of the realm believe that stories that come from the capital are to be believed, so that some seek them out and then share them among each other. I have personally seen those who go down the streets chanting drum-songs and concocting fictitious dramas. And as for real events, they package these as illustrations, print them, and walk the streets singing out sales-chants. Their goals are nothing more than profit. And all the traveling officials and merchants who come to the capital all love the new and the exciting. They clamor to buy a tale, then take it home, and spread it as news [*xinwen*]. There, ignorant bumpkins and unsophisticated youth mistake the tales for truth.[60]

In opinions directed at the court, officials like this one evinced little faith in the ability of the populace to understand or engage in political talk. Such deliberate attempts to invalidate the contents of popular talk at the same time reveal the depth of official concern with the power of public talk. These investigations also contain telling details about the identities of participants in more and less covert aspects of the information trade, including capital liaisons, news purveyors, and palace clerks. Behind the scenes, officials' demand for information fueled the whole enterprise.

Communications Liaisons and News Purveyors

Capital communications liaisons, employed by provincial governors, were important players in the information-gathering business.[61] By statute, capital liaisons assigned to the various provinces resided in Beijing and assumed responsibility for the safe delivery of routine documents to the provincial authorities. Liaisons prepared registries for the gazettes that they obtained and sent to the provinces. They also oversaw the distribution of official materials such as imperial gifts and seals of office. Besides these legitimate roles, capital liaisons sometimes operated as information conduits for provincial governors in the capital. Thus, each of the document smuggling rings prosecuted between 1734 and 1746 involved capital liaisons, both working together and on their own terms.[62]

Rather than regarding the liaisons as independent actors, court authorities and the emperor focused on the directing role of the provincial governors. In a 1746 edict, Qianlong lambasted the "several" provincial governors reputed to have ordered the documents leaked from the Grand Council. "These misdeeds," he wrote, "are all meant for the attention of the governors. And the governors even delight in the occasional receipt of these private communiqués of capital intelligence [*jingshi xinxi*]."[63] Still, although Qianlong shamed the governors by name in his edict, the group escaped punishment by submitting a flurry of apologetic memorials.[64] Anhui governor Wei Dingguo (1678–1755) pleaded that such intelligence-gathering had not come at his initiative. Besides, he didn't pay attention to these unauthorized reports: "When I peruse the gazettes [*dichao*], although in places the liaison has copied side notes [*pian bao*], because it is a long-standing practices, I did not pay attention or investigate."[65] With such a casual dismissal, both court and official in the Qianlong era evidently viewed information networks structured around the relay of capital news to the field post to be routine aspects of the political life of a late imperial official.

Both Kuixu and Yentai, in exposing the persistent leak of documents from the palace into the gossip and news circuits for the capital city, had pointed out gazette publishers, as well as capital liaisons, as notably suspect participants in the information trade. They may have hinted at patronage ties between liaisons and distant officials, but their warnings also attested to the hunger of the local audience for court news. Gazette publishers in Beijing, like patron-supported liaisons, apparently possessed the means to purchase or otherwise obtain documents from the palace. Gazette publishers numbered among the clients in both of the schemes to purchase "ordinary" documents at fairly low rates. In other cases, clerks knew publishers to be active consumers of stories and documents harkening from the palace. In 1718, palace clerks enticed a local gazette publisher with a memorial attributed to a frontier governor and describing the sensational appearance of a three-headed monster as premonition of an earthquake. The ensuing investigation revealed the document to be a forged composite of stories told in private company among government clerks.[66]

News purveyors with relationships to the state were not always judicious in their dissemination of capital news and sometimes deviated from the sanctioned content of official gazettes. The Beijing publishers who obtained an obvious forgery describing the monster and the earthquake wasted little time before putting the document into circulation in the form of an unofficial news sheet (*xiaochao*). These broadsides, claimed capital police, were the source of worsening rumors about the earthquake's circumstances.[67] In provincial cities, the publishers who contracted to print proclamations on behalf of the provincial government moonlighted by printing and selling popular and unauthorized news. In 1735, a Fujian official reported that news pertaining to events in rural Jiangxi had recently captivated the residents of the coastal community of Zhangzhou. He blamed a local printer who had heard rumors from a Cantonese traveler and decided to print this information to earn some side cash. When the printer heard that arrest was imminent, he rushed home and chopped up the printing blocks into small pieces.[68] In 1774, during an investigation into the distribution of forged notices that falsely reported news of a pacified rebellion in the northeast, most apprehended suspects were local printers in Anhui and Nanjing.[69] The Jiangsu governor thus summarized, "Those who print and sell proclamations [*gaoshi*] are also those who concoct pseudo-edicts and fake official reports."[70] These distortions challenged governance because local officials depended on these published notices to act with authority in criminal cases and other matters involving coordination between capital and locale.

Through the popularization of authorized gazettes, memorials and other artifacts of the official communications system became equivalent to news in popular judgment. In the mid-eighteenth century, an array of individuals spread across the empire referred to a circulating forgery as "a page of news" (*yi zhang xinwen*; *xinwen yi zhi*), "a news treatise" (*xinwen gaozi*), and a "newsworthy memorial" (*xinwen zougao*).[71] Official gazettes were distinguished by their connection with the state and regarded as more authoritative sources when compared with ordinary talk or less formal forms of news sheets (*xinwen zhi*) and broadsides (*baodan*). More expensive than popular broadsides, gazettes were relatively rare news sources for local commoners. Still, these portable texts could circulate to unexpected recipients after their initial purchase. Somewhat later, in the early Jiaqing reign, a disillusioned, impoverished, and mentally confused former tobacco seller acquired a court gazette from a patron at his native-place lodge in central Hubei. He used the gazette as the source and inspiration for an unsolicited letter to the emperor asking the monarch to improve his station in life. The man evidently saw these publications as bridges between his everyday world and the worlds of official elites and even the emperors themselves.[72]

Not all news responded to court politics, nor did all unsanctioned exchanges of news result in criminal inquiries or bureaucratic scandals. Throughout the dynasty, chatty, narrative, and ephemeral news sheets were traded throughout the empire, especially in urban and administrative centers. These local news sheets were hand copied or printed, and they often featured illustrations.[73] Purchasers obtained them "by the sheet" (*yi zhi*) for a few coins at most.[74] News sheets were everywhere in bustling Chinese cities, according to foreign observers like the long-time Canton missionary Robert Morrison (1782–1834), who described them in the *Chinese Repository* as "a slip of paper which is published when any extraordinary circumstance occurs which the printer thinks will excite interest."[75] Topics covered by local news sheets included didactic stories and anecdotes, as well as stirring tales of local crime and sensational events.[76]

If the central state viewed the dissemination of news sheets addressing local affairs as innocuous, then the circulation of political news demanded special scrutiny, first for its potential to disrupt the social order and second for the disturbing frequency with which such stories could be traced to actual or faked imperial documents. Suggestions of an authentic connection to the state increased the perceived value and newsworthiness of a document. Although state agents framed their anxieties in terms of the potential to mislead undiscerning commoners, it is clear from a closer look at the interests of the court, as well as the details of document leak cases, that elites were the most active consumers of court news and leaked documents. In the early seventeenth century, one capital official had written poignantly that a proposed ban on the private copying of documents and compilation of gazettes would "make the world deaf and blind, casting us into eternal night."[77] In the Qing, literati consumers, aware of the state's scrutiny of information scandals, managed to navigate these contexts in sophisticated ways. The sophistication of elite avoidance of negative political attention increased as the eighteenth century wore on, and especially when the Qianlong emperor inaugurated the Imperial Four Treasuries project, a library compilation which legitimated invasive searches of literati libraries and writings. Thus the magistrate Wang Huizu (1731–1807) advised his sons not to record "current events" (*shishi*) in their diaries and reading journals, so as to prevent reprisal from the court or from personal enemies who could disingenuously cite the matters of hearsay (*ershi*) that diarists credulously recorded.[78] Once recorded on the page, the reasoning went, an opinion was no longer confidential.

◆ ◆ ◆

Over an approximately sixty-year period, from the late seventeenth through the middle of the eighteenth century, structural transformations in how documents were exchanged and processed within the central bureaucracy influenced the ways that historical actors secured and interpreted political information. In the first part of this period, the Kangxi emperor's use of confidential channels drew attention to lapses in trust within the bureaucracy. The open secret of palace memorials compelled field officials to exploit illicit sources in their pursuit of court and frontier intelligence. The intrigues of the succession struggle during Kangxi's last years and after his death drew attention to court documents, but also convinced the court to label the information trade as subversive and dangerous as it closed down access to palace discussions and documents. The formation of new rules and procedures in the second half of the Yongzheng reign and the first decade of the Qianlong reign eased this crisis. While the emergence of new and poorly understood institutions like the Grand Council generated an outbreak of information security problems, the Qianlong court treated these cases as expected events within a complex and interest-driven political system.

The exchange of political information activated a political community whose interests did not necessarily align with those of the court.[79] The Qing information order powerfully supported the agendas of imperial power. Yet the spate of "information scandals" documented in the archival record emerged around the same time that the high Qing emperors developed the signature institutions of the information order, namely the palace memorial system and the Grand Council. Originating from the court's extensive use of publicity, both elite and popular audiences determined imperial documents, even if illegally obtained, to be newsworthy. The widespread attention paid to stolen and forged documents offers an alternate view to the common portrait of imperial power effortlessly realized through secret communications, surveillance, and censorship.

Elite interests motivated the illegal information trade, but bureaucratic subordinates were the ones who accepted payments and drew on social networks to mobilize action. Provincial governors, seeking to preserve their positions, protect loyalty networks, and interpret often-intense communications with the emperor, commanded extensive intelligence networks spreading to the imperial capital. Capital informants could be family members, but often they were formal subordinates, including capital liaisons. Clerks, scribes, and other employees of the metropolitan bureaucracy were willing to take risks and sell stolen documents and overheard information.[80] Infiltration schemes were planned in private homes and during holiday visits. In some cases, native-place ties supplied the social networks that coordinated document smuggling. In others, clerks in opportune positions provided documents, making office positions more relevant than social relationships. Throughout the empire, financial payoffs, more than political motivations, encouraged printers, scribes, and publishers to enter the information trade.

CHAPTER 3

State News in the Marketplace

FOR MOST OF THE QING DYNASTY AND ACROSS MUCH OF THE EMPIRE, the central state did not dominate the particulars of the gazette trade. Instead, the copying, distribution, and sale of official news involved both state and commercial realms. Government clerks prepared approved versions of official texts, which were distributed according to the court's rules for public distribution. Editions put out by different publishers could vary in appearance, and to a certain extent, in content. Such flexibility allowed the state to outsource complex publishing tasks. Commercial management reduced expenses and lessened the burden of bureaucratic oversight. The court experimented with various forms of supervision to reduce the risk of politically motivated interference, eventually settling on a minimalist model by which urban authorities rather than the central state enforced a limited set of regulations for publishers.

The central state's retreat from direct management led to a capital-centered gazette trade that grew in step with the demand for political news. Traditionally, gazette publishers worked at the fringes of state institutions, establishing copying and printing houses adjacent to palace gates, provincial yamen, and examination yards. By the middle of the nineteenth century, a dozen publishers hummed along in Beijing's commercial Southern City, producing a daily circulation of thousands of printed gazettes. Highlighting the transformation of state texts into products of the urban marketplace, late nineteenth-century Beijing gazettes were affixed with brand identifications and even advertisements. In the provinces, too, independent publishers established relationships with local authorities to publish provincial gazettes and other documents. Both the capital and provincial gazette trades involved collaboration between state and merchant.

Intersections of Government and Commerce

Though the prominent role of commerce in the Qing communications order may seem surprising at first, the state's choice to outsource news publishing is consistent with its comportment in other areas, such as local governance, taxation, and customs collection. As China's population swelled over the course of the dynasty, the Qing court resisted expanding the state payroll and restricted the reach of government agents into social life and commercial activities. At the imperial level, the central state held monopolies on salt and customs collection. In reality, these monopolies amounted to licensing schemes by which the state sold to merchants the rights to produce and transport salt and to collect customs revenues on behalf of the throne.[1] At the local level, magistrates used subordinates and local gentry to compel the payment of land taxes across a district and turned a blind eye to tax farming activities among these groups.[2] Administrators entreated local populations to handle low-stakes investigations and policing in relative independence through their participation in the local mutual surveillance system (*baojia*). In these ways, the Qing state contracted with the commercial realm for services impracticable within the government bureaucracy. Informal relationships preserved the limited size of the bureaucratic state and prevented excessive incursion into commerce. News was no exception. The addition of political communications, in both its legitimate and illegitimate guises, reminds us of the diversity of irregular economic activities entered into by agents working with, if not for, the state.

Looking outward from the case of gazette publishing, these insights can be applied to revise the categories that structure the history of publishing in late imperial China. Most bibliographic treatments of late imperial publishing divide imprints into "government" (*guan*), "commercial" (*fang*) and "private" or "household" (*si* or *jia*), ignoring significant overlaps between these boundaries. More recently, book historians have begun to break down the fictive boundary between the latter two; in considering official news, we have the opportunity to reassess the boundaries between state and commercial publishing.[3] In reality, while the Qing court supported an Imperial Printing Office (Wuyingdian) in Beijing to compose showpiece editions, most printing of routine government texts, including administrative forms, gazettes, and proclamations, was done in the commercial marketplace.[4] Even in the case of display pieces, provincial officials turned to the market to reprint editions for local circulation.[5] Eager to locate indigenous origins for newspapers and journalism, Chinese scholars of the history of news have long recognized the predominance of commercial publishers in the late Qing gazette trade.[6] However, the field has not recognized the wider implications of these commercial connections: that the true scope of "government publishing" was far more diverse in terms of genre, format, production, and distribution than this category would seem to allow.

No merchant accounts survive to document the work of commercial gazette publishers. Even as scholar-officials devoured official news on a regular basis, they refrained from comment on the exigencies of these enterprises. Further attesting to the informal nature of these commercial relationships, the archives offer only limited evidence pertaining to the state's dealings with gazette publishing. Cases where the involvement of scribes, publishers, and couriers with criminal enterprises elicited state attention survive to the exclusion of records of more routine interactions. In using such archival cases as sources, we must avoid falling prey to the rhetoric of state actors and the tempting presumption that publishers traded in secrets, forgeries, and rumors. Material remnants—over thirty thousand gazettes, dating between the eighteenth and early twentieth centuries and scattered in libraries around the globe—are useful reminders of the unceasing regularity of the gazette trade.[7] To supplement these sources, I draw on the commentary of nineteenth-century European visitors, who wrote prolifically but selectively about Chinese state texts. These accounts are most useful for their identification of prices, locations, and material techniques in the gazette industry. Scrutinizing each level of evidence, we find clues to trace the path of capital news throughout the Qing empire—journeys that had as much to do with the street as they did with the state.

Gazette Publishing in Beijing

Commercial involvement in the gazette trade looked somewhat different between Beijing and the provinces. In Beijing, commercial publishers collaborated with metropolitan clerks and institutions to publish gazettes sold in the city and distributed by government couriers further afield. Over time, the state implemented a series of regulations to dissuade publishers from participating in local and trans-imperial black markets in leaked documents and unsanctioned news. Whereas the early eighteenth century had witnessed frequent incidents where leaked documents made their way into gazettes, by the nineteenth century, publishers generally followed established routines for obtaining approved documents. Unlike provincial gazette publishers, who assisted more generally in the printing needs of the local state, nineteenth-century Beijing gazette publishers specialized in official news and rarely sold other scribal or print products.

The Capital Information Trade

In Beijing, the physical structures of the city determined spaces of interaction between state and commerce. In the telling of the twentieth-century art historian Osvald Sirén, "Walls, walls, and yet again walls" formed the skeleton of the capital city.[8] Since the conquest of Beijing, the Qing state had divided the capital city and its population according to the walls that bounded the urban core.[9] A square city wall enclosed the Northern City, which housed the palace and imperial family at its center within a walled Imperial City. The bulk of metropolitan offices, including the Six Boards, Grand Secretariat, and Censorate, lay within the Northern City, but south of the palace.[10] By law, the Northern City was the jurisdiction of the Manchu banners and the state offices, and Chinese residents were relegated to the Southern City. This district had been walled off during the mid-sixteenth century as a measure of protection against Mongol raiders. The Southern City housed the majority of the Chinese population and the capital's commercial and entertainment zones. Most officials and examination candidates chose to sojourn and reside in the compact streets and alleyways adjacent to the gates of the Northern City. Housing religious, commercial, and entertainment centers, including the growing Liulichang publishing district, the area around the "three southern gates" (*qian san men*) formed an official-commercial nexus in the city.[11]

Before the rise of Liulichang, capital gazette publishers concentrated in closer proximity to government offices. Late in the Ming dynasty, capital communications liaisons had begun to contract with commercial intermediaries out of practical concerns for expediency and cost-effectiveness. Since liaison postings were unsalaried prestige appointments, the incumbents were

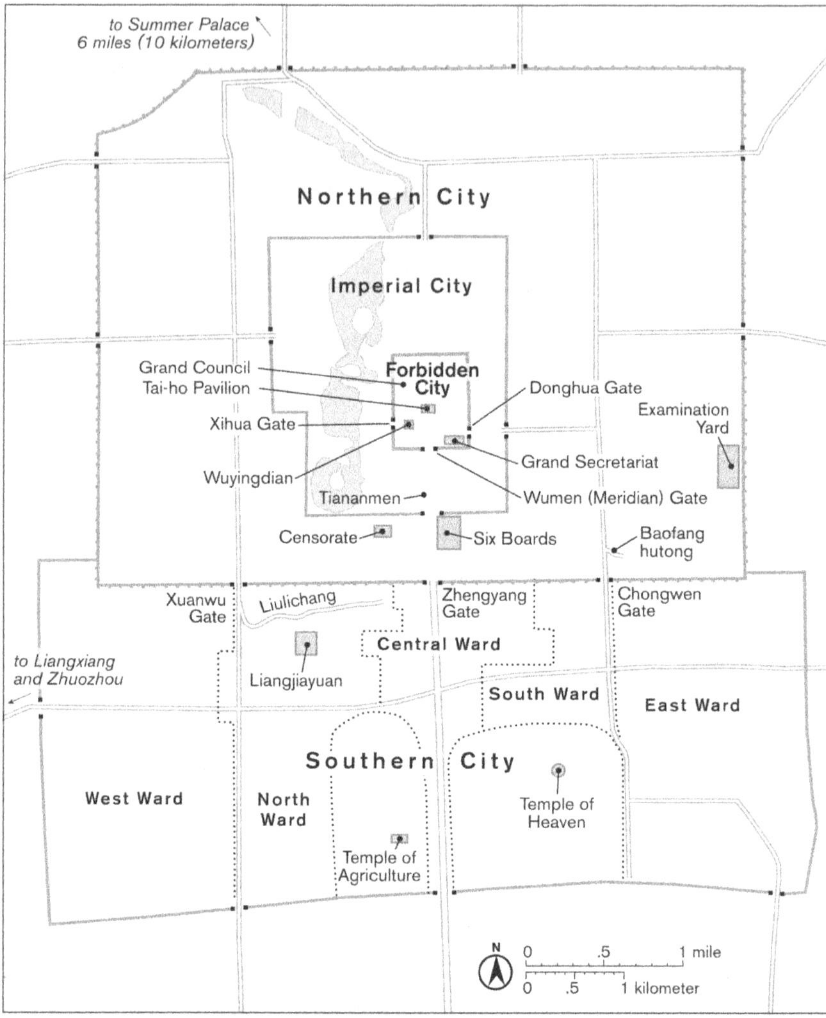

MAP 3.1. Qing dynasty Beijing, showing sites mentioned in this book

motivated to avoid investing personal time and funds in the gazette compilation process. Instead, liaisons selected commercial agents to assemble packets of gazettes—mostly scribal, but some printed—which the liaison would then dispatch by courier.[12] Early gazette publishers were not large enterprises and perhaps served the needs of one or two provinces with a small staff of copyists. By the mid-Qianlong era, three publishers were stationed at the eastern (Donghua) and western (Xihua) gates of the larger palace complex. Here, they were close to the Grand Secretariat, clerical offices, and the walking paths of clerks as they entered and exited government offices. At least one other publisher was located in the southeastern corner of the Northern City, on an alley called Gazetteer's Way (Baofang Hutong) (map 3.1).[13] This site lay not far from the imperial examination yard, allowing publishers to solicit subscriptions from degree candidates and expediting side enterprises of printing examination lists and related announcements.[14]

Owing to their location, commercial gazette publishers had extensive contacts among metropolitan clerks. Gazette publishers cultivated relationships with clerks who worked in the Six Sections, where imperial communications were processed, recopied, and filed. These interactions could take place in a variety of settings. When the gazette copyist Yang Tianyi happened to see on the street a palace clerk with whom he was acquainted, he asked the clerk if an imperial response had been published in a recent case concerning grain storage. Upon return to the office, he included this updated information (though it later proved false) in his day's jottings.[15] Another scribal gazette publisher had a staff of four, including two managers and two scribes. This entire staff hailed from southern cities like Shaoxing and Suzhou, and they relied on native-place ties to establish business relationships that smoothed the flow of documents out of government offices.[16] While copyists often hailed from suburban Beijing, all eighteenth-century gazette publishers that were identified in the archival record were from southeastern provinces like Jiangsu and Zhejiang, perhaps associated with printing and bookselling in those areas.

Documents for Sale

In principle, as long as the documents involved were authorized, the Qing state considered it legitimate for commercial publishers to pay clerks for access to documents. However, in the late seventeenth and early eighteenth centuries, recurrent sales of unauthorized, leaked, and unreleased documents convinced the court to implement new regulations defining which documents could be bought and sold. The court only sanctioned the publication of documents that had received imperial review and had been properly copied and filed. It banned publishers from access to file copies and document summaries that were held in outer court offices during the period of imperial review.[17] Since they were based on documents that lacked the vermillion inscription that marked an imperial decision, these transcriptions became known as "black copies" (*heiben tongchao*).[18] So-called evening notes (*wantie*) were extracts from clerical registers of edicts designated for release the following day, as well as excerpts of courtroom conversations. Palace officials worried that these unvetted transcripts included both inadvertent and planted inaccuracies.[19] In their condemnations of these activities, metropolitan officials pointed out that leaked documents, often suggestively called "short reports" (*xiaochao*), were fodder for the capital rumor-mill on topics such as provincial appropriations and bureaucratic infighting.[20]

Through the 1730s, metropolitan government clerks earned a modest side income for providing documents to Beijing gazette publishers. For instance, gazette scribe Yang Tianyi paid his palace contact five hundred cash per month for documents in the early Qianlong era.[21] For clerks, the potential profits to be earned in selling leaked documents and overheard secrets or in tampering with the documentary system were much larger in consequence of the risk of detection and punishment. In 1736, two commercial publishers and the capital liaisons for eight provinces paid six clerks more than fifty taels per month for unpresented memorials, allowing the clerks to hire four copyists to keep up with this lucrative business.[22] Such income, when split six ways, would inflate the salary of even a highly placed clerk by nearly fivefold over the course of a year.[23] It was becoming clear that clerks, who might well have established relationships and personal interests among the bureaucracy, were susceptible to bribes and other payments in exchange for palace information.

Outsourcing the Gazette Trade

In response to cases of documents leaked to gazettes, the state took measures to reduce the likelihood of improper collusion between clerks and printers. These moves in fact expanded the presence of commercial agents in the gazette trade. In 1741, officials in the Grand Secretariat noticed that the gazettes published by the publishing house (*baofang*) of Yang Tianyi included an unreleased draft memorial relating to regulations on grain stores. In response, Grand Councilor Necin (1708–1749), who served concurrently as head of the Board of Appointments, ordered no further exchange of payments between clerks and gazette publishers.[24] Thereafter, palace officials first approved documents for release, after which they were reproduced by hand or in print outside of palace walls. By separating the process, the state established distance between official business taking place within the palace and the presumably chaotic process of publishing daily gazettes. Publishers seem

FIGURE 3.1. Drying paper for use in the imperial bureaucracy, from Michel Benoist's pictorial album, *Art of Papermaking in China* (Art de faire le papier en Chine, ca.1775). Bibliothèque nationale du France.

to have complied with state regulations, as the number of reports of leaked or advance documents in the archival record diminished after this time.[25] In this way, it proved easier to enforce limits upon the information trade if it mainly involved commercial rather than state agents.

The state's decision to outsource the publishing process can also be understood as a practical response to the material and labor constraints of the era. During China's sixteenth- and seventeenth-century commercial print boom, most book publishing took place either in the Yangzi River delta or closer to the southern forests where paper production took place.[26] The northern capital, surrounded by arid mountains, lacked the skilled labor and natural resources necessary for extensive papermaking, printing, or publishing.[27] Paper for official use and for palace-supervised publishing products was imported from southern suppliers (see figure 3.1 for a French missionary's illustration of the production process). Although these prices were nominally fixed by the central state, suppliers often pressed local officials to pay inflated prices to meet capital quotas.[28] Paper production and transport, as well as the carving and maintenance of print blocks, were line items that the state preferred to leave to the commercial realm.[29] Capital publishers likewise dealt with shortages of skilled labor and materials. In the Kangxi era, print publishers routinely omitted the given names of memorialists, presumably to avoid carving complex and rare characters found in names alone.[30] One eighteenth-century bibliophile wrote that capital publishers often used wooden movable type to print gazettes, casually exchanging a homonym character whenever the font of a given character was exhausted.[31] The relative shortage and expense of publishing supplies in the capital also helps explain why printed items, from gazettes to imperial compendia, were typically paid for and reproduced in the individual locale, not supplied directly from the capital.[32]

The Gongshen Tang: A New Look for Gazette Publishing

Midway through the Qianlong era, the court switched tactics and decided to place gazette publishing under state auspices. In 1760, it implemented the Gongshen Tang joint publishing model in hopes of limiting abuses in the production and distribution process. These abuses were different from the leaks to private publishers that had taken place earlier in the dynasty. Critical officials attributed gaps and inconsistencies in the distribution of gazettes to commercial publishers' privileging profit over their public mission. In addition, they saw capital liaisons as inadvertently and sometimes purposefully facilitating the breakdown of gazette distribution through negligence and misappropriation of state funds. By establishing a state gazette publisher, the court could now order capital liaisons to jointly manage the task of copying, printing, and distributing gazettes, the first two tasks having previously been subcontracted to commercial publishers.

During the tenure of the Gongshen Tang, which remained operational until at least 1820, the court maintained more formal control over gazette publishing than at any other time in the Qing dynasty.[33] However, even the state concern retained elements of collaboration between the state and commerce. No surviving bureaucratic regulations explain the operations of the Gongshen Tang, but scant archival records indicate that it ran more like a business than a government office. Capital liaisons pooled their province-supplied budgets in order to purchase equipment and materials and pay employees, who worked on a contract basis. In 1803, an argument and brawl broke out when the liaisons gathered to debate finances.[34] Beijing's urban ward (*cheng*) officials treated this as they might handle a financial dispute in another capital business and simply established a payment plan to clear the personal debts owed.[35] Tellingly, the Gongshen Tang, like its commercial successors, was located together with other commercial bookstores and print shops outside the Zhengyang Gate in the Southern City.

Although the publishing house had been set up to improve official behavior, the capital liaisons charged with running the Gongshen Tang soon ceased to responsibly oversee the enterprise. The liaisons readily accepted tips and payments from those seeking out privileged palace information.[36] Soon, they hired workers to replace themselves as managers of the publishing enterprise. In 1820, a rumor leaked from the palace occasioned an investigation of the clerks and gazette copyists who made their way between the publisher and the palace on a daily basis. Investigators questioned Shao Yucheng, employed as manager of the Gongshen Tang. Shao, a native of Shaoxing, had been in the position for twelve years. He affirmed that the Gongshen Tang received documents approved by the Six Sections and then printed up the gazettes and provided the capital liaisons with a supply to send to the provinces. In other words, their practices had nearly reverted to those of the pre–Gongshen Tang era, with a commoner replacing the capital liaisons as manager.

Gongshen Tang utilized wooden movable type to print gazettes. In the past, some commercial publishers also sold printed gazettes, but in this case, the Qianlong court may have specially ordered the use of print as a security measure. Any scribe could forge or alter a manuscript gazette. But print required the hiring of skilled compositors, carvers, and printers. More specifically, movable type met the demands of gazette publishers because their assigned contents were relatively short, formulaic, and predictable. In particular, gazettes reproduced the circumscribed vocabulary of the bureaucracy, which therefore necessitated a limited corpus of type. The Gongshen Tang and later publishers often employed simplified variants for visually complex or dense characters that might be difficult to carve or recognize in the movable-type format. These techniques also solved material constraints. Around the same time, a palace official supervised the production of two hundred copies of an expansive collection of recovered texts using movable type. Although these types were carved from hardwoods, they did not require the sourcing of large pieces of timber as were required for solid woodblocks and could be reused thousands of times before requiring replacement.[37]

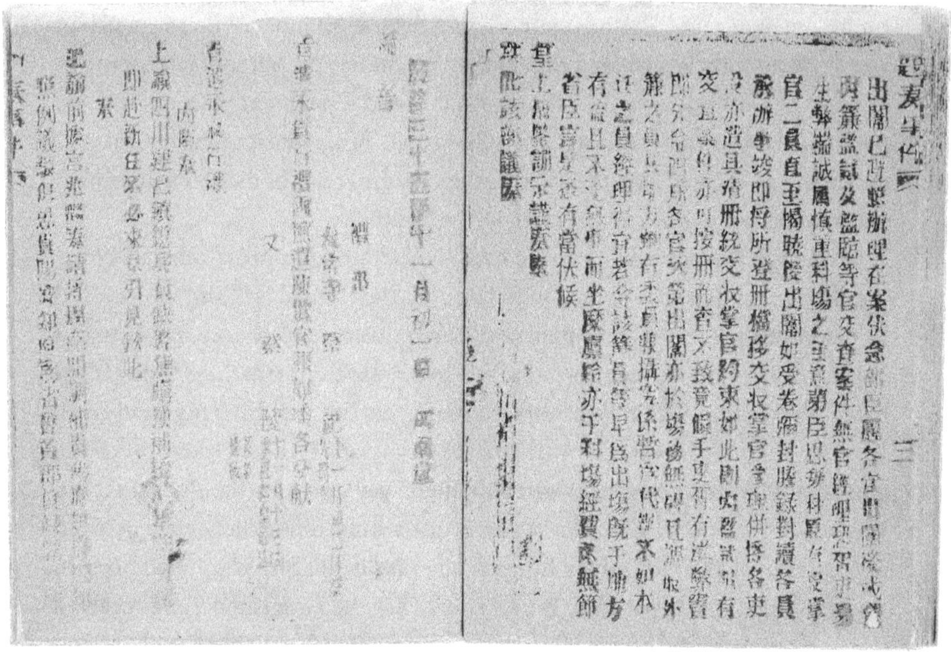

FIGURE 3.2. Pages from a Gongshen Tang gazette, dated December 17, 1770 (QL 35/11/01). Note the name of the publisher in the first column and the remnant impressions of shoulders of wooden blocks. The dark impression in the bottom left of the facing page is a blank column marker used to fill in gaps. Courtesy of the East Asian Library and the Gest Collection, Princeton University Library.

Movable type met the demands of serial publishing in ways that woodblock printing could not.

In combination with wooden movable type, the printers of the Gongshen Tang may have used the process of wax transfer (*la ban*). In this process, a wax stereotype was first created by laying a sheet of wax onto wooden type set in columns in a frame containing a single page or two facing pages and then imprinted from wax to paper to produce gazettes in small, rapid runs for official consumption.[38] The wax transfer process was not widely used in Beijing before this time.[39] Wax printing was used in Guangdong and the surrounding region by local printers and provincial gazette printers to print ephemera and provincial circulars and to reprint capital gazettes.[40] Knowledge of this technique may have come to Beijing via southern print workers.[41] In this era, when Beijing faced a shortage in qualified carvers and print workers, newly arrived southern craftsmen were one possible source of inspiration.

The Gongshen Tang editions incorporated visual details that made their gazettes recognizable products of the official imprint (figure 3.2). Each Gongshen Tang gazette reminded readers of its provenance with a masthead bearing the issue's date and the publisher's name. Center margins proclaimed a new title, *Memorialized Matters* (Tizou shijian), and included page numbers that showed each page to be part of a composed pamphlet rather than divisible into parts. The wide proportions of the pamphlets, with sixteen columns per facing page, invited readers to fold them in half, foreshadowing the slim profile of later editions.[42]

Capital Gazette Publishing in the Nineteenth Century

The fact that the Gongshen Tang was located not within or proximate to the palace but rather just beyond the gates to the southern city was symptomatic of the ongoing march of official publishing outward from the imperial center.[43] Outside the "three southern gates" of Beijing, the government publisher and its staff shared their neighborhood with booksellers and publishers, as well as tea shops, opera houses, and guildhalls. In Liulichang, just to the west of the Gongshen Tang, a growing population of booksellers and commercial publishers sold administrative texts to be employed by officials, clerks, and others who worked in connection with the state. The most prominent Liulichang publisher was Ronglu Tang, which sold stationery, accessories, official directories, law books, forensic guides, memorial collections, and even custom editions of one's own writings. Demand boomed in the nineteenth century as the population of office-seekers and clerical staff grew progressively larger. Powered by a primary audience of aspirant, expectant, and serving officials, the sale of government directories (*jinshen lu*)—guides to the state and its personnel that promised up-to-date information useful for official service and networking—was an important growth area for nineteenth-century capital publishers.[44]

Gongshen Tang's move to the new location came in the context of a significant revival of Beijing's commercial gazette publishers. By the early 1850s, four main publishers were located in the Outer City, all within the jurisdiction of the city's Northern Ward, which stretched between the Xuanwu Gate and the Zhengyang Gate from the southern wall of the Northern City to the southern wall of the Southern City. Most proprietors in the mid- to late nineteenth century hailed from Shandong, such as Zhang Yixing, a native of coastal Zhaoyuan, who ran the Gongli Baofang located in Liangjia Yuan, not far south of the Liulichang book markets.[45] Rather than the court, these publishers (Gongli Baofang, Gongxing Baofang, Tianli Baofang, and Juxing Baofang) interacted regularly with urban authorities. Ward offices maintained registers of the locations and personnel of publishers and the contents of the gazettes they produced.

Rather than competing for business, the capital gazette publishers cooperated among themselves and with their official contacts to exchange and print state documents. Thus, when one city official feared that an edict had been left out of the day's copy, he went to see Zhang Yixing of the Gongli Baofang and asked him to distribute the updated document to each of the neighboring publishers.[46] In 1859, a former metropolitan scribe (*tiexie*) ran the Liben Tang, a manuscript publisher located near the Donghua Gate to the palace complex. With closer ties to the state than other commercial publishers, this business functioned as a clearing house between the palace bureaucracy and the other print publishers.[47] The proprietor, Zhang Tonghe, visited palace offices daily (perhaps accompanied by staff) to copy authorized documents. Employees of each print publisher then came to the Liben Tang to procure the day's material. When Zhang ran into trouble with the authorities, he produced a record book that documented which items he had copied from the palace.[48] The clear records maintained by publishers, bureaucratic contacts, and supervising officials indicates the maturity of commercial gazette publishing in this period.

After capital liaisons lapsed from direct involvement with gazette publishing by the mid-nineteenth century, city authorities took over supervision.[49] For a time, the court remained too weak to enforce regulation of the gazette, freeing commercial publishers to use their contacts to obtain information. Later, political imperatives and an expanded readership for gazettes spurred renewed interference. When, after 1860, foreign agents began to scrutinize the court gazettes for mistakes and misprints, the court asked city police and censors to enforce more stringent rules for the formatting, content, and publishing of gazettes.[50] Still, these new rules were not particularly restrictive.[51] They instructed publishers to print texts in their entirety, even if this required expanding the issue beyond its typical length of ten pages. In fact, publishers continued to split lengthy memorials across multiple issues after a simple notice that the item was incomplete (*wei wan*).[52] Compared to the vicissitudes of the commercial market and the growing public demand for information, state regulations had only a limited impact on the gazette trade.

As the number of publishers in the city proliferated, their circulation grew larger. Nineteenth-century publishers handled a larger load of subscriptions, dealt with more involved state regulation, and maintained more consistent business records than their predecessors. In 1859, the publishers included Juxing Baofang, Juheng Baofang, Hecheng Baofang, and Liben Tang. By the end of the century, more than ten commercial gazette publishers operated in Beijing, with a combined circulation of several thousand copies per day (in the early 1870s, individual publishers seem to have printed about two hundred gazettes per day).[53] These shops clustered in the Liulichang area. In addition to these formal establishments, denizens of Beijing could solicit complete manuscript gazettes near the Donghua Gate (see map 3.1).[54]

Gazette publishing happened in the open, not behind closed doors. British diplomat Rutherford Alcock (1809–1897) described the cluster of gazette publishers in Liulichang as "the Paternoster Row of the Chinese Capital," an allusion to London's publishing and bookselling district.[55] When paying a visit to the nearby home of a friend in southern Beijing, the bureaucratic functionary Wang Zhonglin (1816–1878) recalled sitting for a spell, "watching the printers hunting for characters and filling their blocks."[56] Close proximity aided collaborative efforts among publishers to share the load of printing and distributing documents to be sent to the provinces, the capital's offices, and to private purchasers and subscribers.

The Price of a Beijing Gazette

The visual and material characteristics of late nineteenth-century gazettes attest to the expansion of the capital market. They were slim booklets enclosed in distinctive yellow covers, "a pamphlet stitched in a dingy yellow wrapper . . . some seven inches in length by four in width."[57] Late Qing gazettes commonly bore the name of the publisher on their covers, and some even featured stamped cover illustrations representing the gazette's connections to official life (figure 3.3). Publishers continued to use wooden movable type to produce a rapid and readable product, although they disposed of the wax stereotype technique. They also worked more economically with paper and ink than had the printers of an earlier era. In contrast to the spacious margins of Gongshen Tang gazettes, the late Qing publishers filled narrow pamphlets with print and even folded single sheets into the pamphlet when texts exceeded usual page limits. These techniques reflect publishers' efforts to keep costs low.

FIGURE 3.3. Cover of a Beijing gazette. Illustrated covers were more common in the late nineteenth century. The pictured official holds a banner bearing an auspicious phrase. Collection of the National Palace Museum.

Gazette publishers made it easy to obtain and read the news in a variety of formats. The commercial publishers produced specific editions for circulation to provincial officials, as well as for capital audiences.[58] In Beijing, consumers could choose between the daily "palace notes" (*gongmen chao*), a simple list of audiences, duty assignments, and ritual assignments, and more comprehensive versions that included edicts and memorials. Some offered "digest" versions earlier in the day and more comprehensive editions in the evening. Consumers could also purchase print or manuscript editions. Manuscript editions came in a variety of styles, from those written in neat standard print to quick editions in varying hands. At least one gazette publisher offered consumers the option of repackaging a year's gazettes in twelve handsome cloth enclosures with bone clasps.[59] Many consumers subscribed to gazettes on a monthly basis rather than buying individual copies. Monthly subscriptions offered consumers a discount from the price of an individual edition.[60] For the capital resident, leasing a gazette for the day was an economical choice. Gazette carriers delivered, picked up, and redelivered leased copies throughout the day (figure 3.4).[61]

FIGURE 3.4. Depiction of a gazette seller in Beijing. Sketched by William Simpson for the *Illustrated London News*. Copyright Illustrated London News Ltd/Mary Evans.

Individual purveyors set their own prices, varying according to format, without interference from the state. For the majority of the nineteenth century, individual issues of the printed gazettes went for seven or ten copper cash in Beijing.[62] A monthly subscription cost between 250 and 400 copper cash.[63] One official diarist recorded paying a few thousand copper cash per year for gazettes in the 1860s and 1870s.[64] Similarly, in 1878, Juheng Baofang charged a purchaser 3,746 cash for a year's supply including twelve cloth book covers so the pamphlets could be repackaged into neat monthly sets.[65] Often produced on higher quality paper and considered more legible than their printed counterparts, manuscript gazettes were expensive, going for between 5,000 and 9,000 copper cash per month.[66] The expense of a printed gazette compared favorably with other comestibles of an up-and-coming Beijing resident; for example, a cheap opera ticket sold for about 100 cash in the same period.[67] By contrast, manuscript gazettes were more expensive than even substantial books, and their price exceeded most personal budgets. Manuscript editions were distributed to government offices and sold to foreign agents at inflated prices. In 1895, Beijing's gazette purveyors decided to fix prices for shorter and longer pamphlets and sent out a "joint notice" to this effect.[68]

◆ ◆ ◆

Beijing, as the seat of the imperial government, played host to a dynamic publishing industry that expanded significantly over the course of the dynasty. Beijing gazette publishers worked with state information and sometimes on behalf of state interests. At the same time, they were not state institutions, nor did they face the strict bureaucratic controls that we might expect. The story of the city's vibrant news publishing industry helps us visualize the everyday relationships and processes that powered the work of the imperial state. Simply put, the metropolitan and territorial bureaucracies could not have functioned without commercial collaboration. These collaborations often tested security concerns, but they ultimately proved beneficial to an imperial state that sought to minimize its fiscal burden and intervention into private affairs. Moving outward from the capital, the business of official news remained a matter of the street, although its rhythms, personnel, and texts looked somewhat different.

State News in the Empire

Stemming from Beijing, gazette publishing linked disparate locations throughout the empire. The business of copying, printing, and distributing gazettes brought about interactions between imperial elites and commoner populations. Only a portion of the empire's gazettes were produced in Beijing and sold in the city or delivered to provincial capitals for the use of high officials. The majority were recopied and printed in local jurisdictions. The substantial business of provincial gazette publishing mirrored and complemented the distribution of capital gazettes. In provincial cities, publishers assisted in the printing needs of the local state. In addition to gazettes, they reproduced proclamations and documents related to the provincial examinations.

State News as a Local Enterprise

Most official recipients received capital gazettes via the government courier system; others relied on commercial publishers. Within the state courier system, the exchange of news mirrored the administrative hierarchy, with the effect that regional powerholders received information first. Gazettes were published in the capital. Then, under the eye of capital liaisons, they were delivered from Beijing to each provincial capital, reprinted in the provincial capital, and then delivered to subordinate offices. Residents of the suburban districts surrounding Beijing were in an awkward position because the system required materials to travel first to the more distant provincial seat of Baoding, then backtrack to the capital suburbs.

By the early nineteenth century, commercial outlets emerged in Beijing and its suburbs to proffer gazette and mail deliveries to officials stationed in field posts. These schemes, which operated under official radar, were known as the "Liangxiang post" (*Liangxiang bao*) and "Zhuozhou post" (*Zhuozhou bao*) for their association with those towns, which served as key transport hubs in the southern metropolitan region.[69] The manager of one such enterprise received between two and three taels per month from each of his official clients. He thus cleared total earnings of over sixty taels per month simply for supplying gazettes more quickly than government couriers.[70]

In the provinces, most gazette publishers were located in administrative seats, where they based themselves at travel junctures and adjacent to government offices. In Guangzhou, a gazette publisher was located next to the offices of the Guangzhou prefect. There, the publisher printed provincial gazettes and reprinted court gazettes using a wax impression technique that ensured a quick process but low-quality imprints.[71] Another mid-nineteenth century publisher was found a few streets to the east, flanked by the official school and the provincial examination yard.[72]

Provincial gazette publishers interacted with both local officials and their counterparts in surrounding jurisdictions. The staff of the publishers based in Anqing and Nanjing, the provincial seats of Jiangxi and Jiangsu, respectively, routinely exchanged documents and information.[73] Traveling officials often took up gazettes upon their arrival to new jurisdictions, from provincial capitals to county seats. In nineteenth-century Shanghai, a gazette seller's location adjacent to the west gate of the city wall, where roads branched to adjacent Jiangnan cities, played into the connections between news, travel, and the courier system.[74]

The arrival of the capital gazette to a provincial gazette publisher triggered a process of scribal copying and printing to serve the needs of local residents and officials. According to the American missionary and diplomat Samuel Wells Williams (1812–1884), "thousands of persons" throughout

China in the mid-nineteenth century were employed in "copying and abridging the Gazettes for readers who cannot afford to purchase the complete edition."[75] Employees involved in the process from copying to delivery derived income from sales and tips, not government stipends.

Customers in provincial cities obtained hand-copied editions and excerpts from the gazettes more commonly than their capital counterparts. Some editions available in early nineteenth-century Canton, for instance, came in a neat, scribal hand; others were written in scrawled characters. The copyist's name was never included. In both the capital and the provinces, publishers often made corrections and amendments to the day's copy. On slips of red paper, publishers added by hand or printed a last-minute notice or proclamation. Smaller pieces of paper were used to blot out mistaken characters or miswritten names. Copyists wrote the dates and sometimes summaries of the day's business on the standard stamped covers of their gazette pamphlets. In these ways, scribal and print formats intermingled even within individual issues, and even as printed products grew more dominant in the marketplace (see examples in figure 3.5).[76]

Provincial gazette publishers sourced labor and supplies locally as they reproduced court gazettes for subscription or on order. Canton reprints and manuscript editions evoke the commercial networks that supported print culture in South China and maritime Southeast Asia. Canton was a major urban market for the rural papermaking enterprises located in hinterland Guangdong and Fujian. In Canton, paper firms (*zhihang*) controlled by natives of nearby Foshan sold a wide range of paper products transported by waterways from the mountainous interior. Through the entrepreneurship of Foshan merchants, southern paper was sold and used throughout the empire. Both papermakers and these intermediate suppliers often left their mark on the page, in the form of stamps that served advertising and branding purposes, and some gazettes bear theses stamps. These stamps promised the "purest white" and "highest quality" paper and reminded consumers of the brand (*hao*) of their maker, should one want to purchase a supply. When consumers and publishers purchased sheathes of paper from paper suppliers, a certain proportion of the product retained the papermaker or supplier's stamp.[77]

The print methods used by provincial gazette publishers show the integration of official news publishing into a wider market for printed ephemera. In South China, provincial gazette publishers employed a wax printing method somewhat less sophisticated than that employed by the Gongshen Tang to

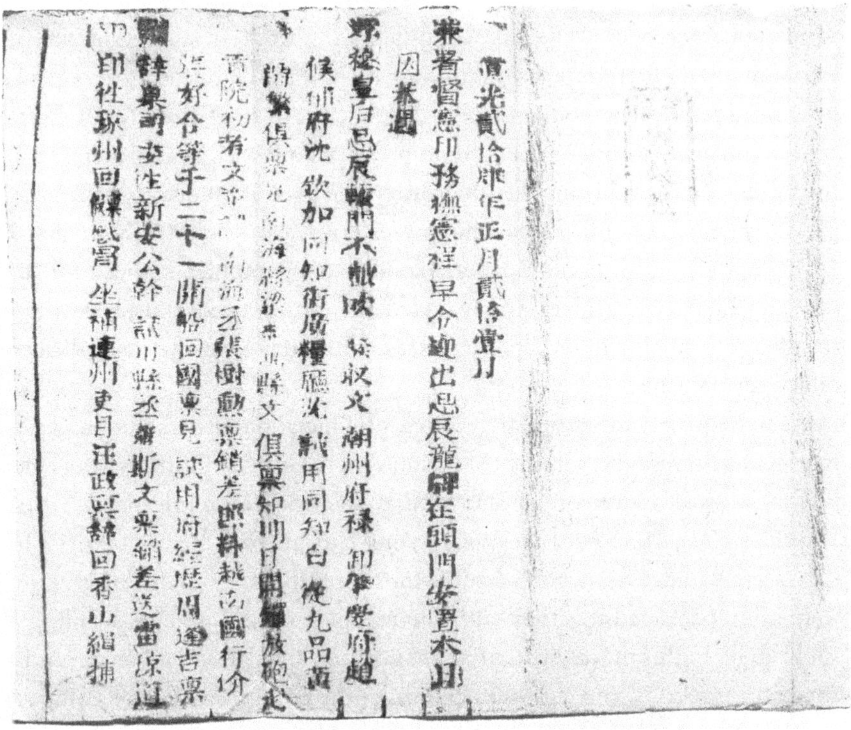

a

FIGURE 3.5. Manuscript and print formats in provincial editions of the Qing gazette. (a) Provincial gazette (Dufu xian yuanbao) published in Canton, dated March 9, 1844 (DG 24/01/21). Caleb Cushing Papers, Courtesy of the Library of Congress; (b) Table of contents of manuscript gazette, dated September 15, 1833 (DG 13/08/02). Courtesy of Staatsbibliothek zu Berlin.

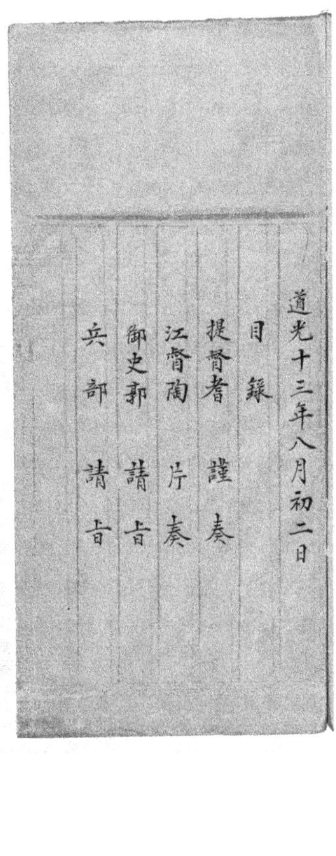

道光十三年八月初二日
目錄
提督者 謹奏
江督陶 片奏
御史郭 請旨
兵部 請旨

b

print capital gazettes. Whereas Gongshen Tang workers laid wooden type into frames and took impressions on wax off of these composed text layouts, provincial print carvers often inscribed characters in relief directly onto wax-covered strips of wood.[78] This method produced a less elegant product than the former. In the mid-nineteenth century, the poor print quality of Suzhou gazettes made them infamous among Western readers based in Shanghai.[79] A single, wafer-thin piece of paper, folded into a pamphlet, sufficed for the provincial gazette. Printers simply added columns at need; thus, a slow day resulted in a small slip of paper, whereas a busy day's gazette needed to be folded several times.

As well as reprinting capital gazettes, provincial publishers put out separate local editions representing the business of the local authorities. As a rule, provincial gazettes were much shorter than their capital counterparts. Titled *Yuanmen chao*, *Yuan bao*, *Du fu xian yuan bao*, and other similar variants, they seem to have been published in most provinces.[80] Provincial gazettes were often packaged together with the recopied capital gazette, forming a supplement to this more substantial publication. They described recent audiences, transactions, and communications of the provincial seat in a compact list-like format. Daoguang-era provincial gazettes from Guangdong often began with a list of incoming and outgoing correspondence (*fa shou wen*) between the governor's yamen and various local officials and subordinates in terse form.[81] Following this section, the gazette listed the governor's daily schedule, including official visitors to the governor's yamen.

Besides gazettes, provincial publishers obtained contracts to produce a variety of official and unofficial texts. They published proclamations (*teng-huang*) as they were issued by provincial administrators, and afterwards repackaged these documents into books for sale.[82] The triennial examinations constituted the high season for a trade in announcements related to the examination results. One early eighteenth-century education commissioner in Sichuan, Sui Renpeng (1703–1738), described that immediately after the announcement of examination results, messengers working for the provincial communications liaison flooded the examinations yard and pressured successful recipients to purchase gazette subscriptions. Sui perceived that economic pressure had motivated the hiring of unscrupulous individuals and the use of extortionate practices, and suggested a devoted budget for gazette publishing to be managed by the provincial liaisons, and the imposition of stricter rules against disruptive subordinates.[83] As late as 1899, a

Shanghai newspaper article decried the proliferation of heralds who harassed candidates exiting the Suzhou examination grounds to purchase official notices at extortionate prices.[84]

Even as commercial schemes introduced discomfort for local scholar-officials, the state preferred to leave provincial gazette publishing and distribution outside of state management. Rather than embracing the measures proposed by Sui Renpeng to ameliorate the rent-seeking behavior of printers and heralds, Beijing officials called the proposal preposterous. Board secretary Zhang Tingyu (1672–1755) wrote that to argue that messengers should be paid out of official budgets so that they would not press for tips was ridiculous. Such trivial matters should not be added to the administrative or financial burdens of the bureaucracy.[85] In allowing heralds to continue hawking gazettes and examination notices at inflated prices, the court suggested that regulating local social order was the business of the district official, not the central state. Furthermore, profitable collaboration with official business should be encouraged, not quashed.

Economic Possibilities and Limitations

Whereas the gazette industry in Beijing had a national reach, the provincial gazette publishers were distinctly local enterprises. The staff of gazette publishers in Beijing typically originated from wealthy regions with established publishing industries, including southern Jiangnan and, as book publishing spread across the empire, coastal Shandong. They brought expertise, connections to suppliers, and contacts with government clerks to their work. Careful not to jeopardize their official contracts, Beijing's gazette publishers apparently restricted their output to gazettes and examination-related materials. Provincial gazette publishers, by contrast, handled a more diverse workload. They processed the routine work of the local administration and took on side jobs as well. Provincial publishers thus interacted more closely with the interests and needs of local society than did the government-oriented capital publishers.

Was news publishing a profitable enterprise in late imperial China? Was it considered a reputable profession? In the early twentieth century, editors, journalists, and publishers would become important fixtures of the urban cultural scene. The publishers of prominent newspapers earned significant returns from the swelling circulations of mass newspapers. Meanwhile, journalists became embroiled in political affairs that attracted national attention.

For the majority of the Qing period, news publishers did not attract such expansive interest, nor did they net profits substantial enough to gain them notice in local communities or from the state.[86] News publishing, even state news, proceeded at a rapid pace and produced crude imprints on cheap paper. It did not connote the prestige associated with showpiece editions. While publishing apparently required only minor capital contributions, it likewise earned limited returns. Prices were low, and many editions were shared by multiple readers, either informally or through borrowing systems. And while the staff of gazette publishers may have offered timely tips based on official sources to their friends and acquaintances, they do not seem to have carried this work over to become journalists after the expansion of Beijing's newspaper industry in the late nineteenth century. Instead, former gazette workers faded into anonymity as vestiges of an earlier age of economic interactions between the state and street embedded in the Qing information order.

◆ ◆ ◆

"These gazette publishers are all worthless individuals," the metropolitan official Yang Kaiding wrote scornfully in 1756.[87] Yang felt that the authority and security of state documents was threatened by the incipient commercialization of gazette publishing, and he sought to eliminate the common agreements between officials and commercial publishers to copy, print, and distribute gazettes. Yet while Yang bemoaned the debasement of official communications, the growing audiences for official news clearly cared more about timely access to information than proper handling. In fact, the publishing of state-related texts was an area of commercial innovation and growth. The contrast between Yang's scorn and the flood of quasi-official publications available to purchasers illustrates the larger tensions in the interactions between the official and commercial worlds, especially present in the streets, offices, and shops of Beijing. The thirst for usable information—called "indirectly official" by a British Legation staff member—was so great that it was impossible for the state to encompass all stages of the compilation, printing, and publishing process.[88]

Publishing for the state was by no means dominated by the state. Instead, Qing officials entered into flexible relationships with commercial agents who sourced materials, copied texts, and printed documents for state use. At times, publishers and consumers alike were able to circumvent court regulations. The growth of the gazette industry over time derived not from the expansion of government business or personnel—pamphlet lengths remained stable and the Qing kept stipendiary positions fixed—but rather from the expansion of the ranks of individuals interested in state activities. The officials, students, and expectant officials who populated provincial cities filled the demand for gazettes and could pay the prices asked by purveyors. Thus, the *Glasgow Herald* told readers that in mid-nineteenth-century Beijing, a visitor could be assured of obtaining the Peking Gazette "as regularly on his breakfast table at eight as he found the *Times* when in London."[89]

CHAPTER 4

Official Readers and Political Culture

READING STATE NEWS LAY AT THE CENTER OF THE INTELLECTUAL, administrative, and careerist work that members of the imperial bureaucracy performed on a daily basis. For this reason, Chinese officials remained the most committed readers of state gazettes throughout the Qing dynasty, even as the audience for court news grew to encompass a wider audience. Gazettes kept officials apprised of current events and political agendas. For frequent readers, many of whom recorded details in personal diaries, gazettes represented more than repositories of useful information. Some read gazettes as a counterbalance against more polished state sources. Others learned how to write for the bureaucratic community by studying gazettes. Equipped with details from court gazettes, provincial governors and metropolitan censors formulated policy proposals and engaged in debates. Administrators and their staff picked up details, espoused by their distant counterparts, of techniques for alleviating locust infestations, quelling riots, or calming the people. And many readers were keenly aware of the names, positions, merits, and shortcomings of their colleagues in the tightly networked bureaucratic realm.[1]

Personal and public writings reveal the agendas that official readers articulated through the reading and citation of state information culled from gazettes. Our gaze lingers on readers who became known as administrators and intellectual figures, as well as those who excelled at using gazettes without acclaim. From these examples, an arc of readers' practices emerges, from the politically charged commentary and history writing of the seventeenth century, through the nuanced administrative techniques of the eighteenth century, and ending with the intensely competitive bureaucratic culture of the nineteenth century. Each of these practices represented timely forms of political engagement with state news. If political outsiders and intellectuals were the prototypical gazette readers of the seventeenth century and statecraft officials the representative readers of the eighteenth and early nineteenth centuries, then students, clerks, and would-be officials became more prominent within the emergent bureaucratic public of gazette readers by the mid-nineteenth century.

The Politics of Reading Gazettes

According to his autobiography, gazettes played an important role in the political education of the of the seventeenth-century intellectual Gu Yanwu (1613–1682). Gu grew up in Kunshan, midway between Suzhou and Shanghai, and studied under the tutelage of his adoptive grandfather. Together, they read the gazette sent from Beijing daily in the 1620s, a tumultuous decade when factional battles wracked the Ming capital. The two compared the proposals found in the court gazette with the *Comprehensive Mirror for Aid in Government* (Zizhi tongjian). As Gu grew into his teens and began to socialize with other budding literati of the Jiangnan region, he neglected his grandfather and the court gazette. Gu later regretted that he had not continued the practice of reading gazettes and had thereby lost a grasp on current affairs across the empire.[2] For Gu and other late imperial thinkers who shared his anxieties about the revisionist tendencies of new regimes, the unceasing regularity of the court gazette enshrined it as an authentic artifact of a historical moment.[3]

Gu and his cohort of seventeenth-century chroniclers turned to ephemeral gazettes as source materials out of the desire to retain a sense of history as it really was. Private authors who took to their studios to record the history of the last decades of the Ming dynasty, the war with the Manchus, and the flight of the Ming court southward hoarded court gazettes that were disseminated from Beijing and, later, the Nanjing court-in-exile. One evocative example is Huang Zongxi's (1610–1695) *Jottings on the Veritable Records of the Hongguang Reign* (Hongguang shilu chao). Huang prefaced this book by recounting a disturbing incident. One night, he awoke to hear the scratching sound of a rat chewing on paper. Lighting a candle, Huang saw the rat munching on his stacked copies of gazettes from the Southern Ming court of the erstwhile Hongguang emperor. Seeing his documents so threatened, and reflecting on the other materials that had been lost in frequent moves, Huang resolved to begin writing his chronicle of the Nanjing refugee court.[4] Perhaps two dozen authors wrote histories of the Ming-Qing conflict based in large part on gazette collections.[5] Thus, the hoarding of gazettes naturally preceded the writing of histories that claimed a more direct perspective on a contentious past.

After his youth, Gu Yanwu paid fastidious attention to the court gazette despite the fact that he refused to take office. A colophon to Gu's famous *Record of Daily Knowledge* (Rizhi lu) praised his use of sources, from official sources like the dynastic histories and the Ming *Veritable Records* down to disparate maps, local gazetteers, official communications, and gazettes.[6] Part of a dramatic crackdown on the compilers and distributors of a privately authored history of the Ming dynasty, Qing forces seized portions of Gu's library that had contributed to that work.[7] Although Gu himself could not be collared to serve the Qing state, several of his colleagues participated in drafting of an official history of the previous dynasty. In letters, Gu stated that the court gazettes of the 1620s, the decade when he had read together with his adoptive grandfather, were the most authoritative sources for those years and disparaged changes to the record in later histories.[8] Gu's letter to his nephew Xu Yuanwen (1634–1691), a participant in the state-run Ming official history project, pointed out precedents for using gazettes as unbiased references. He even suggested methods to authenticate sources, by reminding his nephew that movable-type print editions of the gazette had just begun to appear in 1638, meaning that only manuscript editions dating to earlier eras should be regarded as genuine.[9]

The examples and commentary of Gu Yanwu and other seventeenth-century intellectuals inspired later generations of scholar-officials.[10] Eighteenth-century model official Chen Hongmou based an argument for the utility of regular readings in court gazettes (as opposed to deep reading in esoteric or philological texts) on another seventeenth-century political outsider, the poet-philosopher Huang Chunyao (1605–1645).[11] According to Chen, a thorough understanding of current events through reading the gazette made Huang's compositions well grounded in reality with nothing spurious, both solid and practicable in all cases.[12] Chen described this reading practice as lending itself well to political careers, since it allowed one to follow the currents of who was in and out of favor. Reading gazettes introduced the possibility for outsiders to participate in politics through their own writings and correspondence on matters of the day.

Gu Yanwu grounded his reliance on gazettes as historical documents in his pained awareness that new regimes rewrote history. After the seventeenth century, however, gazettes informed a more limited set of historical writings.[13] As Qing rule became more firmly established, gazettes lost the luster that they had held in the context of regime change. Furthermore, by sponsoring archival compilations and tomes of campaign history (*fanglüe*), the Qing state was actively engaged in writing its own history. Official Hang Shijun (1696–1773) therefore made a statement when he retired to his hometown, took up work as a tutor, and doggedly refused to read the court gazette. For twenty years, one contemporary wrote, "If any of his cohort took office, even reaching [the rank of] grand academician, board secretary, or governor-general, Mr. Hang would claim ignorance."[14] Whereas gazettes of the conquest period had reminded literati that historical truth could be excavated from documents, their high Qing counterparts perhaps deplored that the news of their era was so thoroughly controlled by the central state.

By praising reading methods rather than politics, Qing writers navigated the tricky business of lauding those who evaded office and even erstwhile Ming subjects and loyalists. By the eighteenth century, the regular reading of gazettes could be used to manifest reverence to the ruling Qing dynasty. In an honorific biography, the official Yin Huiyi (1691–1748) described how each time his aging mother read the court gazette, she bowed her head to the ground three times to show respect.[15] Such gestures elevated the ordinary gazette to the status of an imperial object deserving veneration.[16] Even in ostensibly private records, such as diaries, most readers followed imperial documentary practice by beginning a new line above the top margin when quoting gazette contents. These practices, however perfunctory, performed gestures of respect. More practically, maintaining documentary standards in personal notes also allowed readers to quote and reuse information derived from gazettes in their own work.

Gazettes and Administration

As private writers distrustful of the dynastic enterprise turned away from gazettes in the eighteenth century, a widening retinue of less skeptical readers put court bulletins to use. During the same period, collecting and annotating gazettes became commonplace practices among serving and would-be officials, in part in response to the expanded availability of state news. As a provincial administrator, Chen Hongmou suggested that every town and village academy should subscribe to the gazette; even poor scholars could afford the cost of the subscription were it shared with their colleagues in the same town.[17] Some, like Chen, became famous for reading gazettes and for recommending others to do so. But as exemplified by the case of Yin Huiyi's mother, gazettes were also common reading material for scholar-officials and their families. When imperial investigators raided the house of a disgraced official in the early Yongzheng era, they suspected that someone had cleared the house of incriminating books and left behind only "ordinary texts" like examination essays, gazettes, contracts, and account sheets.[18] A few years later, when a Manchu military official wrote to impeach his Han subordinate for impropriety in maintaining an annotated personal archive of gazettes, the emperor dismissed the accusation and pointed out that such practices aided comprehension.[19] By the late Qianlong era, the emperor casually scolded a mere government student in Hunan for failing to keep close attention to the gazettes.[20] And at the turn of the nineteenth century, the scholar Yu Zhengxie (1775–1840) consulted gazettes covering nearly two hundred years in writing his literary compilations.[21]

For enthusiasts of statecraft-style learning, establishing a habit of reading gazettes as a young child or student—or having been read gazettes aloud by a parent, guardian, or teacher—was in some ways equivalent to the scholar's trope of having read or been read the classics as a young child.[22] These scholar-officials saw that gazette reading facilitated the intellectual practice of collecting and compiling documentary facts. As dense repositories of information, gazettes helped authors pepper their treatises with evidence. One day, the scholar-official Gong Zizhen (1792–1841) saw dried mud in the Beijing suburbs crack in an unexpected fashion, contrary to his experience growing up in coastal Zhejiang. A nearby farmer described this as a symptom of the differences between northern and southern mud. Gong thought this to be a bit of folklore, but nine years later, he encountered an old gazette that described the same phenomenon.[23] Gong's gazette offered not political wisdom, but solid evidence of natural conditions in disparate parts of the empire. His ability to source seemingly trivial information from the gazettes of years past relied both on the accumulation of stockpiled pamphlets and strategic use of this personal archive as a reference tool.

By applying evidentiary techniques to reading gazettes, scholar-officials could hone their administrative prowess. After evidentiary methods and statecraft perspectives had their heyday in the eighteenth and early nineteenth centuries, these lessons experienced a revival near the end of the dynasty. Early in his career, the military official Du Yu (1854–1916) referred to the words and deeds of his fellow Hunan native Zeng Guofan (1811–1872), a national hero known as both the architect of the post–Taiping Rebellion reconstruction of empire and as a reverent Confucian scholar-official.[24] Du found himself frustrated by acclaimed political treatises like the eleventh-century *Comprehensive Mirror to Aid Government* (likewise Gu Yanwu's political textbook alongside the court gazettes) that were too sprawling to feasibly put their lessons into practice.[25] In his diary, Du recalled that Zeng had recommended reading just twenty pages of the statecraft classic per day, pausing to compare historical and theoretical texts to contemporary matters.

Reviewing the celebrated official's concise instructions, titled "The Duties of an Official," Du found advice on managing the overflow of communications that besieged an official each day:

> 1. Cull through everything; know its origins.
> 2. Punctuate and mark up gazettes.
> 3. Look through and annotate lists of officialdom.
>
> These three items should be considered nightly tasks. As well, they comprise a method for keeping one's mind on the matters of administration.[26]

Zeng's "method" for administration proposed diligent attention to a variety of informational materials to ease the strains of official life. His short description included no mention of Confucian morality, no details of how to adjudicate local disputes, and no recommendations on how to balance straitened budgets. It attested instead to the textual work of the official, who, he asserted, needed to read "everything" on a daily basis—but nothing more urgently than the court gazette and the official rolls. Of Zeng's three recommendations, Du Yu singled out marking up gazettes as "worthy of emulation," observing that it was "a practice with gradually accumulating rewards."[27]

The first recommendation—to read "everything"—spoke to the intellectual foundations on which Zeng's own career rested. A lineage of statecraft thought, extending from the seventeenth century through Zeng's era, promised rewards to those who focused their attention on practical matters of administration. Undergirding their attention to practical (*shi*) matters lay a deep-seated belief that the Confucian scholar-official could best contribute to the moral vitality of the realm through actions in the real world, not by obsessing over archaic texts or theories.[28] Statecraft officials read widely in contemporary affairs to inform their approaches, and their writings attested close attention to the court gazette as an important strategy for understanding the workings of imperial policy across the empire.

Zeng's second item, encouraging officials to parse gazettes carefully, recognized the specialized mechanics of reading official documents, which required close attention to deconstruct tightly bound phrases of bureaucratic language. The memorials embedded in court gazettes detailed criminal and administrative cases with ramifications both for the larger bureaucracy and for the intensely local task of adjudicating cases and disputes in one's own jurisdiction. If the impetus to read widely drew on seventeenth-century intellectual trends, then the recommendation to read carefully responded to the growing complexity of law and administration in the empire. Zeng, like many other nineteenth-century officials, employed legal advisors to do the work of compiling and combing archives and preparing rulings.[29] Yet administrative matters could not be left entirely to subordinates. If the advisor's focus was local, then the official's gaze roamed across the cases that cropped up from other prominent posts: parsing language, drawing comparisons, and reading between the lines.

Reading and Bureaucratic Practices

The popularization of court gazettes for official use relied on two interlocking trends: first, the teachings of statecraft scholarship, which became increasingly widespread but also stripped of its political connotations in the eighteenth century; and second, the dedicated effort of the Qing state to propagate its public image in the circulation of gazettes and other official texts. Gazettes became an authoritative and portable archive of commands, decisions, and precedents that could be cited in the absence of a formal proclamation. Memorialists not only quoted *from* gazettes to establish knowledge claims, they wrote *for* gazettes in conscious awareness of their audience. To write for the bureaucratic community required conscientious awareness of political trends and currents. The uses of political information can be seen in the ways that officials used gazettes and other official documentation in their public writings and career paths.

Crafting an Argument

Official memorialists deployed references to the court gazette as springboards for proposals, evidence to bolster arguments, or as rhetorical devices that called up an audience of gazette readers that stretched far beyond the court. The practice of quoting from the court gazette as a pretext to raise an issue of personal interest can be found in memorials dating to the early years of the Shunzhi reign and thus probably carried over from earlier dynasties.[30] Official memorialists wrote for the bureaucratic community of gazette readers, as well as for the imperial eye. Among the most common strategies was for an author to cite an example from the gazette as an opening premise to offer his own opinions. In 1646, one censor wrote that having read in the gazette that the emperor wished to compile revised tax registers, he felt compelled to submit his recommendations on tax regulations.[31] The metropolitan official Li Zhifang (1622–1694) began his proposal on post transfers with a reference to reading the Zhili provincial governor's memorial on a related topic. Li's argument focused on the impropriety of allowing sub-bureaucratic functionaries to assume acting positions as magistrates during post transfer without provincial approval. He bolstered it with a list of clerks and secretaries who had assumed acting positions in recent years—material clearly drawn from gazettes.[32]

Some authors also used gazette examples to close an essay or memorial after describing their views at length, as when memorialist Shen Tong (1688–1752) concluded a discourse on the community law enforcement system (*baojia*) with the lines "Review the gazette, and you will see that both metropolitan and provincial officials are discussing *baojia* in great numbers. This is why I have sketched out this discussion." Here, Shen validated his commentary by offering a casual reference to the prevalence of his chosen topic in the pages of gazettes.[33]

Other memorialists used gazette materials to lend persuasive touches to their arguments. In a memorial countering a proposed imperial ban on popular liquor production, the metropolitan official Sun Jiagan (1683–1753) quoted from the court gazette proposals for prohibiting the brewing of alcohol that had been advocated by his counterpart and rival Fang Bao (1668–1749). While enemies of brewing argued that spirits contributed nothing positive to society, and potentially wasted grain, Sun pointed out that the state itself garnered burdens when it confiscated liquor and arrested peddlers and brewers. What would be done with the alcohol if it could not be sold? He also noted that most people in North China involved in liquor production were poor peasants with few other options, and warned against increasing these people's hardships.[34]

Sun Jiagan and Fang Bao were longtime contemporaries and opponents on many issues besides alcohol. Thus, Sun did not need to search through gazettes in order to find information about Fang's proposal or points against it. But by referring to Fang Bao's memorial as published in the gazette, Sun suggested that gazette readers might peruse his new counterproposal and critically compare the two documents. In this way, his memorial appealed to an implied (and much larger) audience of gazette readers, as well as to the Qianlong emperor and his advisors, the real arbiters of the proposal. Skilled memorialists such as Sun Jiagan knew that their proposals circulated widely in the gazette and sought to use this publicity to their own advantage. As well, by referring to the gazette in his counterproposal, Sun strengthened an appearance of neutrality. In this way, when Sun wrote a sharp assessment near the end of his memorial, "The recent proposals of the Grand Academicians and Fang Bao are all empty talk and not appropriate to this situation," it appeared less a personal rebuke than a neutral critique based on the review of openly circulated documents.[35]

Capital officials with easy access to gazettes published in Beijing were particularly active in referring to gazettes when they composed memorials. Censors were especially prominent in this regard. Circuit censors reviewed elements of administration in province-sized jurisdictions, even as they remained in the imperial capital. Their knowledge of the ups and downs of territorial administration thus relied on their access to documentary communications that substantiated existing conditions in the provinces. A sample of the relative frequency of censors quoting gazettes in their memorials can be found by perusing memorial collections of the era. The seventeen memorials that quoted gazettes in the early nineteenth-century collection *Memorials of the August Qing* (Huang Qing zouyi) were all authored by capital officials, and the majority by circuit censors.[36] Metropolitan officials read gazettes to find memorials authored by governors and governors-general on topics as varied as personnel administration, tax collection, infrastructure, and disaster relief. In this way, gazettes provided an interface for policy discussions between central and territorial officials. The functionality of the court gazette as a bureaucratic forum therefore relied on the maintenance of effective communications channels between the center and the provinces.

Early Qing officials had urged the court to utilize the court gazette as an instrument of bureaucratic discipline. These priorities guided the development of the gazette's consistent format and verifiable contents. According to the censor Ren Kepu, circulating information relating to official appointments, such as the details of administrative trials and punishments, could reduce the prevalence of administrative crimes.[37] Meanwhile, for Ren's contemporary Zhang Cunren, who had witnessed the tumultuous name-calling moral politics of the late Ming era, the protection of confidentiality trumped the advantages of transparency. Zhang asserted the importance of establishing clear boundaries between matters under consideration in the palace and those items that circulated openly. Gazettes needed to clearly indicate whether an item had already been deliberated upon by the emperor, in order to prevent leaked and undecided matters circulating as fact.[38] By the mid-eighteenth century, clear standards guided the release of official information into gazettes at the palace level, while supervising secretaries and capital liaisons oversaw the preparation and distribution of gazettes in Beijing and beyond. The adoption of such reliable standards increased the utility of gazettes in bureaucratic dialogue.

The gazette's purview thus expanded along with its circulation. By the mid-eighteenth century, not only did a broader spread of officials quote from gazettes, they read in gazettes of more geographically distant matters, spanning the empire and its frontiers. On his deathbed in coastal Zhejiang, the scholar-official Qian Chenqun (1686–1774) took pleasure at the news of Qing victory after a decades-long fight against the Junghar Mongols. Eyes clouded by encroaching blindness, the old man entreated his family to read court gazettes aloud for their accounts of the campaign. Qian's experience of victory with eyes closed compelled him to rise from his bed and pen one last series of commemorative poems to the emperor.[39] Institutional factors also influenced the growing political relevance of gazettes; the inclusion of palace memorials in court gazettes from the 1730s onward built awareness across the empire of emerging modes of governance and communications, particularly the newly formed Grand Council.

The reliable existence of the gazette as a documentary record of policy discussions distinguished Qing political practice from that of earlier dynasties. In the Tang dynasty, individual regional powerholders had installed capital correspondents in Chang'an to gather intelligence. The Song state standardized the production of gazettes and implemented rules for secrecy.

However, in neither the Song nor the Ming dynasty do we have clear evidence of the gazette's uniform availability across the bureaucracy. By contrast, shortly after regulations allowed certain palace memorials to enter the pages of the court gazette, Zou Yigui (1686–1772), a metropolitan censor, recognized the gazette's potential as a bureaucratic forum. Zou urged the Qianlong emperor to employ the gazette as a stage for policy debates within the bureaucracy. Why not, he recommended, publish in full the details of responses to policy proposals, so that readers and authors could understand them more clearly?[40] Zou's proposal suggested that the gazette could convene disparate officials together into virtual yet simultaneous conversation.

Nonetheless, the Qing state never released complete transcripts of all bureaucratic communications. Instead of treating its publications as vehicles for empire-wide discussion, the state prioritized goals of bureaucratic order in its use of curated transparency. The publication of details of civil examination questions, personnel nominations, and impeachments was meant to increase the sense of transparency in the examinations and personnel appointments.[41] The state made sure to circulate details of tax forgiveness programs, thus dissuading the dishonest magistrate who might otherwise go ahead collecting taxes in order to line his own pocket.[42] The dissemination of gazettes mirrored the posting of public notices (*tenghuang*) that notified the populace of acts of imperial policy, also commonly employed in situations that invited potential fraud.[43] In these ways, gazettes exemplified the uses of redundancy within the bureaucracy.[44] Redundant layers of communications helped maintain the accountability of the bureaucracy by supplying information to detect and report the malfeasance of peers. In effect, gazettes allowed officials to police each other's transgressions and to understand differential treatment across distances.

Interactions within the empire-wide forum of political communications shaped the nature of policy discussion for the bureaucratic community. As a result, a political culture of citation and dialogue pervaded in the bureaucracy prior to the translation and adoption of Western models of parliamentary democracy. The influence of the statecraft tradition motivated officials to attend to the empirical details of administration embedded in their peers' published memorials. Memorialists advertised their intellectual and administrative strengths by quoting from each other's work, often in the context of sophisticated rhetoric. Provincial administrators knew that their reports were exposed to the scrutiny of the bureaucratic community, lending them national prominence, but also increased exposure to critique. Censors especially responded to the state's imperative for bureaucratic discipline and accountability by tracking gazette descriptions of deeds and misdoings. Officials and administrative experts thus cited gazettes in explaining legal constraints on behavior for newcomers to the bureaucracy.

Learning by Comparison

In late imperial China, while training to take examinations and enter official life, students focused on the classical canon, supplementing this with commercially published commentaries, crib sheets, and examination guides. Once on the job, officials began to gather expertise from practice and experience and relied heavily on local subordinates and assistants. Indeed, many so-called magistrate's handbooks (*guanzhen shu*) were in fact intended for the secretaries who performed the grunt work of administration. Gazettes played a role in educating both officials and secretaries. For officials, wide reading in gazettes did more than undergird the process of formal training in classical texts. It also offered a clear look at the pitfalls that plagued many careers. Exposés of official misbehavior and corruption reminded officeholders of the dangers of self-serving behavior. Meanwhile, legal advisors employed gazettes as tools for forming recommendations and case judgments. Gazettes supplied timely evidence of evolving legal precedents. In the eighteenth and nineteenth centuries, editors and publishers incorporated cases found in court gazettes into administrative compilations to serve the secretarial market.[45] For both officials and their advisors, reading gazettes encouraged readers to think of official work within imperial frameworks.

Magistrate's handbooks attested to the value of balancing commitments to the central state and the local community.[46] Many handbooks reproduced documents and communications drafted by the authors and their colleagues, such as a printed appeal to local gentry for donations in a flood crisis, or a sample letter recruiting a private secretary. As a result, the court gazette received only passing mention in practical manuals, as when a model document informed its readers that according to the court gazette, similar situations existed in other areas, or that a certain order for the locale had been received from provincial offices and could be read in the court gazette.[47] Given that most memorials reproduced in court gazettes were authored by high officials, the contents of the gazette could feel distant from the various preoccupations of the overtaxed magistrate. In a local post, the temptations to skirt the letter of the law were many; underfunded magistrates could collude with local elements to raise funds from petitioners, taxpayers, and other constituents through the extortion of irregular fees. They might delay handling cases or give each matter a summary acknowledgement rather than a thorough investigation.

Yuan Shouding (1705–1782), the author of a well-known administrative manual, warned that gazettes were full of examples of the folly of such shortsighted decisions. Yuan wrote, "To read the court gazette has benefits. Not only itemized proposals and new precedents, also criminal sentences and completed cases, are entered in its pages. It can be used to [improve] adherence to laws. Whenever provincial officials are censured and dismissed, they enjoy not a whit of leniency even for minor offenses. A bit of knowledge like this makes crime and punishments hugely terrifying. Is this not helpful to the body and mind?"[48] He listed four categories of material in the gazette important for officials: itemized proposals, new precedents, criminal sentences, and completed cases. Capping the discussion, he suggested with an allusion to the biography of the Han dynasty official Jia Yi (ca. 200–169 BCE) that although gazettes offered readers examples of successes to guide administrative work, more prominent were the examples of failures that instructed the official what not to do. By reading gazettes, local officials should notice that the risks and potential consequences of malfeasance were both many and terrifying.[49] Yuan's remarks spoke to the county official more concerned with self-preservation than the vagaries of court politics or the nuances of policy memorials. After all, these low-level officials did not have the right to memorialize, and therefore their names and writings would not enter into the pages of the court gazette—unless they were caught extorting funds, mishandling cases, or in some other abuse.[50] Thus, rather than casting his recommendation to stay out of trouble in moral terms, he simply recommended that officials familiarize themselves with the preponderance of evidence: administrative crime was not worth the risk of punishment.

Beyond deliberate malfeasance, local officials also faced scrutiny when cases that they adjudicated came up for review as a result of post transfer or when subjected to an appeal process. A magistrate could be punished for ruling according to the wrong statute or using outdated information to guide his reasoning. Yuan Shouding's reminder to review proposals, precedents, sentences, and leading cases published in court gazettes applied to the concerns of legal advisors, who handled the majority of the local caseload as well. Legal secretaries, such as Fang Yurun (1811–1883), consulted gazettes to assist in drafting judicial decisions and compiling precedents and regulations.[51] Indeed, Wang Huizu, a celebrated legal secretary turned magistrate, attested to these uses of the gazette in his own administrative guide: "One should discuss laws and precedents, becoming rooted in their basis; one should read the court gazette to see their realization, review the imperial rescripts that are used to rule those below, and write judicial rulings in order to make appeals to those above."[52] He appealed to local officials and legal advisors to keep in mind the wider universe of judicial and administrative decisions and precedents. A narrow focus on one's individual situation and jurisdiction could mislead the local official into believing that the activities of the wider state did not matter. In fact, reading the rulings of counterparts in distant locales could offer a convenient shortcut in a confusing situation.[53]

Administrative Knowledge outside the Bureaucracy

The proliferation of gazettes in Qing China made available a new repository of administrative information that was national, rather than local, in scope. Beginning in the late seventeenth century, administrative and legal compendia were published that employed publications like gazettes as source material. Because they utilized gazettes, these publications claimed, they could be trusted as comprehensive and authoritative records. The compendia adopted thematic and even creative takes on law and administration, including catalogs of precedents (Li Zhen, *Overview of Established Precedents*, 1715), "rejected cases," (Li Zhen, *Overturned Decisions of the Kangxi Reign*, 1720), and criminal cases (Zhu Qingqi and Bao Shuyun, *Conspectus of Criminal Cases*, 1834). Gazettes also supplied material for detailed disquisitions on disaster relief (Yang Ximing, *Complete Guide to Disaster Relief*, 1823) and the salt administration (Wang Shouji, *Essays on the Salt Administration*, 1873). Finally, compilers employed gazettes to complete surveys organized by geographic region (Li Yingjue, *General Surveys* of 1896 and 1902, focused on Anhui and Zhejiang respectively) and period (Chen Tao, *Memorials of the Tongzhi Restoration from the Capital and the Provinces*, 1875).[54] These texts preempted the work of combing archival documents for reference cases and allowed readers to place their own actions in the wider legal and bureaucratic empire.

By and large, the authors of gazette-derived administrative texts were not high officials. Instead, they were administrative specialists, booksellers, private secretaries, and professional authors. Yang Ximing, who wrote about famine relief, was a private secretary, and Wang Shouji, author of the compendium on the salt administration, was a low-ranking specialist. Chen Tao, who published memorials espousing the "spirit" of the Tongzhi Restoration (Tongzhi Zhongxing), described himself as a capital denizen who habitually copied out items of interest from the court gazette.[55] Non-official readers not only studied and digested the ideas contained in gazettes, they also marketed their publications to the official community. Late seventeenth-century publisher-editor Li Zhen, for example, ran a bookstore and print shop in Beijing oriented to the capital's official community. Perhaps through an office-holding relative, Li obtained access to government archives, the records of which he used to supplement the "daily papers" (*ribao*) that were the main sources for his legal compendia.[56] Gazettes allowed individuals at a distant remove to read and write about recent cases. The Zhejiang-based editors of *Supplement of Leading Cases* (Cheng'an xubian, 1757) quoted from archival files for local cases, but borrowed their entries for cases in other provinces from the court gazette.[57]

Throughout the dynasty, official memorialists understood themselves to be writing for colleagues in the bureaucratic community. But their readership was more widespread. If the bureaucratic community comprised mainly individuals with the right to memorialize the throne, then the bureaucratic public included lower officials, like local magistrates, who found in gazettes a guide of what *not* to do in one's official career. It also included secretaries who read gazettes as a strategy to improve their administrative acumen. Some officials, secretaries, publishers, and other authors took up the information they found in gazettes and repackaged it into new publications. In writing these texts, they contributed to the empire-wide forum of bureaucratic discussion. Their activities therefore contributed to the intellectual vitality of the bureaucratic public, a population that grew more significant in the last century of the Qing dynasty.

Career Motivations in the Nineteenth Century

The third item in Zeng Guofan's list of recommended practices had instructed officials reading the court gazette to annotate lists of personnel transfers. With this, Zeng admitted to the importance of networking, a less celebrated though essential aspect of official life. Knowledge of who served in what post, who received what degree, and who hailed from what jurisdiction aided arts of sociability, whether in the civil examinations ladder, as a capital official, or during official travels. Those who regularly reviewed the lists of audiences and appointments in gazettes could welcome new officials and learn who was in favor at court. Attention to the incidents that landed officials in hot water instructed readers to hew to a moral path and provided hints of the changing realities of the bureaucratic state.

By the nineteenth century, as the fiscal power of the central state declined, would-be officials vied against intellectual rivals, but also against power-hungry degree purchasers to enter and rise through the ranks of the bureaucracy. More than any intellectual trend, social connections defined readers' encounters with state news. Zeng Guofan's recommendation to mark up personnel records reminds us that even committed Confucian scholar-officials organized their political lives in the context of a complex and increasingly challenged bureaucratic system. A strong tradition of sociologically inspired scholarship in Qing history has examined the career patterns of officials and the internal structures of the bureaucracy, revealing connections to the changing fiscal fortunes of the dynasty.[58] The constraints of under-funded positions and an overtaxed system tempted officials to stray from moral mandates despite fear of punishment.[59] For the larger bureaucracy, such scholarship indicates the dueling strengths of rationalizing agendas and autocratic power in the eighteenth century, followed by the weighty consequences of a bloated system in the nineteenth century.[60]

The documents of the personnel administration published in gazettes evolved in pace with the state's use of office-selling and other schemes for irregular appointments. Throughout the dynasty, gazettes included extensive records of the personnel administration, including perennial aspects like the nomination and appointment of new officials and the granting of sick leave and retirement, as well as less routine events like the censure and dismissal of corrupt officials. Beginning at least in the mid-Qianlong era, the personnel information supplied by gazettes extended to purchased appointments and expectancies. Monthly lists (*fenfa dan*) recorded the dispatch of new officials to provincial posts. These lists included individuals who purchased expectant positions and then awaited an assignment; to choose one's destination commanded a lofty price.[61] Appointment lists were important enough to readers that late Qing newspapers reprinted them regularly. The lists are important sources for understanding the emergence of the bureaucratic public, an expansive group that included holders of purchased degrees as well as ranked officials who joined the bureaucracy by more traditional means.

Personal connections made these lists matter. For official readers, the named individuals were not anonymous functionaries but relatives, friends, and rivals. Officials therefore followed gazettes for references to the careers of social contacts. Such information likewise proved invaluable in navigating careers. In both temporal and geographic journeys, official careers brought elite men into situations in which social relationships were of the utmost importance. Private writing by officials, especially in diaries, but also in poetry and informal jottings, reflect the widespread interest in maintaining and cultivating social interests. Such agendas can already be discerned in the writings of Southern Song dynasty elites, who read gazettes to maintain awareness of distant friends. Tracking counterparts created a sense of shared political awareness among office-holders.[62] In the eighteenth century, official Hu Juqing (1685–1749) expressed self-conscious anxiety about his predilection for reading the rolls. Hu viewed his obsessive perusal of personnel roles to be a symptom of his own inability to find spiritual satisfaction. In his diary, Hu recalled the Tang dynasty poet Yao He (b. 781), who had written, "A day spent scanning the rolls, in the end costs the spirit a year." Yao's words motivated Hu to pledge to put the gazettes out of mind.[63]

Keeping current on the postings of bureaucratic counterparts was both a necessary and maligned component of official work. The presence of personnel details in the gazette fueled the importance of networking as a component of political careers and therefore imperial political culture. The image of examination students and expectant officials jockeying for position as they read the latest personnel reports from Beijing looms large in the reports of foreign visitors and in late Qing fiction.[64] In these stories, officials and would-be officials so hungered for positions that they engaged in comical and criminal hijinks to cultivate relationships and favor, conspicuously among examination supervisors and board officials. Such depictions cropped up markedly in the late nineteenth century, when the number of qualified degree recipients had grown in stark excess of available posts, and when willing purchasers challenged lifelong students for official positions.

Li Ciming: A Late Qing Official and His Gazettes

Perhaps no individual epitomizes the hungry pursuit of social information in the gazette more than the nineteenth-century capital official Li Ciming

(1830–1894). Li's diaries showcase the techniques that he and other Qing officials used to organize political information in order to make it useable on the road and for years to come. The entries in Li's diaries are nearly as extensive as any library collection of gazettes today.

Born in 1830, Li Ciming arrived in Beijing as a young man with limited connections and lacking a provincial or metropolitan degree. After selling off family land, Li had amassed a considerable sum of money, which he gave to a friend to help him purchase eligibility for a metropolitan board position.[65] In Beijing, however, Li was told that because of a clerical snafu, he would have to pay an additional sum to take up the position. He soon found out that a longtime acquaintance who had brokered his purchase had actually taken a cut of the fees.[66] He hung about in the city and soon received a low-paid training position (*xingzou*) in the Board of Revenue through the patronage of the board secretary, Zhou Zupei (1793–1867). Li's expenditures almost always exceeded his meager salary, and he was forced on occasion to pawn his winter coats. Returning home to Zhejiang, Li earned money by mortgaging family land and working at the recently established provincial publishing bureau. After several tries, he obtained a provincial degree in Hangzhou in 1870. He then returned to the capital and received a small salary bump when he became an expectant official.[67]

While based in the capital, Li Ciming needed to master the details of a wider and ever-shifting retinue of resident and sojourning officials. Gazettes served his purposes perfectly. Li's comprehensive diary records attest to his commitment to the gazette as an information source during the course of his rise. He began to include occasional notes from gazettes in the mid-1850s, before he began his official career.[68] By the early 1860s, he wrote in his diary every day, and most days he included a record from the court gazette. Like many diarists, Li began his entries with a note of the date and the day's weather, before continuing to detail meetings, visits, recreation, and reading. Gazette records, marked with triangles or circles, concluded most entries.[69] He indulged wide-ranging literary, philosophical, and historical interests by reading and taking notes from many different texts in his diaries. Yet he did not systematically mark or separate these reading entries and book notes from the main content of his daily entry. Only for his notes on the court gazette did Li take care to separate the notes from the main entry and annotate them for easy reference.

Li Ciming remained a consistent follower of the gazette for his entire career. Changes in his practice of recording gazette items over the years reflect his rise through the metropolitan bureaucracy. In the early Tongzhi reign, while he served as an unsalaried Board of Revenue functionary, his gazette transcriptions sometimes made up the bulk of the day's lines. Li occasionally recorded purchases of monthly subscriptions to the court gazette or the palace digest (*gongmen chao*) in his encyclopedic diaries.[70] Most likely, Li read gazettes while in the board office, and the fees he recorded represent his contributions to the office subscription.[71] Thus, while Li had regular access to gazettes, he did not keep them in his home. Lacking a personal archive, Li copied a tailored archive of gazettes into his diaries.

By reading and chronicling personnel details, Li constructed a personal archive of information about ranked officials throughout the empire. His early entries, beginning before his move to Beijing, concentrate on the opening pages of the gazette. The court digest recorded information involving official appointments and careers, including promotions, demotions, transfers, requests for sick leave, and so on. With his careerist ambitions, Li sought to find out which positions were in flux, which officials were favored, and who might be a useful ally. While ranked officials like Zeng Guofan recorded this information primarily concerning family members and friends, the undistinguished junior official copied from the digest indiscriminately. Maintaining information about the bureaucracy became more important while his career was on hiatus. At home in Zhejiang, Li borrowed a recent issue of the *Directory to Officialdom* (Jinshen lu) to keep up with the latest capital and provincial appointments.[72] With these notes, the diary became a comprehensive index of the highest-level provincial and metropolitan officials in the bureaucracy.

Li's recording practice evinces his efforts to maintain a structured personal archive notwithstanding changes in access to political information. While away from the capital for a long period, Li Ciming often lost timely access to the gazettes, and his reading schedule and diary entries reflected these transitions. In the capital, because he read gazette issues on the same day that they were published, he did not date these daily entries. However, at home in the southeast, Li recorded items from the court gazette at infrequent intervals, and introduced these entries with precise annotations of the dates of the gazettes.[73] During the years that he spent away from Beijing, he skimmed several gazettes in a sitting, rather than reading an issue each day. Like other officials stationed in the provinces, Li often read gazettes at a substantial delay. In the summer of 1867, he recorded gazette entries at a delay of about one month after their capital publication.[74] Within his longer entries, he marked the specific date (for example, "the twenty-second") in small characters after the individual extract. This practice ensured an accurate reference date for individual items even when he read gazettes in larger batches. In longer annotations, as when he introduced his shorter daily entries, Li made sure to visually mark the reference so that the gazette entries could be readily noted when flipping through the diary's pages.

Reading gazettes for personnel details was a careerist activity, but it also nurtured relationships separated in years and miles by the demands of official life. The day after he borrowed the *Directory* to supplement his gazette readings at home in Zhejiang, Li Ciming received a piece of bad news. On this rainy morning, he awoke late. A friend came and told him that he had just seen the latest gazette sent from the capital, which stated that Zhou Zupei, who had served as a mentor to Li in his first years in Beijing, had passed away two months prior.[75] After Zhou's death, Li composed a commemorative inscription, and Zhou Zupei's son also paid him to write a short biography of his father.[76] Though for the most part, Li's records of the details of officials with whom he might cultivate favor appear in a utilitarian light, his experience of Zhou's death reminds us of the emotional ties that crisscrossed the Qing bureaucracy.

In the winter of 1871, Li Ciming journeyed back to Beijing to resume his official life, having finally obtained a provincial degree. He spent his initial days back in Beijing receiving guests, looking for appropriate lodging, and trying to reacquire his Board position. On his very first full day in the capital, Li visited each of the heads of the six boards. A few days later, he found out that arrangements had been made for him to resume his board position. Li's knowledge of the contours of the metropolitan bureaucracy had paid off. While away from the capital, he had read the gazettes at a delay, but once returned he soon obtained the most recent news. Seven days after reentering the capital, Li sat down for a marathon session with the court gazette. He copied nine pages of entries covering the past six weeks of the gazette's issues into his diary. The next day, Li returned to his habit of recording gazette items at the end of each day's diary entry, and he stopped itemizing dates, since as a capital resident he enjoyed the privilege of reading issues as soon as they were published.[77] As Li earned more, he began to spend more, renting a lavish home and employing several servants. Li finally landed a metropolitan degree in 1880 and then became a censor.[78]

The case of Li Ciming is an instructive reminder of how social transitions affected the lived experience of officials and their encounters with political communications. Although Li was perhaps the late Qing bureaucracy's most devoted reader of court news, he led an undistinguished career in the capital, and his own writings were featured in the court gazette only a few times in the span of his lengthy tenure.[79] Instead of defending contested truths, he hoarded names and social information from his reading of court news. Yet Li Ciming alone could not be blamed for the abandonment of the idealized intellectual prescripts that guided officials in their readings. Like his late nineteenth-century contemporaries, Li contended with a bureaucracy in crisis: an underfunded and overstaffed state teeming with anxiety.

◆ ◆ ◆

None of the readers profiled here simply "read the news" in their perusal of court gazettes. Instead, they constituted political lives through their engagement with the information contained in the court's daily dispatches. Few readers could be as cynical of power as Gu Yanwu, as attentive to administrative details as Chen Hongmou, as sophisticated at building arguments as Sun Jiagan, or as meticulous in mapping the bureaucracy as Li Ciming. Still, if these men were exceptional in reputation, their practices were more typical. Administrative, political, and careerist approaches to state information were predominant modes of political engagement among Qing officials. To be sure, officials made careers through their navigation of civil service examinations, their acquisition of personal relationships, and their handling of administrative complexities. Moreover, successful careers required keen political awareness, including attention to the changing imperial temperament and the ideas and personalities current within the bureaucracy.

In reading gazettes, officials made meaning of the activities of the state and encountered the living institutions of the dynasty. Incisive and creative readings of state news informed multiple facets of official work. Copied into personal records, gazette jottings became individualized archives that could be referenced for details of events, personages, and appointments. While gazettes never offered comprehensive coverage of imperial news, they did reward careful reading with valuable insights, including statements of changing court policy, notices of the promotion and demotion of officials, and tantalizing snippets of official language and attitudes. And in their own writings, made public in gazettes, officials contributed to a lively political forum that spanned the vast distances of empire. Along the way, a wider community of readers came to constitute the bureaucratic public: those who gathered and analyzed political communications for personal and political goals. Still, among an expanding reading population, officials were best equipped to benefit from reading communications authored by their counterparts across the empire. Their stories form a point of contrast with the gazette's significant foreign readership.

CHAPTER 5

The Qing Gazette Goes Abroad

THROUGH THE MEDIUM OF GAZETTES, THE QING COURT ADDRESSED the state, the empire, and the world. The heads of East Asian tributary states read Chinese gazettes throughout the late imperial period as dispatches of state business.[1] The Western audience for gazettes, meanwhile, evolved over time, as did the meanings that Western readers assigned to Chinese state news.[2] As early as the seventeenth century, resident missionaries introduced the gazettes of the Qing dynasty in their published correspondence. From there, scholars and diplomats added their opinions and gazette translations were published widely. Western interpreters wrote about Chinese state news in personal and diplomatic correspondence, newspapers, and journals. Gazettes remained the paramount source for Europeans intrigued by contemporary Chinese politics through the nineteenth century, when a booming number of Western newspapers published gazette translations in response to readers' interest in the wars and rebellions then consuming the Qing empire.

In the early eighteenth century, the French missionary Cyr Contancin (1670–1732) wrote of the Qing gazette that "nothing is printed in it which has not been presented to the emperor, or which does not originate from the emperor himself."[3] The missionary's statement called to mind the image of monarch with brush to paper, writing directly to the realm. Eventually, however, European interlocutors began to argue that gazettes revealed the Qing state's shortcomings more than its assets. If Contancin referred to the court gazette as a metaphor for the primacy of the emperor's word throughout his subject territories, nineteenth-century readers suggested that the limitations of the Chinese gazette expressed the faltering authority of imperial rule in China. Nearly two centuries after Contancin praised the value of the court gazette, the French consul Camille Imbault-Huart (1857–1897) addressed a Paris geographical society concerning the Chinese state publication. In these waning years of Qing power, the consul claimed, gazettes had become useless as tools for comprehending Chinese modes of governance or public life. In fact, Imbault-Huart argued, power was so haphazardly and carelessly apportioned in China that no "politics" remained for observation.[4]

Transitions in the political role of newspapers and media in Europe led readers to think differently about Chinese news. Scholarship on the relationship between print, politics, and the state in Europe makes up a major and avid field of recent inquiry. These studies demonstrate that the idea of "news"—and the formats in which European audiences received news—transformed by the mid-nineteenth century from an oral and manuscript-dominated trade to one of mass print. In the late sixteenth and seventeenth centuries, a print revolution intersected with military and religious conflicts, motivating individuals, publishers, and governments to begin writing and distributing news reports for public audiences.[5] Amid conflict fissuring the continent in the eighteenth century, European governments began to pursue new techniques of press censorship and control. In response, informed readers found ways to gather information from foreign accounts.[6] As readers moved away from state publications, preferring private sources, national governments used official gazettes to try to counter the influence of the political press.[7] The changing relevance and accessibility of news—and state news in particular—thus influenced how Europeans understood the state papers of the Qing empire.

Generally speaking, European interest in China developed in three phases: the seventeenth century augmentation of the sea trade and the arrival of missionaries, the advent of public interest in the age of the opium trade, and the early-nineteenth century formation of scholarly awareness of Asia. The arrival of goods and products from China helped encourage broader popular interest in Asian topics.[8] The political questions of the day—Who should rule? What qualities defined the national community? What divided king from common man?—motivated inquiries into foreign systems of politics and empire. With the expansion of trading and imperialist agendas in Asia, new forms of technical and diplomatic expertise directed inquiries into

Asian states and empires. Where Jesuits and Enlightenment interlocutors had devised views of the Chinese monarch and "Oriental despot," British state agents offered pointed critiques of the nineteenth-century Qing state. By the second half of the nineteenth century, Western readers encountered stories from Chinese gazettes in the context of a booming commercial press, moving news of China into wide exposure. Widening consumption of the news from China made the Peking Gazette a household name and an ideal souvenir, but also encouraged superficial engagement with Chinese news. Following how readers in international contexts read Chinese state news over the longue durée thus reveals transnational intersections of print, politics, and power.

From Missionary Knowledge to State Information

In 1673, from his station in Changshu, a Dutch Jesuit wrote teasingly to a fellow missionary, "Why did father Pereyra not sent news from Peking? He must realize that I could avenge myself by not sending wine!"[9] As the Qing court began to release gazettes for public circulation in the mid-seventeenth century, representatives of Christian missions in China eagerly sought out these dispatches for news from the imperial court. At first, gazettes were most readily obtained in the capital, but print and manuscript editions could also be purchased in Canton and other cities.[10] They were so plentiful, in fact, that a Canton-based doctor employed by the French East India Company (Compagnie français pour le commerce des Indes orientales) used pages from locally printed gazettes to wrap up a collection of minerals for transport back to Paris.[11]

In their correspondence, the missionaries transcribed, translated, and interpreted the news from China for their correspondents.[12] Translated gazette dispatches traversed oceans and continents, swapped for food, books, gifts, and news of other nations.[13] Gazettes provided information on several topics of crucial importance for missionaries: imperial edicts pertaining to Christianity; meteorological, astronomical, and natural phenomena; and information on local officials with whom they might come into contact.[14] Missionaries searched for the appointment details of nearby magistrates and provincial governors so that they might rush to offer gifts and form relationships, thus influencing the officials to favor their presence.[15] Given the volume of information available, one needed to read strategically; veteran missionaries taught new arrivals how to skim the gazettes for memorials originating from the Board of Rites, since these documents might pertain to religious policy.[16]

Cyr Contancin Introduces the "Gazettes of China"

Through missionary exchanges, events occurring in China became the subject of intense interest in Europe. In 1726, the Yongzheng emperor ordered the execution of the Portuguese Jesuit João Mourão (1681–1726). Mourão had confessed to conspiring with a faction of imperial clansmen, including several Christian converts, to undermine the legitimacy of the emperor's claim to the throne.[17] The execution was not a secret matter. Gazettes circulated by the Yongzheng court detailed accusations of treachery together with the missionary's induced confession.[18] Tales of the execution traveled throughout China and, thereafter, via its southern ports to Europe. That year, the incident became the subject of conversation in a weekly meeting of the Propaganda Fide, a papal-sponsored missionary council in Rome.[19] The missionary Cyr Contancin, recently exiled to Canton, transcribed gazette accounts in his reports to European correspondents and explained that these unassuming pamphlets represented the direct will of the Yongzheng emperor. A letter published in the London *Daily Post* described Mourão's ignominious demise and mentioned that the man's confession had been "inserted in all the Gazettes of China, which are never published but by the Emperor's Command," and his death sentence "posted up in the Streets and at the Gates of the Merchant Houses."[20] In their ubiquity and their authoritative voice, gazettes testified to the absolute power of the monarch.

Contancin and his colleagues read and interpreted Chinese gazettes during a historical transition in which Qing state texts became the most essential sources for Western Europeans seeking to understand the workings of the state. In an earlier era, Catholic missionaries had lived and worked closely with imperial elites in Beijing. However, a year earlier, in 1725, the Yongzheng emperor had simultaneously banned Christian proselytization and exiled Catholic missionaries in China to Canton and Macao.[21] Not just missionaries, but most Western sojourners remained at a distance from Beijing, the seat of the Qing empire, for more than a century. Separated from capital confidantes, these sojourners turned to official texts rather than personal contacts to describe for their correspondents the nature of the Qing government and monarch.[22] When Contancin trumpeted the authority of the Chinese gazette, he also admitted that in prior years, when imperial policy towards missionaries had been relatively lax, he rarely read the gazettes.[23] Now, appealing for their convenience and proximity to the imperial state, gazettes became the key to understanding Qing power as it worked in the present moment.

In the gazettes that they purchased from local purveyors, the exiled missionaries found information about appointments and natural events, as before. But given the immense power that the Yongzheng emperor wielded over them, they also began to perceive the distinctive qualities of his ruling style. Contancin found much to praise, despite the emperor's proscription of Christianity. "This Prince is indefatigable in his work; he thinks night and day of creating a sage government and obtaining the happiness of his subjects," the missionary wrote in another letter. The missive continued to describe the emperor's exemplary behavior in detail. When a drought left Zhejiang on the brink of famine, Yongzheng ordered the distribution of rice to feed thousands. When floods inundated the north, he distributed monetary relief. When severe heat afflicted the capital, he ordered that debtors and other accused of minor crimes be released from crowded and sweltering prisons. The emperor not only addressed himself to maladies, but also rewarded goodness and economic productivity. He ordered field officials to report the most distinguished farmers in their jurisdictions so that they might receive imperial recognition. For women, he introduced inducements to maintain chastity, even after the death of a spouse. He offered recognition for filial deeds and allowed officials to retire after the death of a parent. Within the bureaucracy, he installed a rigorous system of evaluations to promote the meritorious and push out the corrupt.[24]

For Contancin, if benevolent agendas illustrated the Yongzheng emperor's concern for his people, then the emperor's willingness to present his policies for public scrutiny demonstrated that he had mastered the uses of publicity. In the case of the flood, Yongzheng had not only apportioned relief, but also published an edict that ordered provincial officials to thoroughly investigate the causes for and relief of poverty across the empire.[25] Such public commandments made fallible officials accountable. When some governors blamed the floods on the bad behavior of their subordinates, Yongzheng dismissed their name calling, writing, "Let us think only of correcting our own defects, and the flood." Most remarkable, according to Contancin, was the initiative to allow officials to offer suggestions on the conduct of good government, which the emperor allowed to be submitted in secret, pledging not to reveal the identities of their authors. In these readings, the emperor himself became the most important subject portrayed by the court gazette, an information master who advertised in his public writings the most commendable characteristics of a monarch: charity, responsibility, and administrative diligence.

Contancin had no doubt that what he read of the emperor and his agendas was true. Chinese gazettes, he explained, were not merely news sources to be evaluated with comparison to rivals, but the sole authorized representations of the imperial will. This made gazettes especially useful instruments of governance: "What makes the Chinese gazette useful for the government, is that instead of filling it, as it is done in certain parts of Europe, with uselessness, and often with slanders and calumnies, it includes only that which is reported to the Emperor, and, as the Chinese government is perfectly monarchical, and as every matter of any consideration are therein reported, this gazette contains nothing which does not serve to direct the Mandarins in the exercise of their offices, and to instruct the literati and the people."[26]

The Chinese court gazette, Contancin effused, offered a method for the use of publicity as a tool of the state. By only publishing the emperor's instructions, together with the memorials that had been presented to the imperial government, the Qing state saved its people from the problem of sorting out the claims, accusations, and falsehoods that plagued the European press. In a sense, the gazettes served as textbooks for the Qing official, and Contancin observed that most Qing officials that he had encountered took diligent instruction from the gazette.[27]

In these comments, the missionary criticized the European press at the same time that he praised the Chinese official organ. As Contancin alluded, the use of the term *gazette* prompted Western readers to understand the Chinese gazette as analogous to other official gazettes with which they were more familiar, such as the *London Gazette* or the *Gazette de France*.[28] Although considered official by their association with the state, European gazettes were also closely linked with the personal leanings and networks of the editor.[29] In seventeenth-century Europe, gazettes had originated as collections of documents, correspondence, and testimonies collected by editors with privileged positions close to the court. Through Contancin's day, the *Gazette de France* operated with a license from the crown, but it drew its content from the wide-ranging personal networks and correspondence of its compiler. Meanwhile, published "by authority," the *London Gazette* printed notices of legislation, copies of diplomatic correspondence, and information about government personnel.[30] Yet the composition of the *London Gazette* could be inconsistent, and in the lively political culture of eighteenth-century London, many readers turned to other news sources, thus dulling the official paper's impact in public instruction. The Chinese gazette, by contrast, appeared a refreshingly effective vehicle for political communication.

Enlightenment Readings of Chinese State News

Contancin's letters from Canton were read not just by his Jesuit superiors, but also by the expansive European audience for missionary writings from distant lands. A prominent anthology of correspondence from Jesuit missionaries in Asia and the Americas, *Lettres édifiantes et curieuses*, included Contancin's letters in its volumes published serially in Paris between 1702 and 1776. Each volume of the popular collection was almost immediately reprinted in multiple European cities and languages.[31] The letters from China were among the most influential items in the collection, informing European understandings of the natural sciences, religion, law, and culture in Asia.[32] Quotations from Chinese documents published in the letter collection were for some an innate draw. The English author Thomas Percy (1729–1811), an enthusiast of all things China, noted that in the *Lettres édifiantes* could be "seen many curious extracts from the Chinese Gazettes."[33]

Contancin's reading of the court gazettes also contributed to the general histories of China popular in eighteenth-century Europe. These included *Description de la Chine* by Jean-Baptiste Du Halde (1674–1743), *Histoire générale de la Chine* by Joseph de Mailla (1699–1748), and other eighteenth-century accounts of the Chinese state.[34] Du Halde, for instance, recapitulated Contancin's depictions both of Yongzheng's character and of the direct connection between gazettes and the imperial will.[35] Du Halde's work, which was translated into English and published as *The General History of China*, was influential in spreading ideas about the makeup and ideals of the Chinese state to British audiences, including newspaper readers. In 1733, even before the full work had been published in either French or English, one London pamphlet periodical reprinted the gazette excerpts originally quoted by Contancin, adducing these sources to be the most interesting components of Du Halde's entire project.[36]

Although he reprised some of Contancin's comments, Du Halde's interpretation of the court gazette's significance considered the state and its institutions in their totality rather than the Jesuits' narrow interest in the emperor. The Jesuit missionaries had not translated memorials authored by field officials, preferring to focus on the imperial edicts that signified the monarch's intentions. By contrast, Du Halde was interested in the structures and organization of the Qing state. In a synthetic essay on institutions, he named gazettes to be one of the Chinese state's most essential extralegal institutions for maintaining order within the bureaucracy. Whereas Contancin had praised the diligence of the official readers of the court gazette, Du Halde pointed out that the sheer frequency of administrative crimes in the gazette suggested that even if the sovereign were, as Yongzheng seemed to be, the ideal monarch, the bureaucrats below him were no doubt fallible, suspect to greed and the pursuit of private advancement. Perhaps by reading detailed expositions of the administrative crimes of their counterparts, officials could be "prevented from falling into the mistakes they tended to commit."[37] Still, the gazettes presented clear evidence of the failings of the bureaucracy. This more discerning perspective would be reiterated and sharpened by European readers of the nineteenth century.

The missionary notes on politics, which described the Qing monarchy and state in idealized terms, led French Enlightenment enthusiasts to conceive of the Chinese state as a potential solution to political problems that troubled contemporary European states, including partisanship, unrestrained absolutism, and the moral decline of government. A variety of political thinkers seized on the idea that the Chinese state permitted total transparency of government. Without direct access to Chinese sources, however, these authors uniformly exaggerated the merits of Qing state publicity, idealizing the Peking Gazette as a comprehensive portrait of state affairs, universally received by the reading public. The practicality of such a state institution struck Jean-Paul Marat (1743–1793), who recommended in an essay on criminal law that France adopt a publication on the model of the "redoubtable" gazette of China, which allowed the people to clearly perceive the government's exercise of law and the status of state revenues and expenditures.[38] Marat's opinion was shared by another French essayist who pointed out that the gazette served as a tool for the public, as well as for the state. In China, "the fundamental laws of the State are in the hands of all; the emperor thus must conform to them."[39]

For the so-called sinophiles, especially Voltaire (1694–1778), the Chinese state appeared to be the most rational in the world, not just in its historical and philosophical traditions, but also, as could be read in its news, in its contemporary operations. In a widely reproduced essay on comparative civilizations, Voltaire stated bombastically that the Chinese gazette was "the most authentic and useful journal that we have in the world." Voltaire ascribed the gazette's utility to its reliable conveyance of detailed information on public works and expenditures; in this sense, the Chinese state received praise for its transparency: the distribution of information-filled gazettes allowed readers to come to a more concrete understanding of the workings of state and society.[40] Voltaire's discussions of politics through the example of China were popular reading material across Europe; from Russia, the monarch Catherine the Great (r. 1762–96) praised the nature of the Qing state but also wrote to caution Voltaire about the gaps between public representation and her experience dealing with the Qing court on matters of borderland trade.[41]

Prominent intellectual voices in France engaged with the topic of the Chinese state and its information policies, but elsewhere in Europe, these treatises actually influenced state policy. Given that most current portrayals of China had originated from the Jesuit missionaries, French thinkers' enthusiastic reception of China began to crumble in the late eighteenth century amid an acrimonious split between the Jesuits and other religious orders.[42] In Sweden, politicians Anders Nordencrantz (1697–1772) and Anders Chydenius (1729–1803) were charmed by the accounts of Chinese information policy in translations of Du Halde's *Description géographique*. From there, both authored pamphlets espousing the merits of the Chinese court gazette as a conduit of state information for the general public. Whereas Du Halde had followed his introduction to Chinese gazettes with a stark example of the emperor's willingness to censor information, both omitted this passage from their writings.[43] The pamphlets influenced the drafting of a Swedish Press Act in 1766. Recently, this legislation has been lauded by proponents of government transparency as "the world's first freedom of information act."[44]

Across Europe, even as each of these prominent interpretations devoted attention to the court gazette, they neglected to detail the overall organization of the state information order of which the court gazette was a single component. Why was the focus on the gazette so narrowly defined? Enlightenment-era descriptions of China fulfilled genuine interest in the institutions of a distant and dignified civilization, but they also served as the starting points for meditations concerned more with European than Chinese contexts. Here was a state, European thinkers found, where the political press, by virtue of total state control, was untroubled by the problem of censorship. In this, they defined the Chinese gazette as a perfect vector of information relayed by a relentlessly monarchical state but failed to address its institutional contexts, broader political significance, or whether highly specific portraits of autocracy, such as the gazettes of the monumental yet brief Yongzheng era, could really be taken as a metaphor for imperial power across centuries.

Chinese Mirrors for Kings

As a site for inquiry, China appealed to audiences beyond intellectuals, including the court officials of pre-Revolutionary France. It is for this reason that Henri Bertin (1720–1792), a long-time minister to the French throne, sent an extensive list of questions for the resident missionaries in China to address in the late eighteenth century. Although the French state had suppressed the Jesuit order, King Louis XVI reprised royal support for the China mission in 1777.[45] Excerpts from Bertin's correspondence, compiled by scholar Louis-Georges de Bréquigny (1714–1795) under Bertin's supervision, were published between 1776 and 1791 in another multivolume missionary anthology, the *Mémoires concernant des Chinois*. Nearly five hundred financial supporters contributed to the printing of the anthology, including King Louis XVI, members of the royal family, the nobility, clergy, notable intellectuals, booksellers, and merchants.[46] Like their predecessors, the Beijing Jesuits of the Qianlong era, including Jean-Joseph Marie Amiot (1718–1793), François Bourgeois (1723–1792), and Pierre-Martial Cibot (1727–1780), habitually read the Qing court gazette. Their responses to Bertin's questions about politics and power in contemporary China drew on these readings.[47] Influenced by Voltaire's China-infused doctrines of political power, which emphasized the Chinese bureaucracy's ability to restrain autocratic power, the missionaries further refined the portrait of Qing monarchy sketched by Contancin and his contemporaries.[48]

These last remnants of the Jesuit mission in Beijing attempted in their writings to promote the authority of their access to timely and trustworthy news, as well as their superior ability to interpret that information. In so doing, they rebutted accusations that the earlier Jesuit accounts had presented an overly rosy portrait of Qing rule. Amiot and Bourgeois in particular took pains to document their access to information, asserting that Jesuits based in the imperial capital had better sources than competing missions based in southern China. The pair acknowledged their source materials more explicitly than past correspondents and highlighted items that demonstrated the expansive geographic coverage of these publications. This new generation of missionary correspondents also presented more modest claims concerning the power of the monarchy. Especially in their private correspondence with French court representatives, the missionaries interpreted Qing rulership, as personified by the Qianlong emperor, to be fundamentally supported by the bureaucracy and the emperor's advisors and therefore consultative rather than domineering in nature.

In 1779, Amiot sent ten issues of the Qing court gazette to the royal library in Paris as concrete evidence of the matters he described. The gazettes, print editions published by the Gongshen Tang in Beijing, described matters as trivial as a sedition case against two medicine sellers and as far-reaching as announcements regarding the ongoing Imperial Four Treasuries project (Siku quanshu), an ambitious empire-wide initiative to compile an authoritative library of historical editions.[49] About a decade later, Bourgeois, the head of the French mission in Beijing, translated and annotated a lengthy two-month section of gazettes, which he claimed would showcase a comprehensive and unbiased view of the court publication. In his introduction to the work, he claimed that the gazette's contents originated with the emperor's early-morning meetings with his Grand Council and that this group, not the emperor himself, picked "the most interesting items" for publication.[50] The translation project began with the exciting news of a major rebellion in Taiwan, but Bourgeois's enthusiasm was tempered by a long stream of announcements concerning the triennial examinations, followed by successive brief notices of appointment audiences. Bourgeois soon resorted to summaries, rather than complete translations. About a month in, seeing the predominance of appointment notices in the gazette's contents, he wrote, "There's nothing interesting in the rest of this gazette."[51] During the seventeenth century, when missionaries at local stations prioritized relationships with local officials, appointment notices had been coveted news items. Now, they seemed trivial to foreign readers mainly interested in the monarchy and central state institutions.

As the missionaries sent their correspondence from Beijing, Henri Bertin reviewed the full collection and prepared excerpts for presentation to the French monarch.[52] Shortly before the onset of revolutionary upheaval in France, King Louis XVI received five letters written between 1785 and 1787. Two letters from Canton treated items of interest pertaining to the growing French trading presence in South China; the remainder, authored in Beijing, focused on the character of Louis XVI's Manchu contemporary, the Qianlong emperor. The missionary correspondent praised the emperor's contributions to the public good and concern for the population at large. By building imperial edifices in the Beijing suburbs, for example, the emperor lent employment to people who might be otherwise hungry or displaced. Qianlong received further praise for his ability to support and cultivate distinct cultural values among the diverse populations under his rule. Thus, he encouraged the practice of archery among Manchus but also followed Chinese court protocol.[53] By citing the Qing court gazette as the source of these examples of benevolent rule, the correspondent highlighted the Qianlong emperor's exemplary behavior and the throne's willingness to employ political publicity. As the missionary correspondent wrote, the edicts published in the gazette expressed "the real spirit of governance" in China.[54]

These late eighteenth-century interlocutors emphasized the consultative and rational aspects of Qing rule. In this, they responded to emerging criticism of autocratic government in Europe, leveled via "sinophobic" arguments against the oriental despot and other symbols that had previously functioned as positive exemplars in Enlightenment thought. In this light, the missionaries made clear that the Qing monarch did not act on his own. In fact, he rarely initiated policy. A telling example here was a case in which representatives of the Censorate had lambasted Beijing's street entertainers for their lack of moral discipline. In response, the Qianlong emperor urged his officials to support the practice of monthly morality lectures for the population, and told the capital police not to crack down on street performers, but rather to keep an eye on the contents of their tales and songs. More than illustrating urban life in China, the anecdote exemplified the Qing emperor's mode of interaction with his officials. Rather than independently dictating policy, the missionary correspondents pointed out, the emperor responded to or took the advice of his officials. Therefore, one should not believe "those that say the Chinese monarch is a despot, in all the odious senses that are attached to this word," as he was often described in France for the specific purpose of defining China as a society without change over "thirty centuries."[55] The correspondents thus used news items from the court gazette to undermine the most prominent assertions of the sinophobic critics.

The subsequent lapse of the Jesuit mission in China, combined with the overthrow of the French throne in 1789, shifted intellectual attention in France away from the dynamics of Chinese political power. Still, the Jesuit works, as well as those of their detractors, had important legacies. In the end, the autocratic view of the Qing monarchy, rather than the consultative portrait, proved more persistent. The image of emperor-as-editor, wielding a pen to instruct and control his empire, remained more enticing than the more mundane view of the emperor in constant consultation with councils and institutions. Most importantly, the prominent placement of imperial edicts within court gazettes implied that the emperor truly reigned paramount over the bureaucracy and society. This view would be put to the test by a new generation of British interlocutors in the coming decades.

Chinese Gazettes from Intelligence to Curio in the Nineteenth Century

In the eighteenth century, schools for the learning of the Chinese language had been established in Paris, Naples, and elsewhere in continental Europe. In England, by contrast, no institutional body could claim expertise in Chinese language or learning. Meanwhile, the joint constraints of the "Canton system" and the East India Company monopoly on trade to China confined most British trading activity to a single port on the coast of southeast China. Any communications with provincial officials required recruiting Chinese linguists or missionaries conversant in the local language, and attempts to train British linguists proved abortive.[56] These circumstances created anxiety among British traders, politicians, and intellectuals that the English had no direct means of learning about China on its own terms nor of intercourse with the Qing throne.[57] Political information, in particular, came second-hand.

The failure of the 1793 Macartney mission to move beyond the level of formalities with its Qing counterparts convinced the East India Company leadership that linguistic fluency would be necessary to achieve English goals in China.[58] Toward this end, the company and the English trading community welcomed George Thomas Staunton (1781–1859) to Canton in 1800. Staunton had learned Chinese after accompanying the Macartney mission as a child. But Staunton worked only intermittently as an interpreter over the next decade.[59] In the context of his frequent absence, in 1809, the company hired Robert Morrison, a recently arrived missionary with the London Missionary Society who needed to supplement his stipend.[60] Morrison, a Protestant preacher from northeast England, had begun learning Chinese in London and continued with a local teacher in Canton.[61] Morrison ended up remaining with the company for more than two decades. By 1822, when Morrison once suggested he might take a trip back to England, company records complained of "the conviction of the difficulty & embarrassment we might be placed in, were the Factory left destitute of persons possessing a knowledge of Chinese, Especially should we unfortunately be involved in negotiations or discussions with the local Government."[62] The company now considered an English translator in residence at Canton to be absolutely necessary and was unwilling to rely on Chinese or European intermediaries.

Morrison produced translations of Chinese documents and trained students in the official language for the English East India Company. His translations from the court gazette constituted the company's main intelligence source on the Qing emperor, court, and state.[63] As language instructor, Morrison taught sixteen students between 1810 and 1830, several of whom went on to take up important consular posts.[64] In this role, he pioneered a new style of language instruction for the training of trading and diplomatic officials. By contrast with most contemporary European learners of Chinese who either memorized bilingual dictionaries or followed a classical curriculum dictated by Chinese teachers, Morrison's main textbook was the court gazette. The gazette was an ideal instructional text for interpreters because it contained state documents written in the working language of the bureaucracy, distinct from that used in vernacular language or classical readings. Moreover, in the course of their language instruction, students could translate useful documents to be transmitted to English authorities.

Like the Catholic missionaries before them, English translators felt that access to the court gazette dispelled various types of misunderstanding and enhanced their regard for the conduct of the Qing emperors. Robert Morrison had written about the gazette as early as 1808, in a letter to the London Missionary Society: "Though they have not anything can strictly be called a newspaper, they are all politicians. In Canton, there is a sheet, about the size of a quarto page, published daily. It however contains little further than the removal of public offices—visits to the Viceroy &c. A court gazette from Pekin falls into the hands of some, & the loquacious Chinese, who spend much of their time in chatting parties, soon diffuse reports, and as is general, with considerable additions."[65]

Morrison's familiarity with the "court gazette from Pekin" probably drew on the descriptions published in Jesuit texts and translated into English. In addition, eighteenth-century English newspapers occasionally mentioned the Chinese gazette.[66] Staunton, who served as an informal advisor to Morrison, may also have alerted Morrison of its utility.[67] Staunton had habitually read and translated the gazettes during his first years in Canton. He later published a selection, which he described as "sufficiently copious to convey a pretty correct idea of the ordinary contents of the Gazette." The thirty-seven examples, primarily edicts from the early years of the Jiaqing reign, showcased the emperor's attempt to regain order over the bloated and misguided military campaigns to combat the White Lotus uprising in central China. Staunton, echoing French remarks of the previous generation, commented that these edicts of such evident political importance showed "obvious proofs of an anxiety to influence and conciliate public opinion upon all state questions, which, under a government theoretically so despotic, would hardly have been expected."[68]

Sinological Theories and Useful Translation

In 1815, the East India Company incorporated Robert Morrison's translations into a pamphlet for distribution throughout England. This edition advertised the company's new printing press and showcased the literary talent of Morrison and his students with its translations from the Chinese gazette, legal texts, and literature authored by Morrison, Staunton, and John Francis Davis (1795–1890).[69] The translated gazette items reflected company interests: Qing court policy toward foreigners, Christianity, and opium circulation. In the London journal *Quarterly Review*, Morrison's choice of subject matter received enthusiastic praise.[70] The editors commended this work as "useful" translation, as opposed to the "theories" of continental scholars of China. It seemed unfathomable, wrote the *Review*, that French scholars could ignore the "real stuff of government" published in the Chinese gazette and instead presume that "the common-place maxims of morality drawn from the ancient writings of Confucius were actually the rule of conduct."[71] In its critique of French scholars, the review ignored the fact that French Jesuits had introduced the gazette as a source for timely political intelligence to the European reading public. More importantly, the review anticipated a common refrain among nineteenth-century British interlocutors: the conduct of the Qing government should be dealt with in terms of changing realities, not the ideals of the classical past.

The critical attitude of the review marked a transition in attitudes toward Chinese subjects and texts, not just in England but across Europe more generally. Whereas the writings of eighteenth-century missionaries had been dominated by topics of interest to church and throne, the early nineteenth century saw the formation of academic institutions and learned societies devoted to the study of China. Their intellectual interests had some ties to earlier traditions and the growing field of oriental knowledge. For example, nineteenth-century European sinologists focused on the Chinese language in order to test hypotheses of common origins between European and Asian civilizations, similar to the ways that Jesuit had tried to map analogues between biblical accounts and the history of Chinese civilization. More commonly, however, new colonial and trading interests in Asia motivated research.

The proliferation of institutions devoted to Asia across Europe caused research interests to fragment. In England, the British state funded research on current political institutions, texts, and laws. In France, attention to contemporary topics lapsed as academic institutions focused on linguistics, culture, and classical texts. Sinological projects sponsored by the Russian state represented a fusion of the two models.[72] Such divergences were reflected in the three states' relative focus on Qing documents. In Paris, the most flourishing location for academic sinology, the Société Asiatique merely reprinted Bourgeois's 1788 introduction to the Chinese gazette in its journal.[73] By contrast, the Royal Asiatic Society, associated with the East India Company and British empire in Asia, hosted John Francis Davis to read his translations from the Chinese gazette at three consecutive general meetings in London.[74] The Prussian Pavel Schilling von Canstadt (1786–1837), who headed the Russian Empire's Asia Department, collected a large set of manuscript gazettes, then donated these to the Austrian Imperial Library in Vienna.[75] The majority of Chinese gazettes brought to Europe in the early nineteenth century were placed in state libraries, rather than academic institutions.[76] Chinese court news was thus understood to convey political information and gazettes were not artifacts for scholarship. Besides diplomats and interpreters, newspaper editors also found that gazette excerpts could supply entertainment and edification to their readers.

The Peking Gazette Enters the Western Press

European news readers had begun to encounter regular translations from Chinese gazettes in the first decades of the nineteenth century. In the English-language press, a common term for the court periodical emerged: Pekin(g) Gazette.[77] This translation established an English shorthand for referring to the Chinese publication, on the basis of *Jingbao*, the title that appeared on the covers of gazettes published in Beijing around the same time. The new title established the Qing court gazette as equivalent to the newspapers and state records of other nations, which allowed editors to skip the task of explaining the particularities of the Chinese document to their audiences.

Gazette translations were particularly valuable for European editors to fill in the "Foreign Intelligence" sections that advertised a newspaper's global contacts. These brief descriptions of the activities and policies of the Qing court established China as an accessible, if quixotic, site of interest, not outside the horizons of the ordinary newspaper reader. Items sourced from Chinese gazettes could be seamlessly incorporated into a column of "Foreign News" or "Foreign Intelligence," downplaying the intermediate steps of translation and exchange that brought an item from the Peking Gazette to a reader of, say, the *New York Herald*, which printed a set of gazette translations in 1845 under the headings "VERY LATE FROM CHINA. Highly Interesting Intelligence! CURIOUS STATE OF THINGS IN THE CELESTIAL EMPIRE."[78]

From Canton, Robert Morrison published his Peking Gazette translations in a number of specialized and more widely circulated periodicals. At first, these included the *Indo-Chinese Gleaner* and the *Malacca Observer and Chinese Chronicle*, both short-lived missionary publications based in Malacca. The translations were further reprinted in London's *Morning Chronicle* and the *Asiatic Journal and Monthly Miscellany*.[79] Eventually, Morrison's translations of the news from Beijing became featured elements of the burgeoning China-coast periodical press, including mercantile newspapers like the *Canton Register* (founded in 1827) and missionary publications like the *Chinese Repository* (founded in 1832).[80] European editors seized upon these sources, and summaries of Morrison's gazette translations featured in a growing number of newspapers across Great Britain and Europe. Newspapers traveled by ship from South China to London, where excerpts were printed in prominent papers like the *Times*, *Daily News*, *Morning Chronicle*, and *Pall Mall Gazette*. Smaller regional papers then picked up these excerpts, thus extending the reach of the Peking Gazette.

The prominent placement of gazette translations within China-coast newspapers attests to Western interest in the activities of the Qing state, but also to the practical calculations made by editors. These newspapers were often side enterprises for printing companies that needed quick and regular source material to fill their pages. Early China-coast editors were not journalists in the professional sense that would emerge later in the century, and both the budget and the staff of these newspapers were miniscule. Furthermore, since editors based in Asia received coverage of events in Europe by mail, they had no advantage in terms of speed over other port city residents who carried on correspondence in Europe. To surmount these constraints, a heavy dose of Chinese politics—including copious translations from readily available court and provincial gazettes—fit the bill. Gazette translations appeared under headings including "Translations and Selected Excerpts from the Peking Reporter," "Peking Gazette," and "Journal of the Capital." Morrison was known in Hong Kong and Canton as an able and generous translator of state documents, and relationships with the press formed a valuable side enterprise for missionary and diplomatic translators for years to come.[81]

Not all members of the Western trading community in South China enjoyed the frequent disquisitions on the Qing state and its activities. When the *Canton Register* published a series of stirring reports on the Qing armies' efforts to quell a major rebellion in far-off Kashgar in the late 1820s, some readers rejected the subject as entirely separate from European interests in China. In a memorable letter to the editor, one "B. C. D." wrote, "The practical Truth is that with these people we have no *inter*-est—we are not *con*-cerned; and therefore we have no *sym*-pathos: no fellow-feeling." The reader concluded his dismissal of the lively tales of superstition, murder, and rebellion: "Cave! or your weekly lucubrations will soon become, waste paper."[82] By contrast, Morrison's hints at Russian conspiracy in the frontier rebellion led several European newspapers to feature gazette translations regarding the events.[83]

The occasional relationship between China-coast papers and the European press became more formal after 1842, when Western papers founded in Hong Kong and Shanghai solicited business connections in Europe. They sold and advertised their publications, both newspapers and books published by their parent printing businesses, through booksellers in London and Paris. These affiliations allowed certain papers to rise in prominence as suppliers of Chinese news. In 1851, for instance, the Hong Kong *China Mail* became the Chinese official partner of the London *Daily News*.[84] Meanwhile, a number of Hong Kong newspapers, including the *Mail* and the *Friend of China*, published "overland" editions for European readers, sent via monthly mail transports. These overland editions were frequently quoted sources when European newspapers excerpted from the China-coast press. While trade and shipping information was the signature export of these port city newspapers, they also commonly excerpted translations of Chinese gazettes.

The British Empire Reads China

In the second half of the nineteenth century, knowledge of Chinese politics became the province of a particularly capacious institution: the British Empire. Under the auspices of the Chinese Secretary, a Foreign Office post established after the dissolution of the East India Company's China monopoly in 1834, imperial personnel gathered and processed a vast catalog of gazettes in pursuit of useable intelligence on the quixotic policies of the Qing state. Chinese Secretaries John Robert Morrison (1814–1843) and Karl Gutzlaff (1803–1851) both relayed gazette translations to London.[85] However, it was Thomas Francis Wade (1818–1895), appointed Chinese Secretary in 1855, who systematically incorporated the Peking Gazette into his tutelage of junior staff, oversaw the compilation of a massive archive of gazettes, and positioned himself as one of the most important experts on the politics of the Qing empire through a series of publications based on close readings of the Qing gazette. Wade's long career, capped with his promotion to British minister to China in 1871, ensured that into the late nineteenth century, the Peking Gazette was a key, if increasingly criticized, intelligence source for the British empire in China.[86]

Early in his career, while based in Hong Kong, Wade published a lengthy *Note on the Conditions and Government of the Chinese Empire*, which he subtitled as "Chiefly from the Peking Gazette."[87] In this extended essay, Wade argued that the Peking Gazette portrayed more honestly than any other source the flaws and even the imminent dissolution and collapse of the Qing empire, making it an indispensable, if enigmatic, intelligence source. His basic opinions, supported by cases, statistics, and anecdotes from the gazettes, were that the Qing empire was plagued by major financial and personnel problems attributable to widespread corruption in the territorial bureaucracy and to a paralyzed court incapable of taking up reform. These criticisms reinforced assumptions that not only were Chinese officials universally corrupt and inefficient, but also that the bureaucratic state itself was arbitrary and unjust. After the *Note* was published, first in Hong Kong and thereafter in London, laudatory reviews circulated in the English- and French-language press.[88]

By devising a survey of the empire based on a comprehensive sample of state papers, the project drew on earlier attempts to profile the Qing monarchy through its texts. Wade's conclusions, however, departed from the interpretations reached by eighteenth-century Jesuits. Whereas Contancin and Amiot had praised the comprehensiveness of the Qing gazette, Wade saw room for complaint. In his view, the inclusion of topics in the court publication was so variable and inconsistent that it could not suffice to be even a "satisfactory record of the passing history of the nation."[89] Wade's perspective here was comparable to his official predecessor, George Thomas Staunton, who had publicized his translation of the Qing legal code as reflecting China's total incommensurability with Western standards.[90] Rather than analyzing the rhetoric and exercise of monarchical power, Wade focused on excavating data from the memorials presented by metropolitan and field officials. His interest lay in the state, not the monarch. And although he claimed the documents were insufficient sources for writing a history of the Qing state, they nonetheless allowed him to develop a pessimistic forecast of the dynasty's ability to persevere through a coming crisis.

Wade's *Note* defined the Qing bureaucracy as riddled with systemic weaknesses. These deficiencies were more significant than the shortcomings of a single emperor. While the rule of an ineffectual emperor would end at death, the longstanding institutions of the Chinese state would prove increasingly ill-suited for the modern age. Wade found evidence of breakdown in the way the bureaucratic system encouraged officials who were nominally moral exemplars to engage in corrupt and dishonest practices. Official memorials embodied this, by burying valuable information in pedantic rhetoric in order to gain favor. Memorialists pretended to embed reports from subordinates, but in fact, they omitted salient circumstances under the excuse that they did not fit within this chain of communications. Meanwhile, the gazette featured official initiatives on crucial matters like finance and defense at seemingly random intervals, making it of little service for consequential interventions or reform.[91] The only thing that gazettes reliably published, Wade concluded, were the rampant "official backslidings" found in cases of officials' removal from office for infractions including "corruption; defalcation; concealment of crime; erroneous decisions; remissness in not preventing, or tardiness in repairing, evil; incapacity; mediocrity; inexperience; informality; litigation; malingering; contumacity; presumption; and unpopularity."[92] According to Wade, the state's punitive focus on misconduct encouraged officials to hide information and detracted from the state's ability to work effectively.

Wade suggested that although they failed as historical sources, the Qing gazettes promised careful readers valuable intelligence as to when and how the dynasty might fall. During his tenure as the leading intelligence expert for the British in China, Wade alluded constantly to information in the gazettes that he read.[93] Moreover, gazettes were easily obtained and made useful translation tools. These factors made them ideal sources for the Chinese Secretary and his growing staff. Wade initiated the creation of comprehensive archives of Qing state papers, located first in Hong Kong and later in Beijing.[94] Chinese clerks transcribed gazettes into large bound ledgers; interpreters and student interpreters translated selected items into English; the Chinese Secretary then summarized these items, added commentary and explanations, and sent them to the Foreign Office.[95] Consular translations were published in the *North China Herald* (established in 1850), and after 1860, student translations written under Wade's tutelage made their way into the Shanghai press and then into English-language newspapers published around the world.[96]

Wade, whom one student interpreter called "the chief" and "the overseer of students," liked to have his gazettes translated in the morning so he could read them at lunch.[97] Student interpreters treated gazette copying and translation as necessary chores, as colorfully recorded in the diary of then-student interpreter Chaloner Alabaster (1838–1898). The teenaged Alabaster wrote, "Took up very late & then afterwards onto Wade as usual—we worked away but did not do much today the teachers being remarkable stupid at 12 1/2 down to office & when there wasted my time nicely reading extracts from the Peking Gazette however as it was by Wades order it was alright."[98] Another student interpreter, W. H. Wilkinson (1858–1930), sent his "boy" to purchase gazettes at a local shop, and read them with a language tutor.[99]

With this focus on state documents, comprehending the intricacies of the bureaucratic language used within Qing documents became an imperial pursuit, with important ramifications for the modern study of China. Wade and others found earlier European-authored bilingual dictionaries and reference works to lack useful coverage of the structure and vocabulary of official documents. As early as Robert Morrison's day, Western readers of the Qing gazette had noticed that its written style, like most documents produced by the Qing government, diverged from that employed in either literary texts or vernacular speech. As a result, a complete understanding of these documents required knowledge of what interpreter Thomas Taylor Meadows (1815–1868) called the "business style" and Wade termed the "language of official documents." This official language comprised a large terminology specific to state texts that combined aspects of literary and vernacular construction.[100] By reading gazettes, junior officials gained instruction in the documentary style and also improved their understanding of "the proceedings of the government."[101] Notably, the documentary textbooks authored by Wade, Meadows, and others were the antecedents to the late twentieth-century "Harvard series" of texts on Qing documents authored by Harvard historian John King Fairbank (1907–1991) and expanded by his successor at Harvard, Philip Kuhn (1933–2016). Through this lineage, the imperatives of empire have long informed the study of Qing political institutions.[102]

Although Britain was not the only foreign state to collect and translate Chinese gazettes as objects of political intelligence, its agents were the most systematic sponsors of this pursuit. The chief result of these efforts is the enormous collection of gazettes now held at the British Library in London. American and French representatives also referred to details from gazettes in their correspondence with their home governments and with the Qing state. Some, like the American envoy Caleb Cushing (1800–1879), collected capital and provincial gazettes in their personal libraries.[103] The British enthusiasm for state-funded collection of political intelligence matched but did not parallel its imperial pursuits in other locations, most prominently India. In India, the British empire perfected the art of intelligence gathering on the basis of informants and marketplace intelligence; in China, where these sources were frustratingly unavailable, British agents sought to master the Qing empire by scrutinizing the state's own words, documents, and deeds.[104]

◆ ◆ ◆

The numbers of Western Europeans in China grew dramatically in the second half of the nineteenth century. The opening of new treaty ports stimulated trading connections, while the advantages of steamship travel allowed Europeans to visit East Asia for leisure, especially as part of a world tour. The nineteenth century souvenir trade encompassed art, novelties, and books, among other items. As China grew more accessible—and its ruling dynasty seemed ever closer to collapse—a copy of the Peking Gazette seemed a choice souvenir from a distant empire. To be sure, Western newspapers and states continued to publish gazette translations and curate them as intelligence sources through the end of the dynasty. But after the calamitous Taiping Rebellion, neither the state nor the press analyzed these sources with the intensity or the sincere interest of earlier generations of missionaries, scholars, and interpreters.

In March 1873, the *London Illustrated News* published a set of sketches drawn by the artist William Simpson (1823–1899) after his return from a world tour. The tour had taken Simpson through the Suez Canal, to Ceylon, Singapore, China, Japan, across the Pacific to the United States, and back across the Atlantic to London. On this date, the newspaper focused on Simpson's travels in China, featuring sketches of the "Temple of Pekin," a puppet show that Simpson called "the Chinese Punch," and other exciting scenes.[105] His subsequent travel memoir, enclosed in a yellow cover with red print, symbolizing that "Yellow is the Imperial color in China, and Red the Nuptial," highlighted his "Account of the Marriage Ceremonies of the Emperor of China."[106] Among the scenes of China featured in both newspaper and book was a sketch of a street vendor in Beijing hawking the world-famous "Pekin Gazette," itself a yellow booklet printed in red.[107] Simpson's choice of portrait suggested to readers that the pamphlet and vendor were quintessential elements of the Beijing streets that merited inclusion in an artist's portrait of China.

The repackaging of Qing gazettes as curios capped the century-long depreciation in their value as objects of scholarly and political interest. Travelers brought gazettes home as souvenirs, offered them as gifts, and sold them to used bookstores. The American poet Henry Wadsworth Longfellow (1807–1882) received a set of court and provincial gazettes in a letter from the medical missionary Daniel MacGowan (1815–1893).[108] In the 1890s, the missionary sinologist James Legge (1815–1897) purchased a set of gazettes previously owned by a British consul. Although the London bookstore's catalog labeled the items as "scarce," they were priced as ephemera.[109] At the Pan-American Exposition of 1901 in Buffalo, New York, a copy of the "Ching Pao, the Daily Pekin Gazette, in present continuation of a gazette published in one form or another in China, under Government auspices, since the beginning of the eighth century, A.D." was displayed in a case together with a brick from the Great Wall, the eyeglasses of George Washington, and the sword of Andrew Jackson.[110] Charles Burroughs (1787–1868), a minister in Portsmouth, New

Hampshire, gifted two gazettes to the Massachusetts Historical Society. He labeled one "the only newspaper published in China for population of 414 [million]" and the other "the oldest daily in the world."[111] Burroughs, having never visited China, possibly obtained the gazettes from a family member involved in the China trade. Still, he decided to embellish the origins of his gift. The Historical Society documented the howler that the gazettes had been presented to Reverend Burroughs by the Xianfeng emperor himself.[112]

The annotations inscribed on souvenir gazette collections make clear that by the end of the nineteenth century, most collectors viewed Chinese gazettes as collectible yet quintessentially tired texts of an aging empire. These notes placed value in the antiquity, quixotic qualities, and connections to the Qing state represented by court gazettes. One Australian traveler, "Mrs. W Clark," wrote on the cover of her gazette, "The Peking Gazette, First Issued 911 A.D."[113] After the fall of the dynasty, gazettes lost their luster not merely in foreign collections, but also on the market in China. Sinologist and historian Mary Clabaugh Wright (1917–1970) secured Stanford University's collection of gazettes from a Beijing purveyor selling gazettes by weight for use as wrapping paper.[114] The owner of a set of gazettes donated to Princeton University used their yellow covers as arithmetic pads.[115]

Rather than celebrating the merits of the Chinese state as displayed in its public documents, late nineteenth-century collectors and travelers riffed on the ironies of its dysfunction. In his memoir of the journey to China, for example, Simpson wrote that the "dingy yellow" gazette, despite its palace connections, left the Chinese people wanting for news and "entirely ignorant of what is going on even within the limits of their own country."[116] These criticisms labeled the gazette as a government publication available to the public yet offering no benefits to popular knowledge. In other words, the Peking Gazette was a newspaper containing no news. The artist dismissed the Chinese official gazette's relevance as a news source and introduced it, instead, as a souvenir of an ineffectual state. As Simpson's language demonstrates, public displays of Qing weakness in global media coverage of mid nineteenth-century wars had shattered the once-vaunted global reputation of the Peking Gazette.

CHAPTER 6

Information Wars

IN THE MID-NINETEENTH CENTURY, WAR AND REBELLION CHALlenged the authority of the Qing dynasty to rule in China. These devastating events also disrupted the state's documentary authority and gave rise to questions about the truthfulness, authenticity, and value of state documents.[1] For some, the contested value of official information became an index to the weakness of the central state. After 1860, these existential challenges inspired a new retinue of state actors in China to modify information policy to bolster the legitimacy of the Qing state in a new international climate. Informed by foreign models, officials and diplomats attempted to remake the court gazette into a modernized instrument of public information. These efforts often forsook the balance of administrative and political needs that had previously guided information policy. Not only did the post-1860 Qing state censor and withhold information from gazettes more than ever before, but it also redirected state publicity toward non-official audiences in novel ways.

If the trials of war revealed systematic weaknesses in state institutions, then the rise of modern commercial newspapers challenged the symbolic authority of official media. The rapid expansion of newspaper publishing in the second half of the nineteenth century and especially after 1895 constituted an unprecedented information environment for the consumption of official media. It became common to read state news within newspapers rather than in the yellow pamphlets of the court gazette. Around the world, governments were responding to the growth of the mass press. Many devised new "official" press outlets to counter oppositional and polemical voices. In China, self-styled press pioneers engaged in a debate in which some invoked court gazettes as positive examples of historical Chinese empires' longstanding commitment to public communications, and others dismissed the publications as outmoded relics of a past age. Where did the Peking Gazette belong in the history of the press, and where did it belong in a new era?

Crisis and Censorship

The systemic crisis faced by the Qing state in the mid-nineteenth century was unlike any other military or socioeconomic challenge that it had prior encountered. Stark poverty and inequality spawned rebellions in the empire's southwestern hinterlands, its western frontiers, and even its agricultural floodplains. These rebellions espoused powerful alternative visions that attracted millions of adherents and undermined the authority and legitimacy of Qing rule.[2] They also revealed weaknesses in state capacity, including empty imperial coffers, untrained military forces, a disorganized territorial bureaucracy, and the faction-riven court leadership. In an era when war came on many fronts, the Qing state found itself poorly equipped to orchestrate a centralized response. The eventual response to these epochal challenges involved the substantial devolution of state capacity to local actors.[3] Amid the establishment of extra-bureaucratic bureaus (*ju*), the flourishing of provincial militias, and the proliferation of local activism, maintaining the instrumental and symbolic authority of the Qing court through its imperial communications remained a necessary, if compromised, task.

In the early 1850s, the flow of official news from Beijing stuttered and stilled. Since standard practice required that reports authored by provincial officials could only be published after they had received an imperial response, the widespread disturbances jeopardized the exchange of official news. Disturbances at any point between the affected region and the capital could delay wartime news from reaching its bureaucratic and public readership. Shanghai-area readers found a notice from their supplier on the cover of a monthly packet of gazettes blaming regional disorder for an interruption in the normal stream of gazettes. Not only was riverine travel impossible, but a document courier (*zhechai*) carrying relevant documents had been plundered by bandits.[4] Since both official and commercial networks for gazette distribution branched out from provincial seats, the loss of administrative cities like Nanjing, Suzhou, and Wuchang disrupted the circulation of news to the provincial hinterlands.[5] In Shanghai, the *North China Herald* noted sudden interruptions of as much as three months in the delivery of official news from the capital.[6]

For travelers, the news sources that could be located were suspect. In the last week of 1852, as Taiping forces reached the transport hub of Wuchang, on the Yangzi River, the metropolitan official Xu Pengshou (1821–1866) sojourned from Guizhou, where he had served as an examination supervisor. Passing through Hunan, he found that the edition of the court gazette reprinted in that province had repeatedly disclosed the contents of classified court letters (*tingji*), including those pertaining to urgent military matters.[7] The next year, memorialists again cited the threat of Taiping rebels accessing military details in the gazettes.[8] Since court policy blocked dispatches relating to the movement of troops and supplies from inclusion in open communications, these cases elicited fears that serving officials had colluded with local publishers to disclose censored material or circulate forgeries.

The sense of crisis spurred new forms of state censorship. The Xianfeng court reviewed proposals to disqualify discussions of pressing issues from inclusion in the court gazette, therefore making them off limits from wider discussion in the bureaucratic community. Proponents of censorship identified capital defense and military expenditures as vulnerable topics to be excised. In 1853, the defense of Beijing had become the most pressing issue of the day as Taiping forces moved north. Capital officials submitted memorial after memorial detailing plans to protect the imperial seat from rebel incursion. Some correspondence, especially that which revealed the decrepit conditions of city fortifications, was deemed sensitive and blocked from distribution. Near the end of the year, gazette publishers printed a memorial that condemned the capital's lapsed defenses and featured lurid descriptions of unkempt city guards huddled in ragged blankets and unfit to protect their stations. The court immediately condemned this action as unauthorized and quashed the leaked document.[9] The official responsible for the mix-up, a ward secretary named Wu Tingpu (1803–1873) tried to cast blame on Beijing gazette publishers by pointing out a recent pattern of telling errors: their occasional failure to publish notices of tax remission, imperial appointments, or orders to assemble militias. Could these seeming oversights be intentional? Wu surmised that by excluding such notices, publishers helped some while harming the general population, providing a hint that publishers could be compelled to alter their gazettes for a price. Although the subsequent investigation cleared the publishers of blame, its proceedings were published in gazettes, perhaps as a warning to others tempted to take advantage of the court's distracted state.[10]

Not all defense-related topics were censored. Through the late Qing, publicity remained a potent tool for the state to support certain wartime agendas.[11] Gazettes circulated calls for militia formation and detailed the donations that funded military campaigns against the rebels. These records documented elite support of the state's endeavors. Moreover, circulating evidence of donations provided an orthodox record against which private claims needed to be substantiated. As the Taiping threat approached Beijing, gazette notices concerning public safety proliferated. Many hinged on the identification and arrest of individuals of "suspicious origins" (*xingji keyi zhi ren*) who entered the city bearing rebel paraphernalia.[12] The Taiping advance sparked a campaign to expel vagrants from significant yet under-protected sites in Beijing, such as the grounds of the Temple of Heaven, where urban residents pastured animals. These memorials, authored by city censors and other metropolitan officials, described the facial features of the apprehended individuals in detail, an implicit warning to readers tempted to take advantage of the disturbed state of affairs themselves.[13]

In the balance, confidentiality overtook transparency as a wartime strategy. In the autumn of 1853, Jiangxi governor Zhang Fei (1814–1862), celebrated for his leadership in the defense of Nanchang, proposed that the court speed the exchange of information in afflicted provinces by allowing military couriers to transport standard gazette dispatches. He described recent circumstances as detrimental to public confidence in state efforts; when unpassable roads delayed gazette deliveries, rumors flourished, to the extent that the outdated notices were considered "mere wastepaper" upon arrival. Zhang argued that by recruiting militia couriers, the court could use state publicity to sooth popular anxiety.[14] The court dismissed this proposal out of hand, and a few weeks later, it approved a proposal to eliminate all discussion of military expenditures from open channels.[15] The message was clear: transparency remained a useful administrative tool, but in times of duress it could be readily constrained.

Reporting the Taiping War

When the Taiping Army's shocking march through central China threw the empire into disarray, the troubles of the Qing state emerged into sharp focus in the pages of Western newspapers. Newspaper coverage of the Taiping War benefitted from significant breakthroughs in the speed and frequency with which information could travel between Asia and Europe. Thanks to steam travel, dispatches published by Shanghai's *North China Herald* and Hong Kong's *China Mail* and *Friend of China* arrived with increased regularity to European ports. It took about two weeks for China coverage to reach India and a month or two to reach London.[16] Still, when reporting on anywhere beyond the immediate vicinity of the treaty ports, China-coast newspapers relied on the court gazettes, prizing their authenticity as state records, if not their truthful description of conditions on the ground. One contributor wrote, "We know that the statements in the *Peking Gazette*, garbled though they may be, have really emanated from the Chinese court, and that they have a real existence as official documents: but who can assure us that the papers passed round among a parcel of provincial speculators ever met the eye of the emperor or received the stamp of his signature?"[17] This assertion lampooned the stilted verbiage employed in official notices but maintained confidence in the value of the court paper as compared to miscellaneous rumors and other sources that some observers collected. The "stamp" of the emperor's signature still outweighed local talk in conveying a true sense of affairs.

If authentic, gazette reports spelled trouble for the Qing state. The translators who expressed concern about the disparities between reports presented to the emperor and real conditions added detail to a claim, in circulation among Western critics since the 1850 publication of British diplomat Thomas Wade's *Note on the Conditions and Government of the Chinese Empire*, that the state's troubles originated in the failing integrity of its officials.[18] Time and again, Shanghai-based commentators noted a pattern in reports authored by officials charged with defending lives and territory "in which falsehood is unblushingly resorted to in order to cover a defeat, which was represented to the Imperial eye as a victory."[19] The many occasions when published reports of "bloody and glorious victories" were later downgraded or retracted, represented not the imperial state's commitment to self-aggrandizing propaganda, but, more ominously, the total deception of the emperor by his subordinates.[20] In their attempts to circumvent the penalties that would follow the revelation of malfeasance or defeat, the empire's officials were complicit in undermining the military capacity of the state. When gazette reports occasioned critical comments, European newspapers reprinted both the reports and the criticisms together. Finding victory announcements prefaced with dismissals, readers were urged to skim past the Chinese official dispatches and focus on the conclusions occasioned from them: the state was in breakdown, not least because of the dishonest character of its bureaucracy.

Among Western papers in China, the Shanghai *North China Herald* boasted the most direct connection to official sources because it obtained translated documents from British consular offices. In its local environs, the *North China Herald* commanded adequate sources of local intelligence. But for information on the movement of Taiping forces toward Beijing and its surroundings, where the newspapers had no Western correspondents, gazettes were indispensable if frustrating sources. In December 1853, for instance, the *North China Herald* compared news from a "private letter" with an outdated file of gazettes to speculate that Taiping forces might be approaching the capital.[21] In Hong Kong, with more immediate access to the rumors, placards, and broadsides that filtered out of Canton, the *China Mail* claimed to have been the first to notice the potential threat of the Taiping Rebellion.[22] Both papers, as well as the *Friend of China* (also published in Hong Kong), also printed on-the-ground dispatches from Western sojourners, often missionaries with varying perspectives on the religious features of the rebellion.[23]

Each of these sources had merits and shortcomings. Writers for the *North China Herald* scorned the pro-Taiping agenda espoused in many missionary accounts, and British officials in particular pointed out the importance of keeping abreast of imperial dispatches even if they merely proved the wholesale corruption of the state and its officials. In one official report on the rebellion later republished in pamphlet form, the consul and occasional translator Walter Medhurst (1822–1885) wrote of the gazettes, "The amount of pertinent information contained in them is limited, and withal so vague and defective, that little can be gathered from them."[24] Medhurst saw self-interest at play in the way that officials crafted the illusion of isolated incidents of "thievish vagabonds" in order to protect their positions and hide the presence of full-scale crisis from the view of the court. In this sense, mendacious officials, rather than the court (which Westerners of this period increasingly labeled as incompetent), made the gazettes imperfect sources of wartime intelligence.[25] Still, Medhurst followed Wade's lead in pointing out that the gazettes, despite their inconsistencies, could not be ignored. Not only did they disclose the internal reports that motivated government policy, but also, they helped Western readers better understand the flawed character of the dynasty.

Gazettes Reimagined

To explain the utility of the Peking Gazette, Medhurst instructed his readers to consider the Qing gazette as the counterpart of other authoritarian regimes. Like the "*Moniteur* under Napoleon" and "Russian official journals, under Nicholas and Alexander," the Qing gazette contained "merely such exhibitions of the state of matters affecting the nation as the ruling power and his subordinates wish to appear."[26] Assertions like these framed the Qing state as no different from other autocratic states around the world and made clear that the Qing possessed no unique claim to information control as eighteenth-century interpreters had insisted. Medhurst was not alone in evaluating the Qing gazette by comparison with international counterparts. Reflecting on this tendency, the early twentieth-century Shanghai journalist Roswell Britton (1897–1951) wrote that European interpreters "mistook them for state gazettes such as were familiar to them, or else belittled them for not being state gazettes."[27] These claims were not simply casual mistakes. Increasingly, they reflected a purposeful campaign by Western diplomats in China to redefine the Peking Gazette as equivalent to the government gazettes published by nineteenth-century states around the world.

In the nineteenth-century world, the concept of "public information," meaning legal or government notices presented to the reading public in a state-run press outlet, attained new significance. These institutions responded to emergent principles of public diplomacy and the growing power and prominence of the newspaper industry. Over the course of the century, newspapers established fuller and speedier coverage (aided by telegraphy and railroads), participated in polemical and revolutionary politics, and celebrated their own contributions to modern life. By contrast, government gazettes were press outlets for binding statements of law, court judgments, and other official notices.[28] Gazettes presented the business of the state in the best possible light, in contrast to the variety of opinions put forth in the popular press. In addition to their role as public propaganda, they also defined the official record: gazettes contained legal facts that could be cited as evidence in court and diplomatic proceedings.[29]

Contemporary articulations of public information played into the diplomatic and military conflicts of the era.[30] By the mid-nineteenth century, Western politicians and diplomats had for decades understood the Peking

Gazette to be the best record of the imperial state available to foreign readers. In order to make the Qing court accountable to the expectations of Western powers, representatives of foreign governments began to articulate a narrower interpretation of the political and legal role of the Peking Gazette, as a static publication that presented official decisions with finality, rather than one that documented bureaucratic discussions and decision-making. Such a reinterpretation helped make the Peking Gazette a paper instrument of diplomatic pressure. According to the thinking of French and British representatives in China, if the Peking Gazette could be designated as an official government organ, then rulings and notices published in its pages would carry persuasive force throughout the empire.

Strategies to manipulate Qing information policy emerged amid declining trust in the integrity of the Qing court's commitment to transparency among Western readers. In 1857, James Bruce (1811–1863), the leader of British forces in China, ordered the bombardment of Canton.[31] For weeks, the court gazette carried no notice whatsoever of the conflagration in the south. Was the imperial court really ignorant of the attack? The revelation that the Qing court had kept discussions resulting from the bombardment out of the gazette in order to prevent foreign agents from reading them there seemed first shocking, then all too obvious. In the *North China Herald*, the revelation that the court had censored reports from Canton motivated a general shift in tone. Now the emperor and his advisors became masterminds, not ignorant victims. One contributor explained to readers, "Peking Gazettes containing important political matters are, it is said, suppressed or simulated before they reach the hands of foreigners."[32] Suggestions of suppression and simulation implied that the autocratic Qing court took drastic means to censor the court gazette—a far cry from the also-current claim that the incompetent court lacked the means to stop the exchange of unflattering reports about the government.

Western pressure reflected the belief that if the court gazette were redefined as an outlet of public information, the court would be held accountable for gazettes and the actions and events they documented. In 1860, in the aftermath of treaty negotiations in Tianjin, British officials pushed the Qing court to disseminate copies of the treaty and "notifications" accompanying it to territorial officials in the provinces.[33] After Prince Gong (1833–1898) agreed to an expanded version of the treaty, Western representatives pressed him to distribute gazettes describing the treaty throughout the empire, so that regional officials would adhere to its expectations. He acquiesced, but formally requested that British ships transport more than a thousand copies of the gazettes to Canton and other southern ports.[34] The French version of the treaty included specific provisions for the publication in the Peking Gazette of a notice concerning the punishment of a magistrate charged with the murder of a French missionary.[35] In 1863, American diplomat Anson Burlingame (1820–1870) wrote concerning a shipwreck of American passengers in China, "If I could obtain the insertion of a notice in the Peking Gazette that the prefect of Fah-chan had been allowed to receive a present for this kindness to American citizens, the effect might be encouraging to other officials in similar cases."[36] Burlingame's message encapsulated the sentiment of the new diplomatic strategy: redefined as an official instrument, the Peking Gazette could be used for leverage against the imperial court and recalcitrant local officials.[37]

The Zongli Yamen Steps In

In 1861, the Qing court approved the establishment of the Zongli Yamen, a metropolitan institution charged with deploying new modes of linguistic, legal, and diplomatic expertise to conduct public diplomacy.[38] The Zongli Yamen spearheaded the refusal of Western demands to manipulate the court gazette while simultaneously adjusting information policy to defend the vulnerable court. Zongli Yamen officials, led by Prince Gong, met frequently with representatives of Western nations and pursued a strategy of political expediency with regard to court publicity that set aside principles of bureaucratic transparency. They consistently insisted that although court gazettes were often taken as official record, their contents did not have the force of law unless underwritten by the emperor. Moreover, wary representatives of the Zongli Yamen would not stake their positions on enforcing demands of Western representatives—although they were amply willing to censor court gazettes according to internal priorities.

On several occasions, Zongli Yamen officials pushed back against representations of the gazette as the official organ or court mouthpiece. In the Tianjin proceedings, Bruce produced a purchased court gazette that contained the phrase *barbarian ship* (*yi chuan*) as evidence that Qing officials were disobeying the treaty to which they had just agreed.[39] Guiliang (1785–1862) and his colleagues disputed the fact that the commercially published gazettes should be considered official communications. In their formal response to the complaint, the group determined simply to "exclude all memorials and documents concerning the barbarians" from public circulation.[40] Bruce's pressure did not, in other words, induce Qing representatives to order bureaucratic officials to stop using terms considered injurious to European interests. Instead, it seemed more expedient to eliminate documents pertinent to relations with Western nations from the purview of the wider bureaucracy than to order a change in terminology. This decision effectively redefined foreign relations as the domain of the court, Grand Council, and Zongli Yamen—not the bureaucracy at large.

Thus, when the court fled Beijing following the Anglo-French siege of the imperial summer palace (Yuanming Yuan) in 1860, Prince Gong ordered the temporary elimination of the gazette's "palace notes" (*gongmen chao*) section, which described the emperor's day-to-day ritual activities and audiences. After the court's return, he ruled that publishers would no longer print notices of the arrival of express couriers or sealed memorials.[41] These urgent notices were easily decoded signs of distant crisis or bureaucratic controversy—and therefore reflected vulnerability.

In subsequent years, Zongli Yamen ministers frequently refused demands to publish, alter, or excise various items from the court gazette. In 1861, during the negotiation of the French treaty, Zongli Yamen officials insisted on upholding the longtime rule that edicts be published in the court gazette prior to the memorials that had prompted their issuance. In addition, they maintained that gazettes would continue to be printed by commercial outlets, not official publishers.[42] In 1870, following the murder of several Catholic missionaries in Tianjin, British representatives complained that the court had not published a "General Proclamation" against anti-foreign violence in the gazettes. On behalf of the Zongli Yamen, Mao Changxi (1817–1882) and Dong Xun (1807–1892) argued that the gazette could not be employed in this way, because Beijing's gazette publishers were private concerns. When Thomas Wade exhibited a gazette as evidence that the court had failed to properly record or format Wade's titles, Mao and Dong once again pointed out that gazette publishers were not state enterprises.[43]

In fact, there was no reason that the court could not compel gazette publishers to print specific notices or employ new terminology and formats.[44] Amid the crises of the Taiping War and the Second Opium War, capital officials maintained sufficient oversight of Beijing's gazette publishers to accomplish any of these tasks. The court and Zongli Yamen both censored the contents of court gazettes at various points. But by insisting that the court gazette held no public or official function, Mao and Dong argued that state documents published in gazettes did not necessarily represent court policy. Therefore, the court gazette could not be considered identical to the official organs sponsored by other powers. The idea that the central state would answer for the myriad ways in which its subjects and officials might somehow act in contravention of the statements contained in the court gazette seemed ridiculous—or at least contrary to state interests.

In asserting limits to their willingness to intervene in the court gazettes while also scaling back open channels behind the scenes, the Zongli Yamen acted to protect Qing information sovereignty—its control over the structure and enforcement of official documents and publications. A similar logic led to the decision to omit discussion of relations with Western powers from the court gazette.[45] These calculations sacrificed claims to documentary authority on the basis of transparency for the sake of protecting court interests. More and more, gazettes, onetime bulwarks of public authority, could be misread and distorted to disrupt state activities. In response, the court and Zongli Yamen adopted more restrictive policies on state information and gazette publishing. Censorious policies of this type would face scrutiny in the next decades, as a widening cross-section of intellectuals, journalists, diplomats, and officials began to consider the future role of political communications in the Qing polity.

Documentary Authority in the Age of the Newspaper

As Chinese newspapers were founded in coastal cities—in treaty ports from the 1860s onward and further afield after 1895—the path forward for the press, including its potential role in modern political life and civic education, became the subject of discussion.[46] Scholars of the Chinese press generally agree that it emerged in three stages: first, with periodicals published by missionary initiatives, often involving collaborations between Christian missionaries and their Chinese converts; second, with Chinese-language editions of profitable English-language papers in Hong Kong and Shanghai; and finally, with commercial newspapers often backed jointly by Western and Chinese investors, as well as missionary and official interests. Regardless of origin, the papers established during these three initial stages overlapped in political position.[47] After 1895, when the disastrous Sino-Japanese War catalyzed new political and nationalist opinions, the papers diversified in agenda and perspective. Special-interest papers appeared, including those for women, students, and vernacular readers.[48]

Late Qing newspapers willingly adapted tropes of the global press. Like their European and American counterparts, they participated in a discourse that celebrated the "free" press above all, neglecting to mention that most periodicals, even in the West, could not fit this description.[49] Moreover, writers in Chinese newspapers, in part inspired by their understanding of the political role of the press in Western Europe, defined the mission of a newspaper as not directly aligned with the aims of the state: newspapers could voice criticisms of the state while serving as positive forces for society and for civic education. Recent experience supported the argument that China needed an independent press. Time and again, the Western press in China had revealed that the court-sponsored descriptions of the Taiping War contradicted facts on the ground.

Journalists and advocates of new modes of civic education used court gazettes as a rhetorical foil for the potential advances of the new-style press. *Shenbao* (established in 1872), the most important Chinese newspaper of the era, for example, published a history of the court gazette in which it sidestepped direct criticism but nonetheless labeled the gazette as belonging to the elites of a past age. In a sense, the article premised, "we could say the gazette is a product for those above, whereas new-style newspapers are a product for those below." Earlier in the dynasty, *Shenbao*'s history suggested, gazettes had allowed Chinese scholars to expand their knowledge of administration. Now, new-style newspapers would expand knowledge among the wider populace. Gazettes were not suited for popular education, since they focused on court matters and did not describe the "trivialities" of the rural population.[50] Still, the first generation of Chinese newspapers needed to reconcile their aspirations with the continued existence of court gazettes. If gazettes provided court-sanctioned information from above to below, then newspapers could aid the populace, first by supplying information and opinions from the populace to the official realm, and second by supervising the government's activities.[51]

As newspapers and political journals grew emboldened to question and even criticize the policies of the Qing court, state authority became a central topic in debates over the proper characteristics of the Chinese press. What obligations did newspapers have toward the imperial state? How should official documents and statements be treated in the context of the newspaper? Backlash against the perceived breakdown of state authority in the burgeoning periodical press resulted in the formation of a new form of "official press" (now called *guanbao*) after 1895 and influenced the formation of national press laws in the last years of the dynasty. Calls to restore and revitalize the "official press" acknowledged the necessity of forming links to indigenous political traditions like the publication of official gazettes, but they also dealt with the prerogatives of a transforming media and political environment.

Gazettes in the Newspaper

Rather than immediately supplanting official gazettes, new-style newspapers (*xinbao*) relied on their existing audience and distribution networks. In the absence of concrete press laws, editors and publishers faced ambiguous relationships with provincial and court authorities, as well as treaty port administrations, each of which showed little restraint in suppressing individual press outlets. The newspapers' treatment of official information, including their publication of internal gazette sections, attested to the publishers' broader concerns about their vulnerable relationship to state power. As in an earlier generation of Western-language newspapers, gazette sections both supplied ready-made content—useful for showcasing new printing technologies as well as relieving the work of overtaxed editors—and handily indicated cooperation with the state.

Gazette sections, reproduced with fidelity to documentary sources, appeared in virtually every newspaper established through the end of the dynasty. From the *Church Journal* (Jiaohui xinbao, founded in 1868), which included gazette excerpts alongside a retinue of Christian allegorical lessons, to the *Tianjin Daily Talk* (Jinhua ribao, founded in 1911), where official dispatches were intermixed with entertainment news, official documents found their way into a surprisingly diverse array of periodical publications.[52] In most newspapers, sections for official news (*dichao*) appeared as the issue's first item.[53] If they explained this policy for readers, most publications, like *Shenbao*, framed it as a necessary homage to the court.

Public interest made gazettes essential source material for *Shenbao*. *Shenbao* published a free daily gazette section, which it pledged would remain free in perpetuity. The time needed for transit from Beijing to Shanghai delayed the availability of this section in the newspaper. For example, the second issue of *Shenbao*, published on May 2, 1872, included the court gazette of April 17 at a delay of fifteen days.[54] In 1882, when *Shenbao* began to receive court gazettes shipped by steamship from Tianjin to Shanghai, the delay was reduced to seven days.[55] In addition to the court gazette, *Shenbao* reprinted provincial gazettes from throughout the Lower Yangzi region.[56] Meanwhile, gazette purveyors were the main distributors of *Shenbao* in cities like Beijing, Hangzhou, and Yangzhou, in some cases through the 1890s.[57]

The Shanghai newspaper strove to overtake traditional gazette printers in attracting an audience. The newspaper's circulation spiked on the days that it published the results of the civil service examinations, showing the extent of popular interest in the subject.[58] Two years after its establishment, an editorial described the newspaper's reprinting of the court and provincial gazettes in matter-of-fact terms: "We publish the provincial gazette [*yuanmen chao*] because people are always coming to our office and asking about such-and-such an official or vacancy."[59] Publishing gazette information quickly and efficiently was a priority for the Shanghai newspaper, which paid dearly for rights to obtain court dispatches by telegraph message in the early 1880s.

Gazettes continued to be published in multiple formats alongside newspapers. In Beijing, a number of publishers put out cheap wooden movable type imprints through the end of the dynasty.[60] Both gazette publishers and Beijing newspapers that republished official information paid fees to Grand Secretariat clerks for the right to copy and print this material.[61] New technologies and formats were also introduced for the court gazette. By printing gazettes, companies could showcase their production process without hiring reporters or writing original content. The earliest type-cast (*qian zi*) gazette publisher in Beijing was the Xiehua Book Bureau (Xiehua Shuju), which had printed woodblock editions of administrative and legal texts in the late 1870s and began publishing a daily gazette, titled *Repository of Edicts and Memorials* (Yuzhe huicun), in 1884.[62] Both Xiehua and Beixin Book Bureau (Beixin Shuju, the publisher of a similar gazette compendium) sold monthly digests as well as daily issues.[63] By 1903, some gazette publishers printed advertisements on the covers of their publications for their own products and for the products of bookstores, gambling enterprises, and photography studios.[64]

Novel communications technologies altered how reader—especially official readers—interacted with state texts. For readers located outside of Beijing but with access to urban newspapers, the utilization of steamship transport and, later, telegraph networks to transmit edicts meant faster access to court information.[65] The incorporation of telegraph networks into official communications systems disrupted longstanding routines. When one education commissioner traveled to Guangdong, he obtained gazette notices by telegraph rather than by borrowing the pamphlets from the local officials he encountered on his route through the province, an activity that had previously typified official travel.[66] Officials in distant posts could read edicts and memorials piecemeal via telegraphic dispatch rather than paging through a day's issue.[67] Commercial publications and telegraph dispatches thus brought court news to the immediate notice of envoys, imperial commissioners, and officials dispatched on traveling assignments. In some cases, such access extended the geographic reach of the state, thus reinforcing a sense of connection to home offices and routines, such as when envoys to Europe read gazettes and celebrated new honorary titles together.[68]

Institutional reforms supplied new reasons for domestic readers to comb through published sets of official communications. In 1901, the Qing court implemented curricular reforms in the civil examinations that tested candidates' ability to analyze history and contemporary politics, rather than classical texts.[69] Monthly news digests served the needs of examination candidates who hoped to showcase their understanding of current affairs. These serials packaged together a larger range of documents than daily gazettes, and included tables of contents for easy reference. The incorporation of gazette material into cheap and popular late Qing encyclopedias enabled even casual readers to perform research in state affairs.[70] Some provinces also published reference materials, but commercial publishers were speedier to publish than their state counterparts. While a traditional portrait of the gazette-reading official had emphasized diligent daily study, new formats eliminated these demands for consistent note taking. Compilations brought all of this information to hand, eliminating these tasks and supplanting the standard ritual of reading the daily gazette.

By 1895, a *Shenbao* editorialist claimed that the newspaper deserved credit for expanding the reading audience for state news. The writer opined that by bringing gazettes to an expanded audience (and for no added cost!), the newspaper had rescued the court gazette from obsolescence. Now, it would be hard to find a reader whose eyes did not at least pass over the gazette's contents from time to time.[71] In fact, growing interest in state texts from the swelling ranks of would-be officeholders probably contributed more to *Shenbao*'s circulation than its own publicity had done to encourage attention to state documents, at least through the early 1890s.

Although *Shenbao* failed to acknowledge its debts to the existing market for official news, it did strike a note of truth in pointing out that the changing publishing landscape had transformed readers' encounters with official news. In Beijing, local regulations affirmed in 1873 defined the contents of gazettes, even if commercially published, as solely and exclusively the items released by the Grand Secretariat each day, in their entirety.[72] Publishers were not permitted to add explanatory notices or narrate the sequences of documents. In gazettes, uninformed readers could find themselves confused by an edict presented without its corresponding memorial, among other sources of ambiguity. By contrast, late Qing newspapers developed links to topics in the gazettes within their articles and columns. *Shenbao* often published articles that commented on the daily gazette insert with titles like "Notes after Reading the Gazette."[73] For matters documented by the gazettes or out of the reach of local journalists, the paper told readers to look to the gazette insert for more details.[74] In newspapers, readers might find commentary on current policy and affairs at the same time that they perused the corresponding memorial. This experience established official news as a subject for commentary and interpretation, rather than as a standalone reference.

The Late Qing State and the Press

For most of the dynasty, interpretations of court publicity had been oriented around the relationship between the court and the bureaucracy. Now, two distinct audiences became critical: the empire's population at large, and the representatives of foreign states with which the Qing empire interacted. For this reason, state agents of the late nineteenth century redefined the boundaries and practices of official publishing. In so doing, they participated in a larger trend that envisioned the modern state as more regulatory and interventionist than ever before. Foreign counterparts, especially Japan, offered instructive examples as to the benefits of media control. The growing consensus that the state should participate more directly in the public realm came to a head after the Sino-Japanese War. By 1907, the Qing state would not only initiate a set of restrictive press laws, but also outlaw commercial publication of official gazettes.

Guided by the experience of Zongli Yamen officials, the Qing state dictated new press controls that followed foreign examples. Since the end of the Taiping crisis, the Zongli Yamen had played a central role both in coordinating imperial communications and in collecting information about the outside world.[75] Agents for the Zongli Yamen paid special attention to how international governments interacted with the press. From England, envoy interpreter Zhang Deyi (1847–1918) sent an extensive list of about 250 newspapers, categorized by frequency, topic, and audience.[76] The Zongli Yamen also collected and translated newspapers from England, France, Germany, Russia, and Japan.[77] These efforts were often piecemeal rather than systematic, but convinced Qing official audiences that more stringent policies could be warranted.

Among these foreign counterparts, Japan was paramount. There, the Tokugawa rulers had long refrained from issuing state publicity and banned commentary on government affairs. In 1862, the Tokugawa shogunate started collecting foreign newspapers for official use. In 1867, on the eve of the Meiji Restoration, the shogunate began to publish an official gazette, not unlike the Qing gazette in that it was intended for official audiences but tacitly allowed to circulate more widely. The next year, the new Meiji government established a preliminary set of press laws and began advocating that press outlets should strive to support, not undermine national interests.[78] The Meiji Restoration thus heralded a remarkable transformation in the state's use of publishing. An editorialist for the *North China Daily News* remarked that the Qing government appeared in the Peking Gazette as "an elaborately designed machine, but so huge and complicated that it groans, creaks, and sticks, at every instant." By comparison, news from Japan highlighted the "vigor and activity of the executive."[79] The *Tokyo Daily News* (Tokyo nichinichi shinbun), established in 1872, presented its contents in two columns: a gazette of government pronouncements alongside foreign news.[80] In 1883, Japan inaugurated a stream-lined *Government Gazette* (Kanpō) to promulgate official decisions and laws.[81] When sharp political contestation emerged, the Meiji cabinet became more severe in its attitudes toward the press. It soon implemented strict press laws, which followed French and Prussian models of state making and social control.[82]

The Qing state followed suit in introducing policies that penetrated into the minutiae of gazette publishing. Capital officials had previously limited their surveillance to registering authorized publishers, collecting copying fees, and investigating cases involving the mishandling, omission, or alteration of state documents. City censors and ward secretaries supervised gazette publishing as part of their overall mandate for urban social control, not as a particular concern for information control. The situation began to change in the early 1870s. A set of regulations published in 1873 signaled capital authorities' desire to standardize the output of gazette publishers. By enforcing uniformity, they could help forestall tedious diplomatic conflicts initiated by foreign representatives who combed the gazettes looking for violations of past agreements.[83] The problem and techniques of information control became more relevant as the Qing negotiated domestic conflicts and border wars amid media scrutiny. When the state began using telegraphy for wartime communication during the Sino-French War in 1881, officials were shocked to find intercepted communications printed in Shanghai newspapers.[84] Although the Zongli Yamen oversaw the encoding of telegraph transmissions, these preventative measures were not enough.

By 1895, journalists expressed open frustration with the state's reluctance to release timely information concerning military activities in the Sino-Japanese War, despite the availability of telegraph communications and real-time reporting from the front.[85] More than anything else, the court gazette supplied a series of programmatic policy statements that stubbornly asserted that tributary relationships with Korea would last in perpetuity.[86] The only frontline reports provided depicted the state's flawed process of dealing with administrative failure through protracted reviews of supply lines, troop discipline, and the frequency of deserters. In gazettes, readers saw how the court wasted time in assigning culpability to individual commanders after every battle or skirmish. According to accepted wisdom, reading such condemnatory notices would inspire rising military officials to do better. Yet these depressing reviews offered little to gazettes' wider readership. Since all official communications needed to move through the bureaucratic process before publication, gazette coverage lagged behind the commercial press. Moreover, such coverage lacked the allure of, say, *Dianshizhai Pictorial* (Dianshizhai huabao), the Shanghai illustrated paper that supplied readers with vivid portrayals of naval and land battles.[87]

When unofficial and politicized outlets began to supersede state publicity, a variety of official actors responded by suggesting that state institutions sponsor new-style press outlets. One of the first publications to receive government sponsorship, albeit briefly, was the *Chinese Progress* (Shiwu bao), a political journal founded by the iconoclastic Cantonese scholar Kang Youwei (1858–1927) and his student Liang Qichao (1873–1929), with the further involvement of Wang Kangnian (1860–1911).[88] Wang Kangnian envisioned that if responsibly managed, the press could become a "legitimate branch of the government" with considerable and legitimate power to critique the state. Funding from Zhang Zhidong (1837–1909), a powerful conservative official of the era, meant that the journal hewed a less critical position in reality.[89] Because Liang Qichao would go on to become an influential commentator on the press, literature, and politics, his personal agendas and biases have influenced histories of Chinese journalism. Liang later described the rise of the political press after 1895 as a new era in which citizens freely offered critique to guide the state. Journals like the *Chinese Progress* thus led the march in advancing China's public politics into a modern stage.[90]

However, in 1896, both Liang and his mentor, Kang Youwei, advocated strict state control of newspapers. Early issues of the *Chinese Progress*, like many newspapers and official gazettes of the era, featured ambitious founding essays that located historical precedents for the new political press. After briefly mentioning the current dynasty's policy of publishing gazettes, these essays looked far earlier in Chinese history to argue that modern newspapers could be traced genealogically to ancient traditions. Newspapers, the prefaces loftily proclaimed, contributed to the aims of a Confucian state. With the help of recycled passages from the Confucian classics, the essays explained that modern newspapers, like the ancient traditions of collecting the songs, complaints, and stories of the people, helped the government understand local conditions.[91] New-style official papers would provide civic instruction, a modern parallel to the longstanding practices of gentry-led village instruction on morality, law, and proper behavior.[92] These arguments were in fact novel in hearkening to the ancient past to support visions of a modern state-run press. Earlier in the dynasty, official voices had appealed to administrative principles rather than Confucian-inspired ideals in articulating information policy.

Liang Qichao's introductory essay to the *Chinese Progress* reified existing political hierarchies and defined the court as a source of moral suasion and instruction for the populace.[93] His concluding remarks praised foreign countries with strict press controls. According to Liang, countries like England, Japan, and Germany prevented social disruption through such legal limits. By enumerating examples of effective press control, Liang appealed to official anxieties about the disruptive potential of the press. His essay suggested that by funding state-sponsored outlets, and by establishing press laws, the state could assert control over the public realm. Consistent with these agendas, Kang Youwei recommended a system of pre-publication censorship for all newspapers and nominated Liang Qichao to survey all submissions to prevent the inclusion of "absurd opinions" and "inaccurate reports."[94]

Political crisis stilled this movement toward the creation of a new official press outlet. In the summer of 1898, the Guangxu emperor responded enthusiastically to the newspaper advocates and issued an imperial edict which instructed Kang Youwei to translate foreign press laws and draft a set of regulations and limitations for the press based on the current situation in China. Guangxu wrote, "Editorials authored by the newspaper should serve to raise up popular morals and root out deep-seated corruption. Given these important tasks, newspaper should not invoke petty and slanderous matters to incite trouble."[95] However, soon after this edict was released, the Empress Dowager Cixi removed Guangxu from power in a virtual coup d'état. Kang Youwei himself fled into exile. Thereafter, Cixi condemned newspapers as forces of disorder and banned them from hinterland jurisdictions.[96] Cixi's intervention in the 1898 reform movement, including its invocation of the political press as a positive social force, subdued the effort to find a place for the state in the world of the press.

Government Gazettes

After the failed bid to install the *Chinese Progress* as a state newspaper, a crop of official papers emerged that were funded by provincial and regional administrations rather than the imperial center. Since the Taiping War, provincial governors had been accruing military, fiscal, and administrative power in contrast to the weakening reach of the central state. The heads of some regions, namely the northern Beiyang administration and the central Liangjiang administration, acquired virtual autonomy from the court. Regional administrators forged ahead in developing communications systems independent of court control. This included new document bureaus (*wenbao ju*) that coordinated the transfer of official communications between distant locations.[97] Meanwhile, from the regional centers, they issued government gazettes (*guanbao*)—government-funded publications that claimed to adapt the historic model of court gazettes to meet modern imperatives of offering popular civic education and information about science, industry, and foreign news.[98] *Beiyang Gazette* (Beiyang guanbao), founded in 1902 by Yuan Shikai (1859–1916), the powerful official at the head of the Beiyang administration, soon became the most widely read and de facto "national" gazette and a model for many provincial imitators.[99]

Prefatory essays to early issues of *Beiyang Gazette* laid out what types of information belonged in government gazettes. Accordingly, an official gazette should not include polemical opinions, but only authorized versions of texts, including "[first] amplifications of the Sacred Edicts; second, edicts; third, governance of this region; fourth, educational matters of this region; fifth, military matters of this region; then current affairs, agriculture, industry, commerce, military science, missionary cases, diplomacy, news from other provinces, and international news."[100] This description organized the topics to be covered in the government gazette according to a hierarchy defined by the relative authority of the putative author. It began with the Sacred Edicts authored by past emperors, then the edicts of the present ruler. The second section included various matters of relevance to governance, education, military, and so on, all of which would be derived from official memorials. Finally, the gazettes would cite stories from other publications, both domestic and foreign. A subsequent essay emphasized that government gazettes, unlike commercial newspapers, took on the responsibility of vetting their sources, and published only thoroughly authenticated versions of official speeches, correspondence, and documents.[101]

Most government gazettes aspired to be read by the wider public. While the court sanction for the *Journal of Self-Strengthening* (Qiangxue bao), a short-lived official paper published in the summer of 1896, had specifically defined the publication as intended for officials, *Beiyang Gazette* and other government gazettes defined their audience more expansively.[102] In general, proposals designed to solicit funding for state gazettes echoed the claims long advanced in the commercial press that newspapers were an ideal medium to edify the populace and dispel ignorance. Still, audiences were less enthusiastic than hoped.[103] In comparison to commercial newspapers, which had been profitable enterprises since the 1870s, economic pressures forced official gazettes to solicit funding from government sources, and the gazettes often counted only compulsory subscribers in their paltry circulations. *Beiyang Gazette* tried to drum up subscriptions by recognizing receptive jurisdictions—the May 1903 issue celebrated "that Zaoqiang [a county south of Beijing] can increase its subscription by seventy copies in one day truly attests to a sage county magistrate whose governance cultivates virtue in the people."[104]

The model of the *Beiyang Gazette* and its successor publications in this "vogue" of government gazettes retained signs of the logic that had long governed Qing information policy. A survey of more than a hundred government gazettes published during the last decade of the dynasty showed that edicts and memorials accounted for nearly three-quarters of the contents of the average publication.[105] According to the publications and the officials that sponsored them, official document excerpts served popular enlightenment by presenting for public review the decisions made by state institutions on the people's behalf. Moreover, these documentary selections upheld the modern functions of a government gazette, as exemplified by foreign models, by presenting authoritative versions of laws and court cases for use by legal and administrative entities. Finally, especially in remote areas, publishing excerpts from official communications upheld bureaucratic efficiency. In Yunnan, for instance, regulations instructed provincial institutions to comb through the new gazette and treat all published documents as in effect—even if they had not yet received the document through other channels.[106] These regulations envisioned the provincial gazette as a mobile archive of official work, updated with each delivery of the news. Unwittingly, the use of the government gazette as a redundant system for adding accountability to official communications systems echoed the purposes cited for the publication of court gazettes at the founding of the dynasty.

The reconfigured contexts and new political ideals that inspired the government gazettes of the post-1898 era ensured that they looked and operated differently from their traditional counterparts. Government gazettes—like most late Qing periodicals—espoused commitment to raising popular enlightenment through the circulation of news. They fulfilled this mission by publishing didactic and moral texts, including amplifications of the Sacred Edict, alongside their transcriptions of bureaucratic documents and communications. However, government gazettes established in the provinces presented only a few recent memorials relevant to the jurisdiction in each issue. Moreover, until the very last years of the dynasty, when a centralizing movement gained momentum, these publications reflected provincial and regional power rather than central control. As a result, when readers replaced their court gazettes with these provincial publications, they received a fractured view of national affairs.

Press Laws and a National Gazette

Metropolitan and court officials noticed that the proliferation of provincial gazettes broke down the visage of the imperial state into disparate pieces. In the first decade of the twentieth century, a series of initiatives to establish a national government gazette reasserted the political power of the center. As early as 1898, the censor Huang Guiyun (1858–1903) had warned the court of the deleterious effects of the unrestrained growth of the newspaper industry and the proliferation of papers that distracted focus away from central agendas. Huang recommended that a government publishing bureau be formed and that the publication of misleading rumors in the press should be punished with exile "according to the statute for treachery and deception." He also wrote, "Capitals are the central pivot [*gangling*] of the realm. Official gazettes should therefore be the leaders of all newspapers."[107] Huang would not live to see the establishment of a national gazette or the framing of press laws.

Subsequent initiatives to establish a national gazette focused less on restoring court power and more on reflecting the dynamic reinvention of the central government then underway. After an imperial edict proclaimed the era of "new policies" (*xin zheng*), recently formed metropolitan agencies led the way in reforms to education, military, and administration.[108] In 1901, the newly established Government Affairs Bureau (Zhengwu Chu) suggested that the court gazette could become a more effective instrument of government by featuring more documents originating from metropolitan institutions. In the past, gazettes had published mainly memorials originating from provincial officials and included fewer notices and memorials generated by metropolitan institutions. The court gazette needed to be made more comprehensive in order to document new government policies and thereby bolster central authority. To facilitate this, metropolitan agencies would directly release documents to Beijing's gazette publishers. This argument signaled that the bureau and other metropolitan bodies—rather than the court—deserved credit as the core institutions behind modernizing reforms.[109] The Government Affairs Bureau argued that the publication of a centralized government gazette would fulfill the court's recent command for officials to propose reform measures to help "the masses fully know the proper way" (*zhong jian zhizheng*). This statement connected the pursuit of administrative efficiency to the expansion of popular knowledge (*min zhi*), in agreement with the general trend to shift the imagined audience of government gazettes toward a much larger reading public than its traditional bureaucratic audience.

In the first decade of the twentieth century, metropolitan agencies urged the court to draft press laws. While no national laws were in operation before this time, some locales, such as Guangzhou, had already instituted provisional press laws developed through cooperative efforts between newspapers and local authorities. To prepare to outline national regulations, two new institutions, the Ministry of Civil Affairs (Minzheng Bu) and the Ministry of Foreign Affairs (Waiwu Bu) transcribed and annotated current and historic press laws from Japan, England, and France. These amounted to a thirty-seven-page report.[110]

Finalized in 1907, the resulting Qing press laws were approved by a commission that included both Yuan Shikai and Zhang Zhidong. In spirit, they restrained rather than protected the newspaper industry. The Ministry of Civil Affairs took over regulation of the newspaper industry, thus centralizing state oversight of journalism and publishing. New papers had to apply for government approval and were required to submit their publications for approval on a regular basis. The rules precluded newspapers from publishing slanderous or immoral content, commenting on court cases in progress or influencing their proceedings. They required the use of bylines and instituted fines for violations. In addition, the press laws barred newspapers from publishing edicts and memorials that had not yet been released by the Grand Secretariat or published in state-sponsored gazettes.[111] The laws required that founders register their newspapers with authorities upon establishment, report information about their contributors to authorities, submit copies of newspapers for pre-publication review, and face strict punishments for accepting bribes or publishing government secrets, seditious opinions, false information, and slander.[112]

For some, modernizing the Qing information order required a final step: the elimination of the commercial gazette industry. In his proposal for a national gazette, the censor Zhao Binglin (1877–1927) concluded that the court needed to take control of its information by "making secret that which should be secret, and suppressing the dissemination of that which should not be disseminated." His memorial suggested that the workings of state authority needed to be clarified in the era of the mass press. Eliminating commercial publishers and placing the official press under the direct supervision of the Government Affairs Bureau would further strengthen the "official" character of new government gazettes.[113] This proposal resulted in the establishment of the *Government Gazette* (Zhengzhi guanbao) in late 1906. The order cited the precedent of "various nations" in permitting only state publishers to handle government documents with legal force.[114]

The court's response to Zhao's proposal only nominally outlawed the commercial gazette trade. In fact, some publishers continued to produce gazettes for a few more years, until the abdication of the last Qing emperor in early 1912.[115] And if Zhao had envisioned the *Government Gazette* as speaking for the Qing state in the twentieth century, it did so for just a brief period. When revolutionaries declared the foundation of a new republican government in 1911, they named their government's official publication the *Cabinet Gazette* (Neige guanbao). The swift succession of titles foreshadowed the political circumstances of twentieth-century China and the encompassment of state news under political directives. After the fall of the dynasty, competing authorities in China each issued gazettes. The Beiyang government used the title *Government Gazette* (Zhengfu gongbao). In the early months of the Republic, the Nanjing government used the title *Gazette of the Provisional Government* (Linshi zhengfu gongbao), thereafter retitled *Government Gazette* (Zhengfu gongbao).[116] The frequent name changes, tied to political transitions and disputes, further illustrated that official news, subsumed under the auspices of each regime, no longer represented an interface between the state and the political communities with which it interacted. They now represented the state alone.

Eulogies for the Peking Gazette

In May 1890, the Shanghai *North China Herald* published a lengthy eulogy for the recently deceased "Marquis Tseng"—Zeng Jize (1839–1890), the son of Zeng Guofan, and famous for his own work as a diplomatic envoy of the Qing court. The eulogy detailed Zeng's final moments: "On Friday the heart's action began to show symptoms of failure, and stimulants with proper nutriment only temporarily alleviated the distress. On Saturday morning at 3:30, after having asked to see the manuscript copy of the Peking Gazette, he turned round, as it were to sleep, and his heart ceased to beat."[117] The obituary linked the regular beating of Zeng's heart with his maintenance of the routines and rhythms of official life. In placing the gazette beside Zeng's deathbed, the newspaper situated this celebrated statesman into a scene more reminiscent of his father, who had famously chronicled his reading of court gazettes in his diaries.[118] Did Zeng's death with the gazette suggest the resilience of the Qing information order, born more than two centuries prior? Or did it presage the looming extinction, or perhaps natural obsolescence, of the state's most representative text?

Seventeen years later, occasioned by the announcement of a new national government gazette in 1907, newspapers throughout the English-speaking world carried obituaries for Zeng Jize's deathbed companion: the Peking Gazette.[119] The first such report came from the *North China Herald*. Soon after, papers from the *New York Times* to the Shreveport *Caucasian* recognized the demise of the Qing gazette.[120] Some Western newspapers described the supplanting of the Peking Gazette as the elimination of an outdated vestige of imperial China. The *New York Times* reminded readers that the gazette was merely "an official circular," and continued, "Its contents were news in a way, but not in any way analogous to the one understood by the modern newspaper, and as long as the Peking Gazette lasted there was little sense in hoping for an advance of China into the family of understandable nations."[121] In these sharp comments, the *Times* ridiculed the Peking Gazette's position at the top of lists of the world's oldest newspapers, and celebrated the lapse of this antiquated remnant of the Qing court. In embedding assumptions about the fall of the crumbling dynasty, these death notices established parallels between the dynasty and the gazette.

In articles on the subject, Western newspapers offered inconsistent accounts of the antiquity and reputation of the deceased Peking Gazette—and the Qing state by proxy. Some accounts personified it as a "venerable patriarch among newspapers" and announced both the gazette's hoary (and exaggerated) antiquity and its timely death, with humorous headlines like "Failed after Ten Centuries" in the *Pacific Commercial Advertiser* of Honolulu, and "Died of Old Age" in the *Ocala Evening Star*.[122] Antiquity afforded prestige to the Chinese gazette in other cases, as when the *Chicago Daily Tribune* commented, "When a newspaper has attained the dignity of years and wisdom enjoyed by this reminder of ancient China it is entitled to create a little flutter in the world by a deviation from the serene and innocuous policy of centuries."[123] Even this praise, however, suggested to readers that the gazette, like imperial China, had remained unchanged for centuries.

◆ ◆ ◆

Chinese newspapers had already contributed for years to the task of writing the Peking Gazette into obsolescence. As early as the 1870s, newspapers like *Shenbao* did so by entertaining counterfactuals about the implicit connections between political media and political modernization. *Shenbao* also prominently compared the court gazette to other international counterparts. Its writers decided that although Chinese history had witnessed the "first newspaper" in the early iterations of the court gazette, in the current dynasty, this periodical had failed to live up to its potential. Most importantly, it remained throughout the imperial era the fodder of elites and the mouthpiece of court interests. As a result, it could not hope to edify the public, improve governance, or, ultimately, contribute to the birth of a strong nation.

These negative valuations—like the obituaries that circulated in their wake—must be evaluated in historical context, as evocations of a media environment in search of identity, but also as attestations of widely felt anxiety about how to place imperial institutions in Chinese political history. That gazette readers of the late nineteenth and early twentieth century found evidence of decline in its pages speaks more to the expectations of the readership concerning the fate of the dynastic state than to defects in the publication that revealed the state's faults. Officials, journalists, and other critics redefined the history of the court gazette in terms of contemporary agendas and anxieties, ignoring its longstanding administrative function, widespread audience, and political significance. At the close of the imperial era, critics were ill prepared to recognize the legacy of the Peking Gazette as an instrument of empire and an institution of political culture.

Conclusion

The True Story of the Peking Gazette

IN ACTION AND IN IMAGINATION, THE QING STATE CONTRIBUTED to the rise of public politics in modern China. Government policy mattered, but so did the ways that audiences construed and criticized state activities. In 2021, as in 1907, as in 1644, national governments and states draw legitimacy through curated transparency. They authorize the circulation of selected official documents for public review. At the same time, they censor dissidence, collect intelligence on subjects, and maintain secret channels of communication. In its pursuit of documentary authority, the Qing state enacted both measures to deter wider scrutiny of state information and those that invited its officials and subject populations to apprehend state documents. Both transparency and secrecy were integral to the Qing information order.

In twenty-first-century discourse, often vague promises of government transparency signal the state's willingness to grant access to "an unmediated state" through the disclosure of documents and other forms of government information. As contemporary critics point out, these claims are untenable. Promises of transparency encourage simplistic understandings of the workings of government, the nature of communications, and even the identity of the imagined public. Moreover, they suggest an automatic "virtuous" relationship whereby public access, perhaps with the assistance of media, guarantees democratic principles of governance. Indeed, the rhetoric of transparency is today invoked by national governments that follow vastly different political models, not to mention corporations and other non-state entities.[1]

For the Qing state, curated transparency was not an ideology, but a tactic, a means of seeking legitimacy. State-led demonstrations of transparency—oriented initially toward the Chinese-dominated bureaucracy, but later directed to a wider bureaucratic and public audience—advertised moral governance, accountability, and efficiency to be operating principles of the Qing state. To this end, gazettes publicized personnel details, accounts of officials' errors and accomplishments, and records of the examination system. Displays of transparency were selective. They flattened and idealized state administration. They presented communications between emperor and officials, capital and provinces, as responsive in nature. They suggested that bad behavior faced consequences and that the state took the people's problems seriously, devoting funds and resources to famine relief and other causes. Limitations on transparency such as secrecy and surveillance, meanwhile, were defined as necessary measures for securing the realm and ensuring uniform administration across a vast empire.

Readers of Qing gazettes saw the imperial state at work. Qing dynasty readers could picture themselves on a trans-imperial map of official communications and personages. Gazettes presented the things that the state and its personnel did: organizing military campaigns, fielding ideas for infrastructure, lauding official careers, eliminating political enemies, and quelling social problems. In the mid-nineteenth century, Weng Tonghe, the scholar-official whose dream opened the introduction to this book, could imagine that he and Xiang Zijing, though living nearly three hundred years apart, existed in parallel news environments in life and in the afterlife. After the lapse of the court gazette in the early twentieth century, a succession of government gazettes and state publications took its place, addressing both mass and narrow audiences and adopting new didactic stances.[2] As a result, the political centrality that gazettes possessed in the late imperial era seems unfathomable in modern China.

The story of gazettes offers new perspectives on the evolution of the Qing state and the emergence of political awareness in late imperial China. Recently, scholarship on governance and the state in the Qing period has shifted in focus from the court to the locale and back again. Earlier landmark works on the central state sketched out key institutions and personalities, but they suffered from lack of access to archival sources. With the introduction of new archival sources since the 1980s and 1990s, historians have recognized the complexity of both central institutions and local administration and the ethnic and cultural intersections of the imperial frontier.[3] In the last decade, scholars have revised our understanding of the nineteenth century, replacing stagnation, corruption, and dynastic decline with revitalized agendas and pioneering institutions.[4] I suggest that the Qing state played an active role in managing public information yet limited its participation in the publishing process, especially outside of Beijing. In pursuit of a limited administrative footprint, the state invited forms of participation from the official, commercial, and even public realms.

The story of gazettes also corrects the pervasive tendency in both scholarly and generalist portraits of the Qing state to exaggerate the presence of secrecy and top-down censorship.[5] As we have seen, these stereotypes derive to a large extent from the Qing state's own publicity, repackaged and articulated in the writings of missionaries, journalists, and other critics of empire. After 1860, the Qing court and Zongli Yamen, in fact, endeavored to redefine the court gazette as a modern state publication. Ironically, these efforts narrowed the window of transparency that had been opening progressively since the beginning of the dynasty, frustrating readers and limiting their understanding of foreign engagements and other entanglements. Dissatisfaction with the state's more restrictive information policies activated criticism against the regime and hastened the rise of a critical public sphere.

Conventional perspectives on late imperial society understate the possibilities for political consciousness within and beyond the official realm. Yet much recent scholarship on the Ming and Qing dynasties is indeed concerned with modes of political engagement. In the late Ming dynasty, when writers impugned masculinity and Confucian credentials in public formats, or when commoner populations honored living officials to garner salient advantages, they advanced political goals.[6] Seventeenth- and eighteenth-century elites used commentary on natural spaces and manmade structures to mourn lost possibilities and assembled literary collections to promote subtle and more overt agendas, especially vis-à-vis the Qing dynastic state.[7] In the nineteenth century, when Han literati came together in poetry circles and defended their knowledge of frontier territories, when local elites redefined standards for history-writing and commemoration, or when diplomatic envoys commented on the wider world order, they demonstrated political awareness.[8] The curated transparency of the Qing state ultimately fostered heightened knowledge of imperial agendas, modes of governance, and even the regime's failings and penchant for secrecy.

That the state's claim to legitimacy included even limited forms of transparency makes clear that political awareness was understood as a permissible and even desirable quality in the Qing, particularly among the official population. In the mid-seventeenth century, Qing rulers sanctioned gazette publishing to restore legitimacy with the Chinese-dominated bureaucracy. Gazettes soon became a forum for the "bureaucratic community"—both the high officials whose writings appeared in the state record as well as the minor officials who might learn from these proposals and discussions. Even palace memorials, so often associated with the autocratic bent of the emperors of the high Qing, could be republished in gazettes to stimulate policy debate. Although the Qing court clearly considered high-level bureaucratic officials to be the intended readers of gazettes, the real audience almost always exceeded this imagined community. Throughout the late imperial period, non-official readers obtained state news through personal contacts and institutions. Likewise, most foreign visitors found easy access to court gazettes. Moreover, non-elites worked *with* political information, legally by copying, printing, and carrying gazettes, and illegally by copying, leaking, borrowing, falsifying, carrying, and otherwise exchanging information, usually on behalf of elite or official patrons. Uninvited readers—as well as members of the bureaucratic community—found grounds for criticism of the dynasty and its ruling personages in the pages of gazettes, even if they expressed their disapproval in guarded fashion.

These unacknowledged audiences increased in magnitude in the nineteenth century in two ways. First, greater numbers of men became entrenched in work related to the operations of the imperial government. Their reading of gazettes forced the expansion of the state's audience to include the "bureaucratic public," comprising not only lower officials, but also quasi-officials and affiliates with no accepted voice in intra-bureaucratic modes of communication. Second, by the late nineteenth century, a large number of Chinese and Western newspapers had participated in extending access to state news through inclusion of gazette sections in their publications. With the addition of these two groups, the audience for Qing gazettes was now global and largely anonymous and possessed no valid voice in the state-run political forum.[9] In effect, the state's information policies had fostered the emergence of an informed public.

The case of the Qing gazette encourages us to consider ways that state-organized publicity can inspire critical forms of political consciousness.[10]

The Qing state adapted from past dynasties in China a policy of disseminating government documents and communications to shore up its authority and legitimacy. In so doing, it permitted and even encouraged its subjects to treat state texts as the news of the day. Gazettes made the state legible. By and large, official media portrayed the Qing state as the court wished, highlighting key desirable features and mechanisms. By design, readers learned about policies, jurisdictions, concerns, and officials. Outside state intentions, they identified key phrases, glaring omissions, and failed initiatives. In perceiving the gaps between reality and representation, readers sharpened their political awareness, honed within the distinctive information order of Qing China.

APPENDIX

Collections of Qing Gazettes Worldwide

In researching the history of Qing dynasty Chinese gazettes, I have encountered an astounding number of gazettes scattered in libraries and archives across the globe—by my estimate, approximately thirty thousand issues in fourteen countries.[1] The remarkable spread of these sources first suggested to me that this project would not concern China in isolation, but must consider the ramifications of Chinese gazettes as globally received news sources. Besides this, the sheer quantity of surviving editions makes them an important scholarly resource.[2]

This appendix has two aims. It identifies existing collections of Qing dynasty gazettes, and it describes the general characteristics of gazettes from different historical periods. It is arranged in rough chronological order, beginning with the earliest (and most fragmented) collections, then the Gongshen Tang period (ca. 1760–1820), miscellaneous examples from the nineteenth century, and finally the capital gazettes of late nineteenth century Beijing. Large collections result from major institutional initiatives; single copies were often owned by individual collectors. The cheaply printed gazettes are exceedingly fragile. Many libraries have repaired damaged gazettes, rebound them or packaged them in novel arrangements, or affixed new covers. Conservation work, while essential, distorts our ability to "read" the material sources.

Given the far-flung nature of these sources, I note when items have been digitized for open access. My aim is to be comprehensive, but this survey doubtlessly omits some collections, especially those in Chinese libraries and private collections outside of Beijing. It should be noted that Qing gazettes can be found in flea markets and auction sites in China. However, as their perceived value has risen recently, so has the incidence of forged items.

EARLIEST EXAMPLES

Gazettes of the Kangxi and Yongzheng eras are extremely rare; to my knowledge, there are no creditable claims of gazettes dating to earlier reigns in the Qing dynasty. According to print historian Zhang Xiumin, a copy of the court gazette dating to 1731 (YZ 9) is held in the Austrian National Library. Some Chinese scholarship also refers to Yongzheng editions held in private collections.[3] None have been digitized.

From readers' commentary, especially the Jesuit missionary correspondents, we know that gazettes were published daily in the late Kangxi and Yongzheng eras. Most transcribed and summarized content from the Yongzheng gazettes reprises imperial edicts on subjects such as the distribution of relief and evaluation of field officials. Courtroom matters were apparently discussed; in the preface to *Record of the Yongzheng Reign* (Yongxian lu), an unofficial history pertaining to court drama surrounding the succession of the Kangxi emperor, the author claims to use gazettes as its main source material.[4] Gazettes also published memorials authored by capital and field officials.[5] Official memorialists (particularly censors) freely quoted from memorials published in gazettes. In Li Zhen's 1715 and 1720 publications excerpting from Kangxi-era gazettes, he indicates that the given names of memorialists were usually omitted.[6]

THE GONGSHEN TANG PERIOD (CA. 1760–1820)

A sizeable number of Gongshen Tang gazettes are held in a number of libraries around the world, typically cataloged under the title *Tizou shijian*. Besides their distinctive title, these gazettes feature telltale marks of the Gongshen Tang printing process, particularly remnant column markings and blurry print. Libraries holding Gongshen Tang editions include the British Library, Nanjing Library, National Library of China (Beijing), Capital Library (Beijing), East Asian Library at Princeton University Library, National Diet Library (Tokyo), Tōyō Bunka Kenkyū Shi (Tokyo), and the National Library of France (Paris). The items held in Tokyo and Beijing can be viewed on microfilm, those in Nanjing can be viewed in digital form (in library only), and the Princeton collection is digitized and available online.

Gongshen Tang gazettes are printed in wide-format pages with about fifteen columns of text per page, with three double-sided pages per issue. The phrase *Tizou shijian* is printed in the central margin. Each daily issue is dated. They contain (in order) imperial edicts, records of the examinations (if included), routine memorials (*tiben*) and palace memorials (*zouzhe*) released for circulation, and finally personnel lists (if included). Memorials authored both by metropolitan institutions and by individual field officials are included. In addition to the surviving copies, the missionary François Bourgeois transcribed and summarized a long series of Gongshen Tang gazettes in 1788 (QL 53).[7] Although most surviving Gongshen Tang gazettes date to the late Qianlong and Jiaqing reigns, there are some examples in the British Library collection that bear dates as late as 1841.[8]

PROVINCIAL REPRINTS AND MANUSCRIPT EDITIONS

Most of the provincial reprints in Western collections are from Canton and Suzhou. Provincial reprints of the court gazette were often distributed together with the provincial gazette. Many surviving gazettes from the first half of the nineteenth century are manuscript editions. Western readers evidently preferred manuscript editions because they were considered more readable than printed copies. Libraries holding printed editions are the Austrian National Library (Vienna), British Library (London), National Library of Russia (St. Petersburg), and Shanghai Library; libraries holding manuscript editions are the Shanghai Library, Bibliothèque nationale de France (Paris), Bayerische Staatsbibliothek (Munich), Library of Congress (Washington, DC), Staatsbibliothek zu Berlin, and St. Olaf College (Minnesota).[9] Vienna, Munich, Berlin, and the Library of Congress have digitized their copies.

Manuscript and reprint gazettes were not published under a single title and vary somewhat in appearance. Titles used include *Jingchao*, *Tizou quangao*, and *Tizou quanlu*. Unlike the Gongshen Tang editions, they have separate cover pages, upon which the title and an issue number (e.g. *jing zi jiushier hao*) has been written or printed. The name of the publisher is not noted. They do not include full tables of contents, but do specify a date and the presence of edicts (*lunyin*) on the first interior page. In these editions, the order of contents is typically personnel lists (if included), edicts, rescripts, and memorials.

BEIJING GAZETTES

Late Qing (ca. 1860–1912) Beijing gazettes are the most prevalent in library collections around the world. The British Library Peking Gazette collection is nearly complete for this period and in some cases contains multiple editions for each date. Other sizeable collections of Beijing gazettes include the Chinese Academy of Social Sciences (Beijing), Capital Library (Beijing), Nanjing Library, and Tōyō Bunko (Tokyo). Smaller collections (fifty issues or fewer) include the National Library of China, Shanghai Library, Macao Central Library, Inner Mongolia University Library, National Central Library (Taipei), Academia Sinica (Taiwan), Waseda University Library, University of Chicago Library, Yale University Library, Princeton University Library, Harvard-Yenching Library, Stanford University Library, University of California Berkeley Library, Claremont Colleges Library, Peabody Essex Library (Salem, MA), University of Minnesota Law Library (Minneapolis), Royal Ontario Museum (Toronto), Columbia University Library, New York Public Library, Staatsbibliothek zu Berlin, Cambridge University Library, Bodleian Library (Oxford, UK), Leiden University Library (Netherlands), School of Oriental and African Studies (London), Biblioteca de los Agustinos Filipinos (Valladolid, Spain), Oriental Institute Library (St. Petersburg, Russia), National Library of New Zealand, and the National Library of Australia. The Waseda, Australia, Berlin, and Princeton copies have been digitized.

A sample nineteenth-century Beijing gazette issue is described in the introduction. Generally, these were printed pamphlets of ten pages apiece. The late nineteenth-century gazettes have covers noting the title and often include the publisher, issue number, or an illustration. The first interior page is a dated table of contents (*mulu*), which lists edicts (*yuzhi*) followed by the important memorials included. These memorials are listed according to the position of the memorialist. Within the main text, records of court audiences are customarily included prior to the edicts and memorials. The narrow pages have seven columns of characters, although wider pages to allow for longer texts were also often folded into the pamphlets.

GLOSSARY

baodan 報單
baofang 報房
Baofang Hutong 報坊胡同
baojia 保甲
baowen 報聞
Beixin Shuju 北新書局
Beiyang guanbao 北洋官報
Bingbu 兵部
bitieshi 筆帖式
bu chao 不抄
buchi jishi bumi 不持幾事不密
Bujun Tongling Yamen 步軍統領衙門

chao 抄 or 鈔
chaobao 抄報
chaobao/chobo (Korean) 朝報
Chen Hongmou 陳宏謀
Chen Yaowen 陳堯文
Chen Zhang 陳璋
cheng 城
Cheng Rusi 程如絲

Da Qing quanshu 大清全書
Datang Jie 大塘街
Dayi juemi lu 大義覺迷錄
Dianshizhai huabao 點石齋畫報

dibao 邸報
dichao 邸抄, 邸鈔
difangzhi 地方誌
Dong Xun 董恂
Donghua Men東華門
Du Yu 杜俞
Dufu xian yuanbao 督撫憲轅報
Duchayuan 督察院
Duji Baofang 杜記報房

ershi 耳食

fa shou wen 發收文
fachao ji ce 發抄記冊
fang 坊 (store/commercial)
fang 坊 (urban precinct)
Fang Bao 方苞
Fang Yurun 方玉潤
fanglüe 方略
fenfa dan 分發單
Feng Pu 馮溥
fengwen 風聞

gangling 綱領
gaoshi 告示
gechao 閣鈔

Gong Zizhen 龔自珍
Gongli Baofang 公立報房
gongmen chao 宮門鈔
Gongshen Tang 公慎堂
gongshi 供事
Gongxing Baofang 公興報房
Gu Yanwu 顧炎武
guan 官
Guan Shuju 官書局
Guan shuju huibao 官書局匯報
guanbao 官報
guanzhen shu 官箴書
Guiliang 桂良

Han gyeong bo (Korean) 漢京報
Han shu 漢書
Hang Shijun 杭世駿
hao 號
Hecheng Baofang 合成報房
heiben tongchao 黑本通抄
Hešeo (Ch. Heshou) 赫壽
Hiyande (Ch. Xiande) 憲德
hongben 紅本
Hongxing Baofang 洪興報房
Hu Juqing 胡具慶
Huang Chunyao 黃淳耀
Huang Erxing 黃爾性
Huang Guiyun 黃桂鋆
Huang Qing zouyi 皇清奏議
Huang Zongxi 黃宗羲
Hubu 戶部
Huidian 會典

jia 家
Jia Yi 賈誼
jiabao 假報
jiao 交
Jiaohui xinbao 教會新報
jietie 揭帖
Jin Yu Lu 金裕祿
jing zi jiushier hao 京字玖拾貳號
jingbao 京報
jingbao zhaichao 京報摘抄
jingbao zhi xiaochao 京報之小抄
jingchao 京抄
Jingdu chao zhi 京都抄紙
jingshi 經世
Jingshi xinxi 京師信息
Jinhua ribao 津話日報
Jinshen lu 搢紳錄
jinshi 進士
Jinzou Yuan 進奏院
jishizhong 給事中
Jiwen Baofang 集文報房
ju 局
juan 卷
Juheng Baofang 聚恒報房
jun 君
Junjichu 軍機處
juren 舉人
Jusheng Baofang 聚陞報房
Juxing Baofang 聚興報房

"Kan jingbao" 看京報
Kang Youwei 康有為
Kanpō (Japanese) 官報
kechao 科抄
keya 科衙
kouyu 口諭
Kuixu 揆敘

la ban 蠟版
langzhong 郎中
Li Ciming 李慈銘
Li Zhen 李珍
Li Zhifang 李之芳
lizhi 吏治
Li Zicheng 李自成
Liang Qichao 梁啟超
Liangjia Yuan 梁家園
Liangxiang bao 良鄉報
Liansheng Baofang 連陞報房
Liben Tang 立本堂
Libu 吏部
ling xia hao bu 領下號簿
Linshi zhengfu gongbao 臨時政府公報
Liu Ke 六科
Liu Yinshu 劉蔭樞

Liubu chengyu 六部成語
Liulichang 琉璃廠
Lü Fengchun 呂逢春
Lu Zhenyang 路振揚
lüebao 略報
lüejie 略節
lufu zouzhe 錄副奏摺
Lüli Guan 律例館
lunyin 綸音
Luo Guoshi 羅國士

mai chao zhi baofang mai chao zhi shuban 買抄之報房賣抄之書辦
Mamboo (Ch. Manbao) 滿保
Man Han Piaoqian 滿漢票簽
Man Piaoqian 滿票簽
Mao Changxi 毛昶熙
min zhi 民智
Minzheng Bu 民政部
mizou 密奏
Mu Yaonian 穆堯年
Mujišangga (Ch. Mujixianga) 穆緝香阿
mulu 目錄

nan bian zhenwei 難辨真偽
Necin (Ch. Naqin) 訥親
Neige 內閣
Neige guanbao 內閣官報
Neige huichao 內閣匯抄

pian bao 便報
pingbao 評報

Qian Chengzhi 錢澄之
Qian Chenqun 錢陳群
Qian Men 前門
qian san men 前三門
Qian Wu 錢鋈
qian zi 鉛字
Qiangxue bao 強學報
Qiangxue hui 強學會
qijuzhu 起居注
Qijuzhu Guan 起居注館
qing'an zhe 請安折
Quehui 慤惠

Ren Kepu 任克溥
Ren Meihe ji 仁美和記
ribao 日報
Rizhi lu 日知錄
Ronglu Tang 榮錄堂

Sanyou Baofang 三友報房
Shandong Tangwu 山東塘務
Shangyu neige 上諭內閣
Shen Tong 沈彤
Shenbao 申報
shi 實
Shilu 實錄
shishi 時事
Shiwu bao 時務報
si 私
Si lun bu 絲綸簿
Siku quanshu 四庫全書
Sui Renpeng 隋人鵬
Suishou dengji 隨手登記
Sun Guangsi 孫光祀
Sun Jiagan 孫嘉淦

Taicheng Baofang 台成報房
tangbao 塘報
tanting 探聽
tenghuang 謄黃
ti 題
Tianbian dichao 天變邸鈔
Tianfu Baofang 天輔報房
Tianhua Baofang 天華報房
Tianli Baofang 天利報房
tiben 題本
tiexie 貼寫
tingji 廷寄
titang guan 提塘官
Tizou quangao 題奏全稿
Tizou quanlu 題奏全錄
Tizou shijian 題奏事件
Tokyo nichinichi shinbun (Japanese) 東京日日新聞

Tong Yangliang 佟養量
Tongshun Baofang 同順報房
Tongwen Baofang 同文報房
Tongxing Baofang 同興報房
Tongzheng Si 通政司
Tongzhi Zhongxing 同治中興

Wai ji dang 外紀檔
Waiwu Bu 外務部
Wang Aoyong 王鰲永
Wang Chenfeng 王宸倖
Wang Fuzhi 王府之
Wang Huizu 汪輝祖
Wang Kangnian 汪康年
Wang Zhonglin 王鍾霖
Wanguo gongbao 萬國公報
Wanli dichao 萬曆邸抄
wantie 晚帖
Wei Dingguo 魏定國
Wei Guan 魏琯
wei wan 未完
weigao 偽稿
wen 文
wenbao ju 文報局
Weng Tonghe 翁同龢
Wenxuan si 文選司
Wu Sangui 吳三桂
Wu Tingpu 吳廷溥
Wuyingdian 武英殿

Xiang Yuanbian 項元汴
xiaobao 小報
xiaochao 小抄
Xiehua Shuju 擷華書局
Xihua Men 西華門
xin zheng 新政
xinbao 新報
xingji keyi zhi ren 形跡可疑之人
xingzou 行走
xinwen 新聞
xinwen gaozi 新聞稿字
xinwen yi zhi 新聞一紙
xinwen zhi 新聞紙
xinwen zougao 新聞奏稿

Xinyi Baofang 信義報房
xu 序
Xu Pengshou 許彭壽
Xu Yuanwen 徐元文
xunchang 尋常

Yang Kaiding 楊開鼎
Yang Tianyi 楊天益
yanlu 言路
Yao He 姚合
Yao Tinglin 姚廷遴
Yentai (Ch. Yintai) 尹泰
yi chuan 夷船
yi zhang xinwen 一張新聞
yi zhi 一紙
yibao 驛報
yicheng shi 已成事
Yikuang 奕劻
Yin Huiyi 尹會一
ying fachao 應發鈔
yizhan 驛站
Yongxing Baofang 永興報房
Yongzheng zhupi yuzhi 雍正硃批諭旨
Yu Zhengxie 俞正燮
Yu Zhuo 俞焯
yuan bao 轅報
Yuan Shikai 袁世凱
Yuan Shouding 袁守定
yuan wai lang 院外郎
yuanmen chao 轅門鈔
Yuanming Yuan 圓明園
Yue Jun 岳濬
Yue Zhongqi 岳鍾琪
Yuzhe huicun 諭摺彙存
yuzhi 諭旨

Zeng Guofan 曾國藩
Zeng Jize 曾紀澤
Zhang Cunren 張存仁
Zhang Deyi 張德彝
Zhang Fei 張芾
Zhang Guoxian 張國憲
Zhang Tingyu 張廷玉
Zhang Tonghe 章同和

Zhang Yixing 張義興
Zhang Zhidong 張之洞
zhao 昭
Zhao Binglin 趙炳麟
Zhao Kaixin 趙開心
Zhao Shenqiao 趙申喬
Zhao Xiongzhao 趙熊詔
Zhaoyuan 招遠
zhechai 摺差
Zhengfu gongbao 政府公報
Zhengwu Chu 政務處
Zhengyang Men 正陽門
Zhengzhi guanbao 政治官報
zhihang 紙行
zhong jian zhizheng 眾咸知正
zhongwai jianjian 中外咸見
Zhou Zupei 周祖培
zhujing titang 駐京提塘
Zhuozhou bao 涿州報
zhusheng titang 駐省提塘
zhushi 主事
Zizhi tongjian 資治通鑑
Zongli Yamen 總理衙門
zou 奏
Zou Yigui 鄒一桂
zouzhe zhidu 奏摺制度

NOTES

INTRODUCTION

1 In most cases, dates are recorded in modern format in the body of the text, with dates according to reign year and the lunar calendar included in notes.

2 In his diary, Weng called Xiang by his courtesy name, Zijing. See "Hsiang Yüan-pien," in Goodrich and Fang, *Dictionary of Ming Biography*, 1:539–44.

3 On Xiang, his family, and their associations in the art world of Jiangnan, see Yang Lili, *Tianlai chuan han*; and Chŏng, *Xiang Yuanbian*. The Weng family collection includes at least three valuable editions once owned by Xiang and his elder brother. Edgren, "Weng Family Rare Book Collection," items 17 (not obtained until 1891), 47, and 57; Tuo, *Changshu Weng shi cangshu*. On how Weng Tonghe shaped the collection with acquisitions at Liulichang and from associates in Beijing, see Edgren, "Weng Family Rare Book Collection," 73; 76–82.

4 Weng Tonghe, *Weng Tonghe riji*, 1:247 (TZ 1/10/17). On the diary's authenticity and value as a source for research on late Qing politics, see Kong Xiangji, *Qing ren riji*, 18–36.

5 Gazettes are not related to "gazetteers" (*difangzhi*, local histories), and the apparent similarity in their standard English-language translation is entirely coincidental.

6 The term *gazette* was apparently first applied to pamphlets of Chinese official news by sixteenth-century European missionaries who recognized these publications as analogous to short digests of political news traded in contemporary Europe. I retain this translation because of its widespread use and the

apt parallels of commercial publishing, political content, and short format, as well as the English-language use to imply an official notice of employment (i.e., *gazetted*). A common theory is that *gazette* referred originally to a certain coin, the cost of a daily newssheet (*gazetta*) in early modern Venice. John Florio investigated these meanings in his 1598 Italian-English dictionary, *A Worlde of Wordes*, as described in Infelise, "News Networks," 54.

7 See, for example, Ji Yun et al., *Qinding lidai zhiguan biao*, juan 62, "Tongzheng Shisi biao."

8 The English-language term Peking Gazette came into common usage in the early nineteenth century. In general, I use the term solely to refer to foreign interpretations or when historical actors do so. I use other terms, such as Qing Gazette, *gazette*, or *court gazette*, when discussing state news within the Qing information order. The term *Beijing gazette* is used for gazettes published in Beijing. The translated title *Capital Gazette* refers to the term *Jingbao*.

9 "China," *Standard*, December 4, 1862. The *Times* had its own China correspondent beginning in 1860. Most English papers borrowed China coverage from the *North China Herald* or the *China Mail*.

10 This is the first monograph in any language devoted to the Qing Gazette. For an influential introduction, see Ocko, "British Museum's Peking Gazette." Good work has been done on gazettes as imperial political institutions, but this scholarship lacked access to the wider global corpus of gazettes. Key works include Zhu Chuanyu, *Songdai xinwen shi*; Zhu Chuanyu, *Chuanbo shiye lunji*; Lin Yuanqi, *Dibao zhi yanjiu*; Huang Zhuoming, *Zhongguo gudai baozhi*; Yin Yungong, *Zhongguo Mingdai xinwen*; and Yao Fushun, "You guan dibao." In the field of the history of journalism, gazettes were often credited as the world's first newspapers yet flawed antecedents to the modern popular press. Representative work include Britton, *Chinese Periodical Press*; Ge Gongzhen, *Zhongguo baoxue shi*; Lin Yutang, *History of the Press*; and Fang Hanqi, *Zhongguo xinwen shiye*. Important recent scholarship includes Mittler, *Newspaper for China*, ch. 3; Lane Harris, *Peking Gazette*; Kong Zhengyi, "Qingdai dibao yanjiu"; Shi Yuanyuan, *Qingdai qianzhongqi xinwen*; De Weerdt, "'Court Gazettes and 'Short Reports'"; De Weerdt, *Information, Territory, and Networks*, ch. 2; Wang, "Information Media"; Li, "News, Public Opinions, and History," 8–17; Liu Yongqiang, "Ming-Qing dibao yu wenxue"; Zhao Ying, "19 shiji xi ren dui jingbao"; Joo, "Remaking a Tributary Relationship."

11 Gu Xiancheng (1550–1612) summoned a putative gazette-reading schoolteacher into a conversation about capital politics in a dream he recorded around 1608. Struve, *Dreaming Mind*, 149–51.

12 In the Qing dynasty, serving officials and emperors alike used the term *dibao* to refer to authorized newsletters but also various reports compiled by palace and bureaucratic institutions. See usage in *KMZZ* 122 (KX 35/11/23), 142 (KX 36/02/20), 155 (KX 36/03/25). The related term *kechao* connoted itemized reports compiled by the metropolitan bureaucracy's Six Sections (Liu Ke). *Yongzheng chao neige liu ke*, 1:93–96.

13 Other title variants used less commonly in the Ming and Qing include *dichao*, *gechao*, *kechao*, *chaobao*, and *yibao*. Struve, *Ming-Qing Conflict*, 21. Beyond gazettes, other terms used for bureaucratic documents lent themselves to political discourse. For example, the term *jietie* referred both to "reference summaries" (a type of note kept within the bureaucracy) and political pamphlets.

14 In early modern Europe, the writers of gazettes and political pamphlets collected and republished dispatches from correspondents. Millstone, *Manuscript Circulation*, 4–19; Ghobrial, *Whispers of Cities*, 96–99. On leaked documents as political news, see De Vivo, *Information and Communication in Venice*, 9.

15 Although many accounts of late Ming news culture emphasize and even celebrate the significance of *xiaobao*, given the lack of original source evidence, we should not overstate their impact. On news in the late Ming, see Wang, "Information Media."

16 Harrison, "Newspapers and Nationalism," 183.

17 See the case of Tu Zhongting in Mokros, "Communication, Empire, and Authority," 1–4.

18 Slauter, "Periodicals and the Commercialization of Information."

19 Bayly, *Empire and Information*.

20 Pettegree, *Invention of News*.

21 Zhang Xiumin and Han Qi, *Zhongguo yinshua shu*, 78–82.

22 See the appendix for a discussion of gazettes in library and archival collections, as well as reprint editions.

23 In June 2020, items claiming to be late Qing gazettes could be found on the bookselling website kongfz.com for prices from 295 yuan to 7,100 yuan (between $41 and $996).

24 Both edicts, worded identically, can be found in *QSL-TZ*, 113:522a–523b (TZ 03/08/28). The two temporary appointments, considered less historically significant, are omitted from the *Veritable Records*. The memorials are also omitted.

25 Imperial consort Quehui (1668–1743).

26 For the late Ming, scholars depend on references contained within literati poetry, prose, and letters. The well-known *Wanli dichao* embeds entries from the gazette within commentary and notes on news sources. It is not, therefore, an authentic copy of gazettes.

27 Quotations from gazettes in Ming writings suggest a format similar to the Qing gazette. The use of the phrase *dichao* often implied "capital news" rather than "gazette jottings" more strictly. This use of *dichao* can also be found in the late Ming text *Tianbian dichao*.

28 Zhang, *Confucian Image Politics*, 29–35; Dardess, *Blood and History*, 2–8.

29 This work defines political culture as the repertoire of practices, expectations, and ideas that defined how individuals imagined, established, and negotiated relationships with the imperial state. It does not presume a unitary political

culture to operate across the empire or even its Chinese territories. Instead, it focuses on the ways that common institutions and experiences combined with individual social, economic, and cultural backgrounds to shape understandings of the politics of the imperial state. In emphasizing that political culture takes place in imagined relationships as well as in action, I am influenced by Charles Taylor's *Modern Social Imaginaries*. For an elucidation of Taylor in the shaping of "common political life" in seventeenth-century England, see Peacey, *Print and Public Politics*.

30 On the dynamics of the "print explosion" from the mid-Ming onward, see Brokaw and Chow, *Printing and Book Culture*; and Son, *Writing for Print*.

31 On this problem see Mittler, *Newspaper for China*, 180–87.

32 Heijdra, "Technology, Culture and Economics," 223–40.

33 Rowe, *Saving the World*, 27–28.

34 Ho, *Ladder of Success*, 107–19; Jones and Kuhn, "Dynastic Decline," 112; Kaske, "Fundraising Wars," 81.

35 This expansion is usually attributed to the Taiping Rebellion, as in Xu Daling, *Qingdai juanna zhidu*, 59–73; Bastid-Bruguière, "Currents of Social Change," 538. Recent scholarship moves the beginning of extensive office selling earlier and interprets it as far more prevalent, perhaps an institutional phenomenon of the Qing state. See especially Wu Yue, *Zhongguo de juanna zhidu*, 27–29, 457–69; Zhang, "Legacy of Success," 281–88; Kaske, "Price of an Office," 292–97.

36 Yang Jingting, *Dumen jilüe*, 14:330–31. Yang's preface on bamboo-branch poetry is dated 1845 (DG 25). The full poem reads:

Because I fear people will think I can't read a word
Each day I have the gazette delivered to my door
In a month I only pay three hundred cash
Sometimes I ask my friends to read it to me.

37 Shi Yuanyuan, *Qingdai qianzhongqi xinwen*, 27–31.

38 See Spence, *Treason by the Book*; McMahon, "Dynastic Decline," 240–41; Jones and Kuhn, "Dynastic Decline," 118–19.

39 See, for example, Elliott, *Manchu Way*; Dunnell, Elliott, and Forêt, *New Qing Imperial History*; Crossley, *Translucent Mirror*; and Rawski, *Early Modern China and Northeast Asia*.

40 For approaches to this problem, see Spence, *Ts'ao Yin and the K'ang-Hsi Emperor*; and Chang, *Court on Horseback*.

41 The Manchu official Mujišangga (d. 1865) was reputed to have an extensive gazette collection. Xu Ke, *Qing bai leichao*, 4296.

42 On the Qing as a "plural legal order," see Cassel, *Grounds of Judgment*, 18–20.

43 Silas Wu, *Communication and Imperial Control*; Spence, *Ts'ao Yin and the K'ang-Hsi Emperor*; Elliott, "Manchu-Language Archives."

44 For the concept of "information order" and its links to twentieth-century communications theory, see Bayly, *Empire and Information*, 3–5. For recent takes on this concept in the Chinese context, see De Weerdt, *Information,*

Territory, and Networks, ch. 3; and Halsey, *Quest for Power*, ch. 7. The political importance of imperial communications in Qing China has been described in a number of important scholarly works. These include Wu, *Communication and Imperial Control*; Kuhn, *Soulstealers*; Bartlett, *Monarchs and Ministers*; and Guy, *Qing Governors*.

45 Yoon, "Grand Council."

46 On Song dynasty practices of "qualified transparency" in the personnel administration, see Tung, "Commercialization of Personnel Information," 92–93.

47 After the Qianlong era, *tiben* were not ordinarily disclosed in the gazettes but could be read by those with access to government archives.

48 By tallying the eventual recipients of incoming memorials, Silas Wu recognized "four modes of political usage": secret, semi-secret, semi-open, and open politics. Wu, *Communication and Imperial Control*, 104.

49 Guy, *Emperor's Four Treasuries*; Son, *Writing for Print*, 130.

50 Metzger, *Internal Organization of Ch'ing Bureaucracy*; Zelin, *Magistrate's Tael*; Will, *Bureaucracy and Famine* and "Views of the Realm in Crisis"; Kuhn, *Soulstealers*.

51 See Mokros, "Documentary Authority."

52 The records of the Grand Council show that a substantial proportion of secret communications were released to the Grand Secretariat and thus made open to the bureaucracy. This point is detailed further in chapter 1.

53 For an illustrative anecdote, see the biography of Wu Tingdong (1793–1873). Fang Zongcheng, *Wu Zhuru xiansheng nianpu*, 53a–b.

54 For a similar observation of the stylized presentation of politics in the *Gazette de France*, see Popkin, *News and Politics*, 48.

55 On the process of defining the provincial administrations, see Guy, *Qing Governors*.

56 These consultations were of note to foreign observers, as described in chapter 5. For the longer history of a participatory political culture, see Schneewind, *Shrines to Living Men*, 16–17.

57 Hayes, "Specialists and Written Materials"; Macauley, *Social Power and Legal Culture*; Chen, "Legal Specialists"; Karasawa, "From Oral Testimony."

58 Yao Tinglin, *Shang pu jingli biji*, 79:247–48.

59 For the complementary case of legal publishing, see Zhang, *Circulating the Code*.

CHAPTER 1: THE QING INFORMATION ORDER

1 Li Bin, *Tangdai wenming*, 18–28.

2 That the Tang and Song institutions shared the same name despite their different orientations suggests a conscious repurposing on the part of the Song court.

3 De Weerdt, *Information, Territory, and Networks*, 37.

4 On enthusiasm for court documents, see De Weerdt, *Information, Territory, and Networks*, 48–75; on leaking, see 82–87; on the state's response to political pressure, see 102–3.

5 Ayao, "Transportation," 14–26; Brook, "Communications and Commerce," 582–96; Wang, "More Haste, Less Speed," 92–102.

6 Kelly, "The Anti-Christian Persecution of 1616–1617," 287.

7 The dearth of surviving editions of Ming gazettes limits scholarly understandings of gazette policies and publishing in the Ming dynasty. We know little about the mechanisms by which gazettes were compiled from imperial documents, to whom they were distributed, how this distribution took place, or the ways in which unofficial gazettes diverged from the official record. Struve, *The Ming-Qing Conflict*, 9–11; Fang Hanqi, *Zhongguo xinwen shiye*, 119–86; Yin Yungong, *Zhongguo Mingdai xinwen*, 100–30; Wang, "Dilemmas of Empire," 163–67.

8 This transition paralleled the decline of the Ming postal and relay systems but did not originate from problems within these imperial transport systems. Brook, "Communications and Commerce"; Wang, "More Haste, Less Speed," 114–25.

9 Yin Yungong suggests that Ming readers used the term *dibao* to refer to unofficial papers because they did not strictly distinguish between official and unofficial gazettes. Yin Yungong, *Zhongguo Mingdai xinwen*, 112.

10 Brook, *Confusions of Pleasure*, 171–72. See also examples from the Southern Song in De Weerdt, *Information, Territory, and Networks*, 88–100.

11 Zhang, *Confucian Image Politics*, 11; Wang, "Information Media," 176–80; Feng, "Mushroom Cloud," 74–83.

12 Kelly, "The Anti-Christian Persecution," 287–88.

13 According to Lynn Struve, at least twenty records of the conquest period were composed at least partially from gazette collections. Struve, *The Ming-Qing Conflict*, 10.

14 *Duoergun shezheng riji*, quoted in Shi Yuanyuan, *Qingdai qianzhongqi xinwen*, 34.

15 Yao Tinglin, *Linian ji*, 54. On Yao and his diary, see also Kishimoto Mio, "'Rekineki,'" 53–77; Will, "Coming of Age," 15–39.

16 Qian Huilu, *Xian gong Tianjian fu jun nianpu*, 654–55.

17 Ōki Yasushi, *Minmatsu Kōnan*, 152–61; Kishimoto Mio, *Min-Shin kōtai*, 143–95.

18 Yao Tinglin, *Linian ji*, 54.

19 Wang, a Shandong native who was detested for his collaboration with the Manchus, was killed later that year in the Ming loyalist uprising at Qingzhou. Wakeman, *The Great Enterprise*, 437, 492; NGDK 037303-001 (SZ 01/07/12).

20 NGDK 059949-001 (SZ 01/08/06).

21 Tianjin (Zhang Xin) NGDK 086169-001 (received gazette SZ 02/06/06); Jinan (Huang Huiyin) NGDK 185042-069 (writes memorial SZ 02/06/17); Ningxia (Liu Fangming), NGDK 186748-009 (received news SZ 02/07/21). Other examples include: Yansui (Wang Yan and Wang Zhengzhi) NGDK 186748-005 and

186748-006 (dated SZ 02/09/01 and SZ 02/09/02). The Qing state later established time quotas for dispatches between Beijing and these locations (by foot/horse, in days) of: Nanjing (23/13); Tianjin (4/3); Jinan (9/5); and Ningxia (40/23). Fairbank and Teng, "Transmission of Ch'ing Documents," 23–28.

22 In 1647, Yizhou military commander Tong Yangliang cited the *dibao* for news of Qing military success in the west and the beheading of a false prince (NGDK 008587-001, received SZ 04/6/21); Shaanxi governor Huang Erxing cited the *dibao* in discussion of violations of the order to shave foreheads; (NGDK 016601-001, received SZ 04/09/24). In 1648, Shandong governor Lü Fengchun cited the *dibao* for news of Qing military success in Guangxi and Guizhou (NGDK 008406-001, received SZ 05/05/12).

23 NGDK 186748-004 (SZ 2/9/1).

24 These correspondences predate the earliest records available to the pioneering historian of news Fang Hanqi. Fang Hanqi, *Zhongguo xinwen shiye*, 188.

25 Hucker, "Governmental Organization," 49–52.

26 *Huang Qing zouyi*, 3:1a; Zhao Kaixin, "Ti wei yu xing shi zheng," in *Qing wu chao mizou*, 59.

27 Zhao Kaixin, "Ti wei yu xing shi zheng," in *Qing wu chao mizou*, 59–61. Quote on 59.

28 Lui, "Censor, Regent and Emperor," 87. Memorial of Zhang Guoxian (SZ 3), in *Huang Qing zouyi*, 2:43a–44b; memorial of Liu Wuyuan, *Huang Qing zouyi*, 3:27a–38b.

29 *Huang Qing zouyi*, 2:43a–b.

30 Lui, "Censor, Regent and Emperor," 83–86.

31 *QSL-SZ*, 20:178a (SZ 02/08/26).

32 For standards of review during the Southern Song dynasty, see De Weerdt, *Information, Territory, and Networks*, 80.

33 Wu, *Communication and Imperial Control*; Huang, *Autocracy at Work*. See also Feng Erkang, *Yongzheng zhuan*.

34 Biography of Feng Pu, *Linqu xian zhi*, 14:3–5.

35 Wu, *Communication and Imperial Control*, 7–19.

36 This process, and the problem of unsealed file copies leading to document leaks, were the topic of several memorials in the Yongzheng reign. See *Yongzheng chao manwen zhupi*, 494 (YZ 01/11/10); *Yongzheng chao hanwen zhupi*, 31:4 (YZ 4?); NPM, GZD 0402020378 (YZ 5).

37 This delay was apparently five days until the mid-Qianlong era, whereupon it was changed to ten days for certain matters. FHA, LFZZ, 03-0329-005 (QL 01/04/04); ZPZZ, 04-01-01-0168-036 (QL 13/03/29).

38 Wade, *Note*, 4–6.

39 Contrary to their name, the two offices do not seem to have divided documents according to language. For example, a Chinese gazette copyist in 1859 described that he copied documents from the registry book of the Manchu Registry on a daily basis. NPM, GZD, 406010511 (XF 09/04/24), testimony of Zhang Tonghe.

40 It is unclear where this distribution took place. We do have examples of clerks selling documents to gazette offices located in the city. Proclamations against leaking and fabrications refer to the "gazette copyists for each province."

41 For the postings and their duties, see *Da Qing huidian* (GX), 69:2a–3a. A total of twenty-four supervising secretaries staffed the Six Sections, split equally between Chinese and Manchu appointees. I compared the careers of several eighteenth-century cohorts of supervising secretaries using the database of official biographies created by the National Palace Museum and Academia Sinica (Qingdai Dang'an Renming Quanwei Ziliao Ku) and the *China Government Employee Database-Qing* database project based at the Hong Kong University of Science and Technology. Supervising secretaries typically came to the position after working as board clerks (*bitieshi*) and secretaries (*yuan wai lang*). Chinese appointees normally held the highest civil degree qualifications, and some Manchu appointees had also passed the translation exams. Though relatively low-ranking positions, supervising secretaries had important responsibilities and often moved into the Censorate after successful terms. On the declining political power of the supervising secretaries in the early Yongzheng reign, see Feng Erkang, *Yongzheng zhuan*, 259–61.

42 *Da Qing huidian* (GX), 2:5a–9a (incoming); 2:19a–21b (outgoing).

43 Sun Guangsi, "Liding ke gui shu," in *Sun Guangsi ji*, 262. Summary version in *QSL-SZ*, 133:1029b (SZ 17/03/15).

44 Sun Guangsi defined the contents of gazettes as personnel transfers, altered and finalized regulations, information on completed and unfulfilled transfers of money and grain, and arrests and apprehensions of criminals together with their crimes and personal details. Sun, *Sun Guangsi ji*, 262.

45 Wang Fuzhi, *Emeng*, in *Chuanshan quanshu*, 12:580.

46 Biography of Ren Kepu, *Qing shi gao*, 264:9919–22.

47 Theories of reward and punishment as motivating moral action were central to Qing-era interpretations of Legalist ideas as political strategies. See Metzger, *Internal Organization of Ch'ing Bureaucracy*, 247–60.

48 For comments on the late imperial state's insistence on transparency in the examination system, see Woodside, *Lost Modernities*, 2–3.

49 *QSL-KX*, 17:250b–251b (KX 04/11/07).

50 Sun Guangsi, *Sun Guangsi ji*, 262.

51 Some prominent seventeenth-century intellectual figures, like Gu Yanwu, did concern themselves with public scrutiny and looked to the classics for inspiration. See Delury, "Despotism Above and Below," 315–17. On the most common tropes cited, see Wagner, "Free Flow of Communication," 122–24. For nineteenth-century press advocates, see chapter 6.

52 Mokros, "Spies and Postmen"; Liu Wenpeng, "Titang kao," 87–91. These officials have also been called "courier superintendents" and "postmasters." However, these posts carried only loose associations to the relay-courier post (*yizhan*) system, and the officials were only tasked with managing certain types of communications between offices. My use of the term "capital

liaisons" for the Beijing-based post draws on the historical "capital liaison" offices of the late Tang dynasty. See De Weerdt, *Information, Territory, and Networks*, 79.

53 Zhang's proposal is referred to in a memorial by Li Wei excerpted in the Zhejiang provincial gazetteer. *Zhejiang tongzhi*, 92:7a–b.

54 Wu, *Communication and Imperial Control*; Chuang Chi-fa, *Qingdai zouzhe zhidu*.

55 Bartlett, *Monarchs and Ministers*, 258.

56 Bartlett, *Monarchs and Ministers*; Rowe, *China's Last Empire*, 40–42.

57 Wang, *White Lotus Rebels*, 116–24; Yoon, "Heshen Clique."

58 Wu, "Memorials System of the Ch'ing Dynasty," 50–53.

59 Bartlett, *Monarchs and Ministers*, 157–58.

60 One significant exception was communications from metropolitan boards, at least in the late Qianlong era. For *tiben* in memorials, see *Tizou shijian*, QL 38/07/09; QL 40/07/02; QL 40/10/16 (National Diet Library, Tokyo).

61 Bartlett, 211–16. The FHA has published a facsimile edition of the QL Suishou dengji, and holdings for subsequent reigns have been digitized.

62 The Suishou dengji only records transmission information after QL 8. I selected the following periods to survey transmission pathways: QL 20/7 (1755), QL 40/7 (1775), JQ 18/9 (1813), DG 6/9 (1826), DG 15/5 (1835), DG 28/2 (1848), XF 3/11 (1853), and TZ 10/7 (1871). QL records: *Suishou dengji dang*, vols. 8 and 32. JQ, DG, XF, TZ: FHA.

63 Chuang Chi-fa, *Gugong dang'an shuyao*, 342–43; Bartlett, *Monarchs and Ministers*, 157–58.

64 Volumes of the Wai ji dang from the nineteenth century are held at the Taiwan National Palace Museum Library. These patterns vary over the course of the dynasty. For example, the volumes for DG 14 contain short summaries of each memorial, but the volumes for DG 23 and thereafter contain much lengthier transcriptions. I have not been able to examine Wai ji dang volumes for prior to JQ 13. They are held at the FHA and not currently open to researchers.

65 NGDK holds several of these registers from the Shunzhi reign and a few from the Kangxi and Yongzheng reigns. The NPM possesses records from the Qianlong (1 volume), Jiaqing, Daoguang, Tongzhi, and Guangxu reigns. Several hundred volumes in Chinese and in Manchu are held at the FHA and are not currently open to consultation. The FHA also apparently holds a sort of style sheet for the Silun bu (*Silun shiyang*). Chuang, *Gugong dang'an shuyao*, 342.

66 Liu Guilin, "Qingdai neige silun bu," 60–64.

67 Bartlett, *Manchus and Ministers*, 265.

68 This text circulated in manuscript and print editions from the early Qianlong reign through the end of the dynasty. Glossaries were not palace editions but were published by Beijing publishers specializing in administrative texts, similar to the directory publishers of Liulichang.

69 *Liubu chengyu*, 1:23a; 5:13b.

70 Shen Qiliang, *Da Qing quanshu*, 6:6. For a useful overview of Manchu dictionaries and the distinctions among dictionaries, glossaries, and thesauri, see Söderblom Saarela, "Manchu and the Study of Language in China," 271–94.

71 The translated terms feature in subsequent editions of *Liubu chengyu* and the late Qing glossary *Administrative Terms* (Gongwen chengyu), 3b.

72 Bartlett, *Monarchs and Ministers*, 170–72; 200–7; see staffing request: NPM, GZD, 402020496 (YZ 13/11/15).

73 FHA, LFZZ, 03-0342-023 (QL 20/12/04). A summary of the policy adapted by the Board of Appointments and Censorate based on Yang's proposal can be found in *Da Qing huidian shili* (JQ), 1014:177a. For a biography of Yang Kaiding, see *Ganquan xian xu zhi*, 6:5a–b.

74 FHA, LFZZ, 03-0342-023 (QL 20/12/04).

75 *Yongzheng chao hanwen zhupi*, 11:468 (YZ 06/01/22).

76 FHA, LFZZ, 03-0334-036 (QL 07/06/09). It is not clear if this arrangement forced commercial publishers to close or simply compelled liaisons to stop purchasing from commercial publishers.

77 NGDK, 179597-001 (QL 11/R3/26); 095883-001 (QL 11/04/14); 050475-001 (QL 11/06/10); FHA, ZPZZ, 04-0101-0138-012 (QL 11/R3/08). This phrase was also used in earlier exposés, i.e. NPM, GZD, 0402020378 (YZ 5).

78 FHA, LFZZ, 03-4681-049 (TZ 03/12/18).

79 The allotments for nine provinces are listed in *Da Qing huidian shili* (GX), 170:20–47. Budgets were not standardized. Allotments for capital liaisons averaged around 1,200 taels per province per year.

80 I am indebted to an anonymous reader for the press for suggesting this interpretation.

81 FHA, Shangyu dang (JQ 24/06/19). Testimony of Shao Yucheng.

82 Mokros, "Spies and Postmen," 33–40.

CHAPTER 2: CHALLENGES TO THE INFORMATION ORDER

1 Kuhn, *Soulstealers*, 220.

2 Although acknowledged in official records, archival documentation from the perspective of a local investigation is not available for any of these cases.

3 Wu, *Communication and Imperial Control*, 42–63; and Spence, *Ts'ao Yin and the K'ang-hsi Emperor*, 213–40.

4 Perdue, *China Marches West*, 197–205.

5 Dai, *Sichuan Frontier*, 78–80.

6 A member of the Plain Yellow Banner and the Aisin Gioro imperial lineage, Mamboo had previously spent seventeen years in the metropolitan court, including a stint as editor of the court diaries. See Cai Xin's funerary inscription in Qian Yiji, *Bei zhuan ji*, 4:796–99.

7 *KMZZ*, 1018 (KX 54/06/06).

8 *KMZZ*, 1010 (KX 54/05/08).

9 On greetings memorials as a Manchu institution and in the development of palace memorials, see Wu, *Communication and Imperial Control*, 45; see also Elliott, "Manchu-Language Archives," 53.

10 Mamboo reported that he had not only shared the report with the Fujian governor-general and military general, but had also gathered civil and military officials in the provincial seat to read the dispatch together and discuss its consequences. Mamboo also planned to send the report to his subordinate officials in Taiwan. *KMZZ*, 1044–45 (KX 54/08/01).

11 *QSL-KX*, 267:626a (KX 55/03/27); *Qing shi gao, lie zhuan,* juan 276. Liu Yinshu had probably solicited information from his capital liaison.

12 Kangxi also scolded Liu Yinshu for impropriety and carelessness in his memorializing practices. McNicholas, *Forgery and Impersonation*, 24.

13 *KMZZ*, 1374–5 (KX 58/03/06).

14 Wang Zhonghan, *Qing shi lie zhuan*, 12:36a–b.

15 Kangxi had thirty-five sons, of whom the eldest fourteen were seen as viable candidates for the throne. On the succession crisis, see Wu, *Passage to Power*. For the ways in which the succession crisis suffused a wide variety of bureaucratic crimes, see McNicholas, *Forgery and Impersonation*, 12–30.

16 *QSL-KX*, 261:574a (KX 53/12/13). Kangxi was not in the capital on this date. More complete versions of Kuixu's memorial apparently have not survived, although the same excerpt published in the *Qing shilu* was also published in at least two biographical accounts. Wang Zhonghan, *Qing shi lie zhuan*, 12:32b; *Man mingchen zhuan,* 4:868.

17 Kuixu published several collections of poetry and prose in Chinese. Hummel, *Eminent Chinese*, 1:430. He also served from time to time as the scribe for the imperial court diaries in these years. See, for example, *Kangxi qijuzhu*, 2065 (KX 53/01/02).

18 See the description of the effects of "tabloid newspapers" written by Zhou Linzhi around 1160, translated in Wang, *Merry Laughter*, 184. The translation of *xiaobao* as "tabloids" anticipates the popular entertainment press of the modern era. I follow Hilde De Weerdt in calling unofficial versions of gazettes and political news "short reports." On the political impact of short reports in the Southern Song, see De Weerdt, *Information, Territory, and Networks*, 86–87.

19 De Weerdt, *Information, Territory, and Networks*, 88–101.

20 Zhang, *Confucian Image Politics,* 7–10; Ditmanson, "Imperial History," 27.

21 *Da Qing huidian shili* (GX), 622:2b–3a and 703:13b–14a.

22 Zhao Xiongzhao was the son of governor Zhao Shenqiao (1644–1720), who had previously served in Jiangnan, so he bore a clear interest in the case. On Zhao Shenqiao's career, see Guy, *Qing Governors*, 292. A full synopsis of the confusion, including the testimonies of the errant clerks, was published in the court gazette. See Li Zhen, *Benchao tibo gong'an*, 1:40a–42a; *QSL-KX*, 271:664a–b (KX 53/03/16); 272:667a–b (KX 56/04/03).

23 In much of the early modern world, clerical posts were "venal" posts available for a price. As a result, clerks sought out opportunities for personal enrichment while on the job. In late imperial China, some clerical posts were salaried, some were paid from superiors' stipends, and some clerks made money from irregular stipends and fees. Kaske, "The Price of an Office," 281–83; Reed, *Talons and Teeth*, 63.

24 Chuang Chi-fa, *Gugong dang'an shuyao*, 298.

25 *Yongzheng chao manwen zhupi*, 494 (YZ 01/11/10).

26 Xiao Shi, *Yongxian lu*, juan 2–4.

27 *Yongzheng chao manwen zhupi*, 494 (YZ 01/11/10).

28 FHA, ZPZZ, 04-01-01-0051-011 (QL 05/06/04); FHA, LFZZ, 03-0331-015 (QL 05/06/04). The Grand Council deliberated and agreed that enlisting social inferiors to solicit and disseminate political information was a reprehensible strategy of factional competition and personal enrichment. *QSL-QL*, 119:740b (QL 05/06/21).

29 Yongzheng also accused a second governor, the Shanxi governor Nuomin.

30 The edict (dated YZ 2/11) can be found in the biography of Mamboo in Wang Zhonghan, *Qing shi lie zhuan*, 12:36a–b.

31 "Yuzhi pengdan lun," in *Yuzhi wenji*, 5:1a–11b. For a somewhat different speech on the danger of factions, see *QSL-YZ*, 22:355b–359a (YZ 02/07/16).

32 Exposés were also reported by Santai, Zhang Zhengyuan, Hiyande, Wang Tang, and Wang Shijun. *Yongzheng chao hanwen zhupi*, 31:4 (not dated, YZ 1–4); *Gongzhong dang Yongzheng chao zouzhe*, 22:850 (YZ 12/04/23), 24:88 (YZ 13/02/02), 27:523 (not dated); *Shangyu neige*, 56:40a–41a (YZ 05/04/22); *Yongzheng chao hanwen zhupi*, 11:468–70 (YZ 06/01/22). Yongzheng issued edicts describing his anger at censors sharing sealed memorials. *Shangyu neige*, 4:10b–11b (YZ 01/02/13) and 84:17b–18b (YZ 07/R07/18); *Qinding taigui*, 2:7a–b.

33 Wu, *Passage to Power*; Huang, *Autocracy at Work*.

34 *QSL-YZ*, 44:646a–647a (YZ 04/05/09); Xiao, *Yongxian lu*, 280.

35 Spence, *Treason by the Book*, 79; *Yongzheng chao hanwen zhupi*, 13:938–40 (YZ 06/11/14).

36 Spence, *Treason by the Book*; Crossley, "*Dayi juemi lu*," 66; 76–79.

37 There were precedents in the publishing projects of the Ming emperors, particularly those of the Jiajing emperor (r. 1522–66), who sponsored publications meant to present an authorized record of disputes between the court and the monarch. See Brook, "Edifying Knowledge," 104. On Kangxi's projects, see Struve, "The Hsü Brothers." Qianlong's most famous project was the *Imperial Four Treasuries* (Siku quanshu). On this, see Guy, *Emperor's Four Treasuries*.

38 Hummel, *Eminent Chinese*, 2:917–19. The compilations included *Edicts to the Eight Banners* (Shangyu ba qi), *Edicts on Banner Affairs* (Shangyu qiwu), *Imperially Selected Memorials on Banner Affairs* (Yuxing qiwu zouyi), *Edicts and Rescripts of the Yongzheng Reign* (Yongzheng zhupi yuzhi), and *Edicts to the Grand Secretariat* (Shangyu neige).

39 *Shangyu neige*, juan shou:8b–9b.
40 "Lettre du Père Contancin," (December 15, 1727), in *Lettres édifiantes* (1781), 21:96.
41 *Yongzheng chao hanwen zhupi*, 11:1 (YZ 05/11/11); see also entries for YZ 05/11/18, YZ 05/11/28, and 06/01/22.
42 *Yongzheng chao hanwen zhupi*, 11:470 (YZ 06/01/22).
43 Huang, *Autocracy at Work*, 117–19.
44 *Da Qing huidian* (YZ), juan 166. Items drafted in 1727 (YZ 5) by the legal commission (*lüli guan*). This schedule of crimes and penalties does not appear in later editions of the *Huidian*.
45 Bartlett, *Monarchs and Ministers*, 9.
46 Bartlett, *Monarchs and Ministers*, 104–6.
47 Bartlett, *Monarchs and Ministers*, 137–56 and 166–68.
48 FHA, ZPZZ, 04-01-01-0138-012 (QL 11/R3/8).
49 NGDK, 197535-001 (QL 11/04/12).
50 NGDK, 050475-001 (QL 11/06/10).
51 NGDK, 179597-001 (QL 11/R3/26); Elliott, "Manchu-Language Archives," 25.
52 NGDK, 197535-001 (QL 11/04/12); NGDK, 050475-001 (QL 11/06/10).
53 FHA, LFZZ, 03-0329-005 (QL 01/04/04); Lü, "You guan Qingdai dichao," 94.
54 FHA, ZPZZ, 04-01-01-0138-012 (QL 11/R3/08); NGDK, 197535-001 (QL 11/04/14); 179597-001 (QL 11/R3/26); 050475-001 (QL 11/06/10).
55 NGDK 016678-001 (QL 06/04/22).
56 Bartlett, *Monarchs and Ministers*, 157–58.
57 For two possible leaks, see a forgery case associated with Youbashi: *Qianlong chao shangyu* 6:76–7 (QL 35/03/13); *QSL-QL*, 856:467a (QL 35/04/04); NGDK, 101787-001 (QL 35/04/08), NGDK, 178575-001 (QL 35/04/09); NPM, JJD, 011680 (QL 35/03/19); and accusations of unauthorized material appearing in printed gazettes by Jiang Ciqi: FHA, LFZZ, 03-0131-047 (QL 38/02/03); *QSL-QL*, 927:471b (QL 38/02/26).
58 FHA, ZPZZ, 04-01-01-0168-036 (QL 13/03/29). It is unclear when the prior rule was set (it does not appear in formal regulations), but metropolitan official Ěsan referred to it as established precedent in 1736. FHA, LFZZ, 03-0329-005 (QL 01/04/04). Yue Jun came from a distinguished family of Qing military men. He was the second son of the famous official Yue Zhongqi. Guy, *Qing Governors*, 225; Dai, *Sichuan Frontier*, 159.
59 FHA, ZPZZ, 04-01-01-0168-036 (QL 13/03/29); NPM, JJD, 002287 (QL 13/05/02).
60 *Yongzheng chao hanwen zhupi*, 8:321–22 (YZ 04/10/26).
61 This section draws on Mokros, "Spies and Postmen."
62 The 1734 case involved eight capital liaisons. Yu Zhuo apparently worked by himself. However, a number of different liaisons were involved in similar smuggling networks later in the year.
63 *QSL-QL*, 264:426a–b (QL 11/04/12).

64 The governors Nasutu (Zhili), Yenjishan (Liangjiang), Chen Dashou (Jiangsu), Wei Dingguo (Anhui), and Chang'an (Zhejiang) were affected. For the apologies, see FHA, ZPZZ, 04-01-12-0049-001 (QL 11/05/04); 04-01-01-0130-058 (QL 11/05/22); 04-01-01-0130-057 (QL 11/05/24); 04-01-12-0050-025 (QL 11/07/10). Historian Pierre-Étienne Will has suggested that this light penalty belies exaggerated characterizations of central security and imperial scrutiny. Will, "Review of *Monarchs and Ministers*," 331n25.

65 FHA, ZPZZ, 04-01-01-0130-057 (QL 11/05/24). One other governor, Nasutu, also referred to the inserted notes as *pian bao*.

66 *KMZZ*, 1318 (KX 57/08/19) and 1613 (ca. KX 57/08/10); Mokros, "Communication, Empire, and Authority," 103–5.

67 *KMZZ*, 1318 (KX 57/08/19).

68 NPM, GZD, 402004620 (YZ 13/03/15). The governor's report failed to account for the contents of the rumors. Yongzheng responded with frustration, "So what was this news that you investigated with such urgency? Please record it as it comes in."

69 *QSL-QL*, 972:1272b–1273b (QL 39/12/07); 972:1279a–b (QL 39/12/13); 973:1295a–b (QL 39/12/29).

70 *QSL-QL*, 973:1295a–b (QL 39/12/29).

71 *Wenziyu dang*, 763, 800, 812, 921, 927.

72 FHA, LFZZ, 03-2442-017 (JQ 11/01); 03-2194-002 (JQ 11/01/06); *QSL-JQ*, 156:11a–b (JQ 11/01/07).

73 Patterson, "Journalism of China," 19.

74 Upon taking office in Shanxi, governor Wang Qingyun bought news sheets for information about his new jurisdiction. Wang Qingyun, *Jinghua guan riji*, 227.

75 Morrison, "Gazette," *Chinese Repository* 1 (1833): 492.

76 See numerous references to news sheets by Robert Morrison in the *Canton Register*. See also a number of local proclamations and news sheets reproduced in Wade, *Wên-chien tsŭ-erh chi*, 2:126–50.

77 Quoted in Wang, "Information Media," 175; see original context in *Wanli dichao*, 1629. On the authorship of the *Wanli dichao*, see Ono Kazuko, "*Banri teishō* to *Banri soshō*."

78 Wang Huizu, "Wu jilu shishi," in *Shuangjie tang yongxun*, 5:7a.

79 Filippo de Vivo's statement concerning early modern Venice applies handily: "In such ways, communication was not just a means of governance; it was one of the practical limits of the state's authority, an object of negotiation rather than a top-down imposition." De Vivo, *Information and Communication in Venice*, 8.

80 Some of these relationships could be mirrored on the regional or provincial scale. In the 1750s, a garrison clerk named Chen Gonghuan continued to supply information on local politics to a former military superior after the superior had been transferred to a different post. "Qianlong nianjian wei Sun Jiagan zougao an (8)," 19–20.

CHAPTER 3. STATE NEWS IN THE MARKETPLACE

1 Wu, *Luxurious Networks*, 32–38; Fairbank, *Trade and Diplomacy*, 48–51; Chang, "The Economic Role of the Imperial Household."

2 Mann, *Local Merchants*, 46–51; Rowe, *China's Last Empire*, 44.

3 Son, *Writing for Print*, 8–10; Chow, *Publishing, Culture, and Power*, 97–100. On commercial publishers' work for the official market, see Zhang, *Circulating the Code* and "Buying and Selling Law Books," 107–8; and Mokros, "Reading the Guides."

4 In 1869, the building housing the Wuyingdian burned down, along with most of its retained woodblocks. Shaw, *Imperial Printing*, 9–17; Zhu Saihong, "Qing wanqi Wuyingdian," 141–46.

5 Zhang, "Buying and Selling Law Books," 116; Yang Yuliang, "Qingdai zhongyang guanzuan tushu," 91; Yan, "Routine Production," 224, 235–36; Wang Yuanchong, "Qingdai shixian shu," 198–200.

6 Chinese scholarship in journalism history has emphasized the commercial status of gazette publishers in order to support an argument for the indigenous origins of an independent press in China. Fewer scholars have investigated the implications of commercial publishing from the perspective of the state. Ge Gongzhen, *Zhongguo baoxue shi*, 49; Fang Hanqi, *Zhongguo xinwen shiye*, 203–6; cf. Mittler, *Newspaper for China*, 176–83.

7 This is my accounting as of August 2020. Despite this large number, the surviving gazettes are limited resources. For example, I have not been able to locate provincial gazettes from provinces other than Guangdong, Fujian, or Anhui.

8 Sirén, *Walls and Gates*, 1.

9 Naquin, *Peking*, 3–6. For the population density of the Southern (also known as the Outer or Chinese City), see Skinner, "Urban Social Structure," 532. Skinner's estimates are based on data from 1917–18.

10 BL, *Beijing neicheng tu*. Wu Changyuan, *Chenyuan shilüe*, juan 2–3.

11 On Beijing's official and examination culture, see Magone, "Once Every Three Years," 169–85; Goldman, *Opera and the City*, 63–102; Belsky, *Localities at the Center*, 64–67.

12 Mokros, "Spies and Postmen," 22–26.

13 BL, *Beijing neicheng tu*. After some twentieth-century alterations, the street once again bears this name. Wang Bin and Xu Xiushan, *Beijing diming dian*, 86–87.

14 Such activities were taken on in provincial cities as well, in collaboration between gazette publishers and communications liaisons. See *Yongzheng chao neige liu ke*, 83:267–270 (YZ 13/11/13).

15 NGDK, 016678-001 (QL 06/04/22).

16 *KMZZ*, 1613 (ca. KX 57/08/10); 1318–19 (KX 57/08/19).

17 *QSL-SZ*, 20:178a (SZ 02/08/26).

18 GZD 0402020378 (not dated, but ca. YZ 6).

19 *Yongzheng chao manwen zhupi*, 494 (YZ 01/11/10).
20 *Yongzheng chao hanwen zhupi*, 31:4 (not dated, ca. YZ 1–4).
21 NGDK, 016678-001 (QL 06/04/22).
22 FHA, LFZZ, 03-0329-005 (QL 01/04/04).
23 *Da Qing huidian zeli* (QL), 51:13b. The best remunerated metropolitan clerks were translation clerks (*bitieshi*).
24 NGDK, 016678-001 (QL 06/04/22). Necin was one of the most exalted figures on the Grand Council at this time. Bartlett, *Monarchs and Ministers*, 174–76.
25 Some accounts from the late nineteenth and early twentieth centuries suggest the existence of an advance "digest" edition (*lüebao*) released each afternoon, followed by a fully vetted edition (*pingbao*) released at midnight. Soong, "Zhongyang zhengfu gongbao," 100.
26 For profiles of publishing in two Fujian regions, see Chia, *Printing for Profit*; and Brokaw, *Commerce in Culture*.
27 Scholars attribute the expansion of the papermaking industry as one cause for the boom in commercial publishing in mid- to late-Ming Jiangnan. However, transport and supply between Jiangnan and Beijing remained a problem. McDermott, "Ascendance of the Imprint," 78–79; Chow, *Publishing, Culture, and Power*, 28–33; Fitzgerald, "Between Paper and Wood," 76–77. On the shortage of labor and wood, see Weng Lianxi, *Qing neifu keshu dang'an*, 104–5; 143.
28 See the case of the Anhui paper merchant described in a memorial by official Min Eyuan (1720–1797). NPM, GZD, 403033458 (QL 42/11/28). For the prices paid by the Wuyingdian, see Weng Lianxi, *Qing neifu keshu dang'an*, 730–49.
29 By the nineteenth century, budgets for capital liaisons earmarked gazette funds for paper, copying, and distribution amounting to about three taels per day. Based on Fujian, in *Da Qing huidian shili* (GX), 170:20–47.
30 Li Zhen, "Xu," in *Benchao tibo gong'an*.
31 Yuan Dong, *Shuyin congshuo*, 1137:571.
32 During the late Yongzheng revision of the *Huidian*, each metropolitan yamen and province was required to remit funds for paper, ink, and labor to the capital to be used in printing the text. Weng Lianxi, *Qing neifu keshu dang'an*, 99–100.
33 Most surviving examples of Gongshen Tang imprints date to the late Qianlong and Jiaqing reigns. However, there are a few Gongshen Tang imprints from the Daoguang reign in the British Library collection. See the appendix for more details.
34 Relationships between liaisons became particularly important during these years. One capsule biography of a liaison published in a gazetteer described an incident when a colleague was falsely accused of a crime, and the liaison stepped in to vouch for the colleague's honesty. Biography of Wang Chenfeng in *Jinan fu zhi*, 55:60a–b.
35 Both the Northern and Southern Cities were divided into five wards that transected the walls of the cities and extended into the suburbs. These were further

subdivided into ten precincts (*fang*). These administrative boundaries remained relevant into the late Qing. Naquin, *Peking*, 360, 418n112.

36 Liu Wenhua, "Jiaqing ershisi nian wang gong dachen tanting guan shi an dang'an." They used these funds to hire subordinates, like Zhao Yuzhan, a seventy-four-year-old former tutor who made copies for the boards on an informal basis.

37 On possible print runs, see Chia, *Printing for Profit*, 31.

38 Since the 1990s, scholars have debated whether or not wax techniques were used in the publication of Gongshen Tang editions. See Zhang Xiumin and Han Qi, *Zhongguo yinshua shu*, 79–82; Pan Xianmo, "Qingchu de yulun yu chaobao," 254–57. Heijdra, "Technology, Culture and Economics"; Ai Junchuan, "*Tizou shijian* bu shi la ban." An interesting effort to reproduce the wax printing process concluded that printers would need to employ a softer brush to avoid completely effacing the relief characters on the wax surface. See Zhao Chunying, "Qingdai 'la ban yinshua,'" 101.

39 Zhang Xiumin's work contains images of wax-printed documents, possibly reprints of memorials or gazettes from 1711 and 1731, held in Rome and Vienna, respectively. These items may well have been printed in Canton. Zhang Xiumin and Han Qi, *Zhongguo yinshua shu*, 79–82.

40 For a description of the method, see Milne, *Retrospect*, 225–29. For references to the prevalence of the wax process, especially in the production of provincial reprints and gazettes, see Mossman, "Peking Gazette" (also reprinted in *China Mail*, Jan. 11, 1866); *North China Herald*, September 14, 1850; *Chinese Repository* 1:414; *Chinese Repository* 19:247–9; TNA, FO 233/58/18, Mayers, "Memorandum on the 'Peking Gazette,'" April 14, 1874.

41 Governor-general Li Shiyao suggested that Guangdong carvers travel to Beijing to ease labor shortages in the *Siku quanshu* project. Weng Lianxi, *Qing neifu keshu dang'an*, 132.

42 On the "ideal ratio" of a book page, see Chia, *Printing for Profit*, 42–44.

43 Liu Wenhua, "Jiaqing ershisi nian wang gong dachen tanting guan shi an dang'an," 47.

44 Mokros, "Reading the Guides," 127–66.

45 "Peking," *North China Herald*, June 9, 1882. A metropolitan official hailing from Shandong attested in his diary that "the majority" of Beijing shopkeepers in the late 1850s hailed from Shandong and especially Dengzhou. Wang Zhonglin, *Wang Zhongjin riji*, 59:526–27.

46 FHA, LFZZ, 03-4578-062 (XF 03/12/22).

47 In 1846, metropolitan official Wang Qingyun obtained a copy of the court annals *Donghua lu* from the scribal publisher Benli Tang, which may also have sold manuscript gazettes. Wang Qingyun, *Jinghua guan riji*, 1:15. Fang Hanqi also refers to a Baiben Baofang outside Donghua Gate in late Qing Beijing. Fang Hanqi, "Qingdai Beijing de minjian baofang yu jingbao," 206.

48 Zhang reported to investigators that this notice had been the fourth item in the office's registry, although he did not know the names of those working

in the Manchu Registry Office (*Man Piaoqian*) on that day. NPM, GZD, 406010511 (XF 09/04/24).

49 Mokros, "Spies and Postmen," 33–40.

50 Although "gendarmerie" has been commonly used to refer to the Bujun Tongling Yamen, I see no reason not to call these forces "police." The nature of the police changed dramatically in the last years of the Qing, but so did other elements of urban administration. Likewise, the city censors who ran the ward offices have been given a wide range of appellations, but most of these obscure rather than reveal the everyday functions of these local officials. See Na Silu, *Qingdai zhongyang sifa shenpan zhidu*, 296.

51 TNA, FO 233/58/18, Mayers, "Memorandum on the 'Peking Gazette,'" April 14, 1874.

52 For example, a lengthy memorial concerning a murder investigation in Nanjing was published across three successive issues. *Jingbao (dibao)*, 1:279–292 (GX 08/03/20–22).

53 FHA, LFZZ, 03-4578-062 (XF 03/12/22); TNA, FO 233/58/7, "Memo," April 4, 1872; Alcock, "Peking Gazette," 252; Britton, *Chinese Periodical Press*, 10. Publishers named in gazette collections, archival documents, and secondary sources include Liben Tang, Hecheng Baofang, Juxing Baofang, Juheng Baofang, Xinyi Baofang, Gongli Baofang, Gongxing Baofang, Jiwen Baofang, Tongxing Baofang, Tianli Baofang, Jusheng Baofang, Tianhua Baofang, Liansheng Baofang, Taicheng Baofang, Hongxing Baofang, Yongxing Baofang, Tongwen Baofang, Tianfu Baofang, Sanyou Baofang, Tongshun Baofang, and Duji Baofang.

54 "If written Gazettes in full form are wanted by outsiders, they can be obtained near the palace gate by the payment of a large sum." Mossman, "Peking Gazette"; *North China Herald*, August 12, 1869.

55 Supervisory officials occasionally complained that the publishers were too scattered for effective policing. An 1865 proposal for the reestablishment of an official publisher akin to the Gongshen Tang received no court response. FHA, LFZZ, 03-4681-049 (TZ 03/12/18).

56 Wang Zhonglin, *Wang Zhonglin riji*, 59:483.

57 Alcock, "The *Peking Gazette*," 248.

58 TNA, FO 233/58/15, "Gazette," April 15, 1872. These gazettes, printed on short white paper in relatively compact and clear font, have also been called the "Shandong edition" because the phrase *Shandong Liaison [Edition]* (Shandong Tangwu) sometime appears at the central margin or on the first page. Given that most courier post editions bear the attribution "joint establishment of the sixteen capital liaisons," the liaisons probably financed these editions together.

59 Osawa Akahiro, "Sūēden ōritsu toshokan no kanseki," 181–82.

60 Britton, *Chinese Periodical Press*, 9–10.

61 Alcock, "The *Peking Gazette*," 252.

62 Osawa Akahiro, "Sūēden ōritisu toshokan no kanseki," 181–82; Britton, *Chinese Periodical Press*, 9–10. Mossman, "Peking Gazette," 119.

63 "Kan jingbao," in *Dumen jilüe*, 14:330–1; Porter, *From Belfast to Peking*, 130; Alcock, "The Peking Gazette," 252.

64 Li Ciming paid 2,000 qian per month for the gazette digest in TZ 2, 500 qian for the *dichao* in TZ 7 (while in Zhejiang), 7,000 qian for the *dichao* in TZ 10, 4,000 qian for the *dichao* in TZ 13, 6,500 qian for the *jingbao* in GX 2, 5,400 qian for the *jingbao* in GX 3, and 2,500 qian for the *jingbao* in GX 4. Zhang Dechang, *Qingji yige jingguan de shenghuo*, 105–218.

65 Osawa Akahiro, "Suēden ōritisu toshokan no kanseki," 181–82.

66 Porter, *From Belfast to Peking*, 130; Britton, *Chinese Periodical Press*, 9–10; Alcock, "The *Peking Gazette*," 252.

67 Goldman, *Opera and the City*, 81.

68 Fang Hanqi, *Zhongguo xinwen shiye*, 214.

69 *Chouban yiwu shimo buyi*, 17–18 (DG 22/06/29). These editions apparently circulated as far as the Nanjing area. For the court response, see *Chouban yiwu shimo*, 57:27b–28a (DG 22/06/29). An English translation is found in Fairbank and Teng, "Types and Uses," 62.

70 Li Jiashan also acted as a broker in degree sales. FHA, LFZZ, 03-3920-010 (DG 04/02/12); FHA, Shangyu dang (DG 04/02/12); Zhu Qingqi and Bao Shuyun, *Xing'an huilan*, 3194–95.

71 TNA, FO 233/58/18, Mayers, "Memorandum on the 'Peking Gazette,'" April 14, 1874.

72 BL, Peking Gazette Collection (DG 29/02/24–29). A single gazette in the collection bears a stamp attributed to its point of sale, the "complete merchandiser" Jin Yu Lu, located on Datang Jie. These gazettes may have been owned or purchased by the missionary Karl Gutzlaff—a small stamp bearing a Chinese translation of his name is affixed to an interior page of one issue (DG 29/03/16–17).

73 FHA, ZPZZ, 04-01-38-0037-015 (QL 17/04/07). Each manuscript publisher employed a few scribes and deliverymen.

74 Milne, "Letter to the Editor," *North China Herald*, November 2, 1850. The publisher was located at Xizang bridge, near the west gate.

75 Williams, *Middle Kingdom*, 1:420. In the early twentieth century, journalist Roswell Britton affirmed Williams' estimate. Britton, *Chinese Periodical Press*, 10.

76 BL, Peking Gazette Collection; BL, THE KING PAOU, or Peking Gazette, (DG 20/12/18).

77 BL, Peking Gazette Collection (DG 11/03/18–19, DG 11/03/20–21, DG 12/03/22–23, DG 26/03/21–22). Tsien, *Paper and Printing*, 221. The stamp of the Ren Meihe firm (*Ren Meihe ji*) can also be found on the gazette collection *Xianfeng san nian shang yu* once owned by the late Qing book-collector and library manager Xu Fang, and now held at Beijing University Library.

78 *Chinese Repository*, 1:414; Davis, *Chinese*, 3:4; Milne, *Retrospect*, 224; Zhao Chunying, "Qingdai 'la ban yinshua,'" 98–101.
79 Wade, *Note*, 3.
80 Far fewer provincial gazettes survive than their capital counterparts. Samples at the Bibliothèque nationale in Paris and the Bayerische Staatsbibliothek in Munich are Daoguang-era imprints from Guangzhou. Because they are packaged inside capital gazettes, these were probably local reprints of the capital gazette. In addition, *Shenbao* published the gazettes of provinces in the lower Yangtze region at irregular intervals between 1872 and 1898. Mokros, "Communication, Empire, and Authority," 304.
81 Bayerische Staatsbibliothek , *Dufu xian yuanbao* (DG 10/10/09); BnF, *Jingchao* (DG 03/08).
82 Shuck, *Portfolio Chinensis*, 79.
83 *Yongzheng chao neige liu ke*, 83:267–270 (YZ 13/11/13).
84 "Gechu baoxi," *Shenbao*, February 3, 1899.
85 *Yongzheng chao neige liu ke*, 83:270 (YZ 13/11/13).
86 I could not locate any names of known publishers in gazetteers or lists of official appointments in the Airusheng *Database of Chinese Classic Ancient Books* (Zhongguo Jiben Guji Ku).
87 FHA, LFZZ, 03-0342-023 (QL 20/12/04).
88 Rennie, *Peking and the Pekingese*, 212.
89 "Newspapers in China," *Glasgow Herald*, February 28, 1866.

CHAPTER 4: OFFICIAL READERS AND POLITICAL CULTURE

1 The most common references to official bulletins in diaries and autobiographies are those that commemorate a new appointment, especially one's own. For example, Yang Guozhen, *Yang Guozhen nianpu*, 138:19–20; Xu Zonggan, *Ziding nianpu*, 148:478–79.
2 Peterson, "Life of Ku Yen-Wu," 125; Delury, "Despotism Above and Below," 123–24.
3 On theories of historical scholarship among Ming loyalists, see Wakeman, *Great Enterprise*, 1085–91.
4 Huang Zongxi, *Hongguang shilu chao*, 2:1. This passage is also described in Brook, *Troubled Empire*, 238–39.
5 Struve, *Ming-Qing Conflict*, 10.
6 Zhang Shao, "Rizhi lu ba," in *Qing jingshi wenbian*, 1:82.
7 Struve, "The Hsü Brothers," 243.
8 Peterson, "Life of Ku Yen-Wu," 242. "Yu Ci Geng shu," in *Tinglin shi wen ji*, 9:9b–10a.
9 Gu, "Yu Gong Su sheng shu," in *Tinglin shi wenji*, 8:15a–b. Gu Yanwu's letters were published and circulated widely after his death.
10 See for example Zhang Chen, *Richu riji*, 105:333–34.
11 Rowe, *Saving the World*, 114, 137.

12 Chen's choice of Huang instead of other exemplary readers (such as Gu Yanwu) is interesting, as Huang, a devoted diarist, was a reluctant examination taker who received his *juren* and *jinshi* degrees in 1642 and 1643 and subsequently committed suicide in the Qing siege of Jiading. He was later celebrated as a Ming loyalist. Dennerline, *Chia-ting Loyalists*, 229–50; Struve, "Chinese Memory," 9–13, 17–23.

13 Draft unpublished histories based on Qing gazettes depict episodes as diverse as imperial campaigns in Xinjiang, a palace invasion, and a set of scandalous murders in rural Anhui. For more details on draft compilations in Chinese libraries, see Mokros, "Communication, Empire, and Authority," ch. 3.

14 Hong Liangji, "Shu Hang jiantao yishu," in *Hong Beijiang quan ji*, 46:14b. Thanks to Daniel Hausmann for this reference.

15 Yin Huiyi, *Yin taifu ren nianpu*, 58–59. This anecdote is also repeated in Mrs. Yin's funerary inscription authored by Fang Bao. *Yin taifu ren nianpu*, 87–89.

16 Some memorialists also claimed to revere gazettes in the same way they would a personally written message from the emperor. Lin Zexu, *Lin Wenzhong gong zheng shu*, 4:5a. Similar claims were made with reference to the Qing legal code. Zhang, *Circulating the Code*, 32.

17 Chen Hongmou, "Ji Zhang Mozhuang shu," in *Qing jingshi wenbian*, 1:81. Chen built his suggestion on his own student experience at the Xuancheng academy. Rowe, *Saving the World*, 27–28.

18 *Yongzheng chao hanwen zhupi*, 8:316 (YZ 04/10/25).

19 *Yongzheng chao manwen zhupi*, 2243 (YZ 12/01/26).

20 "He Shisheng du guo ce an," in *Qingdai wenziyu dang*, 326.

21 See comments in Pan Tianzhen, "Qianlong, Jiaqing jian suo yin ribao," 89.

22 In his autobiography, Wang Wensi (1831–1886) noted that at the age of seven *sui*, he read the court gazette together with his uncle, and discussed with various townspeople the emerging disturbances in South China, weighing the policies and actions of the Qing officials dealing with the British threat. Wang, *Wang Anfu nianpu*, 171:750. For the tropes and realities of early childhood classical education in the life of a seventeenth-century scholar, see Schäfer, *The Crafting of the 10,000 Things*, 31–34.

23 Huo Yanfang and Lu Dongqing, "Gong Zizhen dang'an sixiang," 125.

24 On Zeng Guofan's military, moral, and administrative roles in wartime and post-Taiping Jiangnan, see Wooldridge, *City of Virtues*, 110–49. See also Porter, *Tsêng Kuo-fan's Private Bureaucracy*; Wright, *Last Stand of Chinese Conservatism*; and Hummel, *Eminent Chinese*, 2:751–5.

25 The *Zizhi tongjian*, a political history first printed in 1086, was indeed vast, totaling more than two million characters.

26 Zeng Guofan, "Zhi dao," in *Qiu que zhai riji*, 559:841. Zeng originally wrote the note in the summer of 1860. His letters frequently offered instructions on personal education to his younger brothers. See Liu, "Education for its Own Sake," 76–108. The capital official and diarist Yun Yuding (1862–1917) also commented on Zeng's advice. Shi Xiaofeng, *Yun Yuding cheng zhai riji*, 326.

Other readers of Zeng Guofan's advice on diaries and reading included Liu Dapeng and Yang Changji. See Harrison, *Man Awakened by Dreams*, 11–12; Platt, *Provincial Patriots*, 178.

27 Du, *Yuanmu riji*, 88:353.

28 Statecraft (*jingshi*) was a loose, rather than clearly defined school of thought. Adherents tended to serve in official careers or devote themselves to commenting on issues of public need, such as disaster relief, water works, finance, and administration. It held attenuated connections to the dominant intellectual bent among literati of the time, which stressed philologically minded scrutiny of classical texts. Both approaches emphasized their superiority to the esoteric and theoretical philosophizing that had marked the Ming dynasty. As Chuck Wooldridge points out, the appellation of *shi*, meaning "concrete" or "substantive," was used so extensively in the mid-nineteenth century that the Taiping leadership attempted to coopt this term to legitimate their ideology. Wooldridge, *City of Virtue*, 89.

29 See Chen, "Legal Specialists," 26–34.

30 See NGDK, 185047-002 (SZ 02/05/05), and 185047-020 (SZ 02/05/10).

31 Zhang Mao, "Qing cheng fushui ding'e fangce shu," in *Qing jingshi wenbian*, 1:783.

32 Li Zhifang, "Qing jin zaliu weishu shu," in *Qing jingshi wenbian*, 1:433–4. In another of Li's memorials, he cited his reading in the gazette of Jiangxi governor Zhang Chaolin's memorial on dishonorable practices among clerks, runners, and subordinate officials. "Yan cha jia mao guntu shu," in Li Zhifang, *Li Wenxiang gong zouyi*, 1:7a–9a.

33 Shen Tong, "Baojia lun," in *Qing jingshi wenbian*, 2:1819.

34 Dunstan, *Conflicting Counsels*, 240–44. On the wider distillation prohibition debate, see Dunstan, *Conflicting Counsels*, 203–45.

35 Dunstan, *Conflicting Counsels*, 244.

36 *Huang Qing zouyi* includes 581 memorials in total.

37 Biography of Ren Kepu, in *Qing shi gao*, 264:9919–9922.

38 NGDK, 038852-001 (SZ 2).

39 Qian Yiji, *Qian Wenduan gong (Chenqun) nianpu*, 270–71.

40 FHA, LFZZ, 03-0334-036 (QL 07/06/09).

41 Examination questions were formulated in a secretive process. The publication of questions after the announcement of examination results thus provided a record of recently employed topics and quotes, and revealed the legitimacy of the exam in question as an intellectual test. For a description of the formulation of provincial exam questions, see Williams, "Fraud and Inquest," 92–96. For examination questions in the gazettes, see *Tizou shijian* (Princeton University Library), QL 35/10/18, QL 35/10/23 and QL 35/11/01.

42 For notes on reading of disaster relief in the gazettes, see Hu Erkai, "Qing xu zai gao shu" in *Changsha fu zhi*, 14:75a–76b.

43 McNicholas, *Forgery and Impersonation*, 104–6.

44 On redundancy as an archival and bureaucratic strategy, see Wang, "Dilemmas of Empire," 27–33.

45 On the role of commercial publications in influencing the growing importance of case precedents in Qing law, see Zhang, *Circulating the Code*, 63.

46 Scholars divide administrative handbooks into three types. First, handbooks for magistrates offered basic know-how and the principles of governance for rookie officials. Second, a text might showcase and promote the work of a specific administrator. Third, compilations of regulations, laws, exemplary cases, and documents concerning specific situations (especially natural disasters) guided the hands-on daily work of clerks, secretaries, and other sub-bureaucratic functionaries. Gong Rufu, "Guanzhen de zhengzhi zhihui," 150–55; Will, *Handbooks and Anthologies*.

47 "Qing huomian she qian liujie qianliang," in Huang Liuhong, *Fuhui quanshu*, 3:273.

48 Yuan Shouding, *Tumin lu*, 230.

49 He went on, "As it is said, 'If one does not know how to be an official, one should review past successes (*yicheng shi*).' The gazette contains these successes." The quote draws on an episode in the biography of Jia Yi in the *History of the Han Dynasty* (Han shu). In this anecdote, Jia stated to an interlocutor: "We could say, 'If you are not practiced at official service, consider past successes.' We could also say, 'Where the forward chariot overturns, the rear chariot avoids.' Thusly, the reasons for the longevity of the Three Dynasties can be known from their successes; therefore, inability to adhere to these is a failure to follow the ways of sage wisdom. The reasons for the abrupt demise of Qin can be seen in the lasting ruts of its chariot-wheels. If these are not avoided, the rear chariot will likewise fall."

50 The official Yanchang recorded in his autobiography that in 1883, he followed a case where two provincial officials were suspected of colluding to shuffle appointments but were eventually cleared of suspicion. Yanchang, *Nian shi jilüe*, 173:545; Wu Jing recorded learning of his own removal from office in his chronological autobiography, but he had already retired by this point. Wu, *Ziding nianpu*, 117:203.

51 Fang Yurun, *Xinglie riji*, 58:143–44.

52 Wang Huizu, *Menghen yulu*, 2:225.

53 See Will, "La paperasse au secours de l'homme," 80–84.

54 Li Zhen, *Dingli quanbian*; Li Zhen, *Benchao tibo gong'an*; Zhu and Bao, *Xing'an huilan*; Yang Ximing, *Zaizhen quanshu* (Hangzhou?, 1823); Wang Shouji, *Yan fa yilun* (Beijing?, 1873); Li Yingjue, *Zhe zhi bianlan* (Hangzhou: Liyin zhai, 1896); Li Yingjue, *Wan sheng bianlan* (Anqing: Zhongyun ge, 1902); Chen Tao, *Tongzhi zhonging zhongwai zouyi yuebian* (Beijing: Xiaoyou shanfang, 1875). Li Ciming reviewed a draft of Wang Shouji's work and wrote approvingly of it in his diary. Li, *Yue man tang riji*, 3:1390 (TZ 11/9/27). See also Will, *Handbooks and Anthologies*, 173–74, 540–41, 632–33, 665–68, 960–61.

55 Mokros, "Communication, Empire, and Authority," 190–97. Chen Tao, "Xu," in *Tongzhi zhongxing*. The format and agenda of Chen Tao's compendium is most akin to the *fūsetsudome* of nineteenth-century Japan, which Gideon Fujiwara describes as heralding widening political awareness. Fujiwara, "Channeling the Undercurrents," 320–26.

56 Li Zhen, "Xu," in *Benchao tibo gong'an*; Mokros, "Reading the Guides," 138–39; Zhang, "Buying and Selling Law Books," 105–6.

57 Will, *Handbooks and Anthologies*, 632–33.

58 Ho, *Ladder of Success*; Metzger, *Internal Organization of Ch'ing Bureaucracy*; Guy, *Qing Governors*; Zhang, "Legacy of Success."

59 Ch'ü, *Local Government*; Watt, *District Magistrate*; Park, "Corruption," 979–81.

60 Zelin, *Magistrate's Tael*; Bartlett, *Monarchs and Ministers*; Kuhn, *Soulstealers*.

61 *Tizou shijian*, QL 36/06 (National Diet Library, Tokyo); Kaske, "Fundraising Wars," 84; Wu Yue, *Zhongguo de juanna zhidu*, 207–9.

62 De Weerdt, *Information, Territory, and Networks*, 93–97.

63 Hu Juqing, *Geng fu riji*, 27:475 (QL 14/03/19).

64 Fictionalized depictions include *The Scholars* (Rulin waishi), *Lantern at the Crossroads* (Qilu deng), and *Officialdom Unmasked* (Guanchang xianxing ji). Wu Jingzi, *The Scholars*, 33; Li Lüyuan, *Qilu deng*, 56; Li Boyuan, *Officialdom Unmasked*, 258. For a representative Western account mocking Chinese official attention to gazettes, see Wilkinson, *English Student-Life at Peking*, 91–92.

65 Li Ciming paid for eligibility to hold a Board department head position (*langzhong*, rank 5a). See Kaske, "Metropolitan Clerks," 241.

66 On the degree-purchase scheme and the betrayal by his distant relatives Zhou Xingyu and Zhou Xingyi, see Lu Dunji, *Panghuang qilu*, 16–18.

67 "Li Tz'u-ming," in Hummel, *Eminent Chinese*, 1:493. See also Zhang Dechang, *Qingji yige jingguan de shenghuo*, 33–34, 45–57.

68 See Li Ciming, *Yue man tang riji bubian*, 4 vols.

69 See Mokros, "Communication, Empire, and Authority," 173.

70 For Beijing residents, it was possible to subscribe solely to the *gongmen chao* for a cheaper price than subscribing to the full gazette. Zhang Dechang, *Qingji yige jingguan de shenghuo*, 105–218.

71 At the provincial level, funds for gazette subscriptions were often pooled from the offices and officials who read the gazette. See Selengge, "Zou qing jiang yuan bo tangbing jinxing caiche gui yingwu," (YZ 05/11/24), in Qiu and Liu, eds., *Zhongguo youyi shiliao*, 249.

72 Li Ciming, *Yue man tang riji*, 3:1475. Li also bought copies of the *Directory* in TZ 2, GX 4, and GX 13. Zhang Dechang, *Qingji yige jingguan de shenghuo*, 105–218.

73 For examples, see Li Ciming, *Yue man tang riji*, 3:1496, 3:1503, 3:1505, 3:1509, 3:1534.

74 In 1871, during Li's journey back to the capital, his diaries reflect scant access to the gazettes, with concentrated and lengthy records on the days when he obtained recent gazette issues.

75 Li Ciming, *Yue man tang riji*, 3:1478.
76 Xu, "Li Ciming yu Zhou Zupei," in *Li Ciming zhuanji ziliao*, 1:46–49.
77 Li Ciming, *Yue man tang riji*, 5:2617–2626.
78 "Li Tz'u-ming," in Hummel, *Eminent Chinese*, 1:493; Zhang Dechang, *Qingji yige jingguan de shenghuo*, 45–57.
79 "Jingbao," *Shenbao*, March 31 and April 2, 1893 (GX 19/02/06 and 19/02/08).

CHAPTER 5: THE QING GAZETTE GOES ABROAD

1 See the example of Annam in Lin, *China Upside Down*, 14. A manuscript court gazette (*Han gyeong bo* or *chobo*) was published in Chošon Korea, apparently patterned on Ming dynasty court gazettes. Courant, *Bibliographie coréene*, 2:177–78.
2 Given that this chapter discusses a wide range of European and American perspectives on Chinese state news, I use the term *Western* as a shorthand where appropriate.
3 "Lettre du Père Contancin," (December 15, 1727), in *Lettres édifiantes* (1781), 21:96.
4 Imbault-Huart, "Le Journal et le Journalisme," 50–52.
5 On the early European press and politics, see Pettegree, *Invention of News*; Dooley and Baron, *The Politics of Information*; Dooley, *Dissemination of News*; Raymond, *Invention of the Newspaper*; Koopmans, *News and Politics*; Peacey, *Print and Public Politics*; Kyle, "Monarch and Marketplace"; and the contributions in *Media History* 23, no. 2 (2017).
6 Todd, *Political Bias*; Harris, *Politics and the Rise of the Press*; Censer, *French Press in the Age of the Enlightenment*, and Popkin, *News and Politics*. For a reconstruction of the physical process of assembling news from different sources in eighteenth-century contexts, see Slauter, "Paragraph as Information Technology."
7 Green, "Intervening in the Public Sphere."
8 On Asian ideas and products in eighteenth-century continental Europe and England, see Berg, *Luxury and Pleasure*, 46–84; Porter, *Chinese Taste*.
9 "Pereyra" refers to Thomas Pereira (1645–1708), who arrived in Beijing in 1671. Quoted in Golvers, *François de Rougemont*, 360.
10 When correspondents of the Propaganda Fide specified print editions, they did so to make a distinction, not to comment upon the novelty of the medium. Archives Propaganda Fide, Scritture Originali della Congregazione Particolare dell'Indie e della Cina (Letters Concerning the East Indies and China), vol. 35 (1731), 273r–276v. I am grateful to Eugenio Menegon for sharing the Propaganda Fide archival files. In 1727, Contancin wrote that he received about three hundred gazettes per year, sent to Canton from Beijing. He stated that the print edition published in Beijing contained sixty to seventy pages and included more memorials than the shorter provincial editions. *Lettres édifiantes* (1781) 21:98.

11 Jean-François Vandermonde sent the collection to the Paris Botanical Gardens sometime between 1720 and 1731. The collection, wrapped in gazettes and placed in glass bottles, is preserved at the National Museum of Natural History in Paris. Thanks to Wu Huiyi for this reference.

12 Missionaries copied excerpts from gazettes rather than sending original editions. On the circulation of Chinese books to Europe, see Standaert, "Jean-François Foucquet's Contribution."

13 Golvers, *Libraries of Western Learning,* 3:469–73. See also Menegon, "Interlopers," 47–48. Some Jesuit correspondence, including discussion of imperial edicts, made its way to Mexico via the Philippines before being forwarded on to Europe. See Clossey, *Salvation and Globalization*, 196–204.

14 For portents gathered from gazettes, see Golvers, *Letters of a Peking Jesuit*, 319. Some of these notices made it to the European press, such as the description of an earthquake that struck Beijing in 1720. *Daily Courant*, April 26, 1722.

15 Golvers, *Letters of a Peking Jesuit*, 230.

16 Letter from François D'Entrecolles to Froissard de Broissia (May 10, 1715), describing how missionary Dominique Parennin had described a method for reading the gazette to learn about the actions of the Board of War. *Lettres édifiantes* (1781), 18:398–99.

17 For Mourão's confession, see *Wenxian congbian*, 1:1–14; *QSL-YZ*, 47:717–18 (YZ 04/08/30). On Mourão's relationship with Yintang (the eighth son of the Kangxi emperor), see Menegon, "Religious and Political Martyrdom," 10–12.

18 The year before, Yongzheng's sentence against Sunu, a prominent imperial clansman, was published in gazettes. Letter by Père Parennin (July 20, 1725), in *Lettres édifiantes* (1728), 18:119. On the circulation of reports of Sunu's fate, see Menegon, "Religious and Political Martyrdom," 1–4.

19 Archives Propaganda Fide, Scitture riferite nei Congressi (Letters of Internal Councils), Indie Orientali e Cina, vol. 18, 1726, "Memorie della Cina del 1726," (seconda via), 426r–537v. On the Propaganda Fide's information gathering and exchange, see Menegon, "Interlopers," 46–52.

20 "Extract of a Letter from Canton, dated the 2d of January, 1727," *Daily Post*, December 28, 1728.

21 There had been earlier moments of proscription and exile which also resulted in missionaries in Canton receiving gazettes from Beijing, such as the "Canton detention" of 1665–1671. See Golvers, "Earliest Examples," 325–26 and Bosmans, "Lettres annuelles," 53–58.

22 This is a point of contrast with early modern modes of diplomacy adopted by Europeans in the Ottoman empire. Ghobrial, *Whispers of Cities*, 14–15.

23 "Lettre du Père Contancin," (December 15, 1727), in *Lettres édifiantes* (1781), 21:96.

24 Contancin to Souciet, December 2, 1725, *Lettres édifiantes* (1728), 18:428–63. The papal missionaries of the Propaganda Fide also noted the seemingly omniscient attention of the emperor to the care of his people in an extensive

report on the contents of the gazettes written in 1728. Archives Propaganda Fide, Letters of Internal Councils, Indie Orientali e Cina, vol. 19 (1727–28), "Ristretto di varie notizie cavate dale Gazzette impresse in Pekino nel 1728 in supplimento delle Memorie della Cina del medemo anno per la SCPF," 717r–731v.

25 Contancin to Souciet, December 2, 1725. *Lettres édifiantes* (1728), 18:430–434.

26 *Lettres édifiantes* (1728), 18:434. Contancin's description was widely read and cited. See for example De Mailla, *Histoire générale*, 11:523n1.

27 Contancin to Souciet, December 2, 1725, *Lettres édifiantes* (1728), 18:440–41.

28 In this era, "gazette" could refer to a privately published newssheet, or, increasingly, to a news outlet associated with state authority, funding, and agendas. Infelise, "News Networks," 54.

29 Pettegree, *Invention of News*, 200–7.

30 Pettegree, *Invention of News*, 238; Handover, *History of the London Gazette*; Feyel, "Gazette de France," 443–49.

31 The full title of the collection is *Lettres édifiantes et curieuses écrites des Missions étrangères de la Compagnie de Jésus*. Du Halde edited the China volumes of the collection. Landry-Deron, *La preuve par la Chine*, 25.

32 For the reading notes of Michel Leroux-Deshauterayes (1724–1795), an eighteenth-century French scholar of oriental languages, see BnF, "Recueil des pieces sur la Chine," (excerpt from letter on gazettes on page 102v). On the influence of the *Lettres édifiantes* on Enlightenment scientific discussions on China, see Hsia, *Sojourners in a Strange Land*, 130.

33 Percy, *Hao Kiou Choaan*, 13–16; see Porter, *Chinese Taste*, 162.

34 The full titles are *Description géographique, historique, chronologique, politique, et physique de l'empire de la Chine et de la Tartarie chinoise* and *Histoire générale de la Chine, ou Annales de cet empire*. De Mailla, *Histoire générale*, 11:523n1. The eleventh volume of De Mailla's *Histoire générale* was compiled by Michel Leroux-Deshauterayes and drew extensively on the missionary letters. Irwin, "Notes on the Source of de Mailla," 98.

35 Du Halde, *Description géographique*, 1:550–53. Contancin collaborated to review the manuscript of the *Description géographique*. Landry-Deron, *La preuve par la Chine*, 126–31. For Du Halde's praise of Contancin's writings, see *Description géographique*, 1:ix–x.

36 Brooks, trans., *The General History of China* (London: John Watts, 1736); Green and Guthrie, trans., *A Description of China* (London: Edward Cave, 1738–41); Budgell, "The State of Literature in Foreign Parts, Extract of a Letter from Canton in China," in *The Bee*, 798–802; 848–850; 1016–20; 1224–1229; 1549–1551. On Budgell and his reading of the *Lettres édifiantes* and Du Halde, see Fan, "Chinese Fables," 142–43.

37 Du Halde, *Description géographique*, 2:42–3.

38 Marat, *Plan de Législation*, 85.

39 Quesnay, *Œuvres économiques et philosophiques*, 598.

40 Voltaire, *Essai sur les moeurs*, 1:210.

41 Schimmelpenninck van der Oye, *Russian Orientalism*, 51–52; Chen, *Chinese Law in Imperial Eyes*, 126.
42 Denis Diderot (1713–1784), curator of the massive *Encyclopédie* project, criticized the enthusiastic portrait of China espoused by Voltaire and the Sinophiles. Hung, "Orientalist Knowledge," 262.
43 Rydholm, "China and the World's First Freedom of Information Act," 48–52.
44 Mustonen, *World's First Freedom of Information Act*. Despite this claim, the scope and influence of the law was limited. Fenster, *Transparency Fix*, 23.
45 Hsia, "Jesuit Survival and Restoration in China," 247–48.
46 The full title was *Mémoires concernant l'histoire, les sciences, les arts, les moeurs, les usages, &c. des Chinois, Par les Missionnaires de Pékin*. A final volume was published in 1814. Dehergne, "Une grande collection," 267–98; Silvestre de Sacy, *Henri Bertin*, 172.
47 On the correspondents, see Huard and Wong, "Les enquêtes françaises," 149.
48 On restrained power, see Osterhammel, *Unfabling the East*, 371–76. Amiot described the Chinese gazettes as far better controlled than the "pell-mell" gazettes of Europe, paralleling the comparison between European and Chinese gazettes made sixty years earlier by Contancin. Amiot, "Extrait d'une lettre écrite de Péking le 25 janv. 1787," *Mémoires*, 14:524.
49 BnF, Chinois 2216. For Amiot's notes on these cases, see BnF, Bréquigny 3, 90–104 (letter dated July 5, 1779).
50 BnF, Bréquigny 10, 2. The origins of this claim are unclear. The BnF catalog suggests that the correspondence and gazette copies in this fond were authored by Amiot, but Bourgeois referred specifically to his translations in a letter to Bréquigny, excerpted in Walter, *La Troisième Mort des Missions*, 330–1.
51 BnF, Bréquigny 10, 214.
52 Silvestre de Sacy, *Henri Bertin*, 166–173.
53 BnF, Arsenal MS 5790, Letter of July 14, 1786.
54 BnF, Arsenal MS 5790, Letter of August 1, 1786.
55 BnF Arsenal, MS 5790. Letter of July 14, 1786; the edicts on street performers were published in the gazette on February 18, 1786 (QL 51/01/20). On the changing concept of the "despot" and especially Montesquieu's influence, see Osterhammel, *Unfabling the East*, 340–62.
56 Mungello, *Great Encounter*, 152; Harrison, *Interpreters* (manuscript). See Henrietta Harrison's forthcoming work on eighteenth-century translators for a nuanced view of relationships between Chinese converts and English translators and diplomats.
57 Si, "Breaking Through the 'Jargon' Barrier," 349–52.
58 See Staunton, *Memoirs*, 9–17.
59 Staunton, *Memoirs*, 26–27; 33; 35–36.
60 SOAS, CWM/LMS/South China/Incoming/Box 1B. "Instructions to Robert Morrison," 20 Jan 1807; Su, "Printing Presses of the London Missionary Society," ch. 2.

61 Harrison, *Interpreters*.

62 BL, IOR/G/12/284, Secret Letter of April 18, 1822.

63 In December 1812, the Select Committee sent to London "a Book containing Translations from Chinese Official Documents." SOAS, CWM/LMS. Copies of Correspondence Relating to Morrison. Extract Letter from Canton, dated December 31, 1812; BL, "Official Reports"; BL, IOR MSS D562/14, IOR MSS D562/15, IOR MSS D562/16; *Translations from the Original Chinese*. In 1815, they sent fifty copies of Morrison's translation of an imperial edict from the court gazette (JQ 19/10/02). The committee found the edict to be "an interesting and important, as well as (we regret to observe) a most unfavourable picture of the internal administration of the great Empire." BL, IOR/G/12/20, ff. 505–10, "Extract of Letter from the Select Committee of Supercargoes of Canton," March 12, 1815.

64 Stifler, "Language Students," 80n123.

65 SOAS, CWM/LMS. Journals of R. Morrison, Journal 6. Canton, 1808; Robert Morrison to LMS, Jan 1808.

66 For example, the notice of an earthquake in Beijing in *Daily Courant*, April 26, 1722, and the discussions of gazettes in Budgell's *Bee* in 1733; "Extract from the Pekin Gazette," *Gazetteer and New Daily Advertiser*, Feb. 17, 1769; These references ramped up in the aftermath of the Macartney mission of 1793: "Further Particulars of the Chinese Embassy," *London Chronicle*, Aug. 5, 1794–Aug. 7, 1794; "Chinese Embassy," *Sun*, Aug. 4, 1794; "Chinese Embassy," *Morning Chronicle*, Aug. 4, 1794; "Embassy to China," *The Register of the Times, or: Political Museum* (1794), 1:201–3; "Embassy to China," *Lloyd's Evening Post*, Aug. 6, 1794; "Chinese Embassy," *Whitehall Evening Post*, Aug. 5, 1794.

67 Staunton later wrote, "I was in constant communication with [Morrison], either personally or by letter. I was invariably his *friend* and *advocate*, and, considering the official position I held in China, I might add *patron*." Staunton, *Memoirs*, 36.

68 Staunton, *Narrative of the Chinese Embassy*, xxi; 258–318; on the importance of the White Lotus Rebellion and the Jiaqing emperor's actions at the beginning of his reign, see Rowe, *China's Last Empire*, 182–83; Wensheng Wang, *White Lotus Rebels*. The excerpts translated by Staunton do not refer to the purge of Heshen nor the institutional changes highlighted by Wang, despite the overlap in time period.

69 Morrison had sent a translated item to the Edinburgh *Missionary Journal* in 1813, but as he related, "The following Edict was translated from the Chinese into Spanish, by a Romish Missionary at Macao; and translated out of Spanish into English. I have not seen the original Chinese paper. I have seen several papers in the Pekin Gazette; of which the following is indeed to substance." "China. Edict against Christianity," 18.

70 The *Quarterly Review*, founded in 1809, was one of the two most influential English journals of the time (the other was its rival, the *Edinburgh Review*).

71 "Translations from the Original Chinese," 409.

72 In St. Petersburg, the Asian Museum (established 1818), included an archive of books and documents sourced from the Middle East, South Asia, and East Asia that was closely tied to state pursuits.

73 "Gazettes de l'empire de la Chine," 239–52. See also the serialized excerpts in *Journal Asiatique* in 1833–34: "Gazette chinoise" and "Gazette chinoise (suite et fin)." Prominent French sinologists Jean-Pierre Abel-Rémusat (1788–1832) and Stanislas Julien (1797–1873) also added files of Daoguang-era capital and provincial gazettes published in Canton to the Chinese holdings of the Bibliothèque nationale in France. Courant, *Catalogue des livres chinois*, 130.

74 "Proceedings of the Royal Asiatic Society," 67; "Proceedings of the Royal Asiatic Society," 223; Davis, "Extracts from the Peking Gazette," 386–412. Extracts for 1825 were read on Nov. 4, 1826. "Proceedings of the Royal Asiatic Society," 691.

75 Timkovskii, *Travels of the Russian Mission*, 2:12–13; Schilling corresponded with notable sinologists of the day, including Julius Klaproth (1783–1835) and Stephen Endlicher (1804–1849), librarian of the royal library in Vienna. The gazettes are listed as "Pekinger Staatszeitung" in Endlicher's 1837 catalog for the royal library in Vienna. They remain at the Austrian National Library. See Endlicher, *Übersicht*, 126. Another set of gazettes, possibly belonging to Schilling, ended up in the imperial library of St. Petersburg (now the National Library of Russia). See Iakhontov and Krol, *Kitaĭskie rukopisi*, 176–77. Schilling also gifted gazettes dated to 1823 to Alexander von Humboldt. *Allgemeine preußische Staats-Zeitung*, May 10, 1830.

76 A file of gazettes purchased in Canton by scholar Karl Friedrich Neumann (1793–1870) is now located in the Bavarian Staatsbibliothek in Munich. Muffat, *Die königliche Hof- und Staats-Bibliothek*, 1:81; "Professor Neumanns Sammlungen aus China," 81–82. On Neumann, see *Allgemeine Deutsche Biographie* 23:529–30.

77 Titles used in German included *Hofzeitung* and *Pekinger Staatszeitung*.

78 "Very Late from China," *New York Herald*, January 20, 1845.

79 The *Asiatic Journal and Monthly Miscellany* was a London journal founded in 1816 under the auspices of the East India Company.

80 After John Slade became editor of the *Canton Register*, he and Morrison shared translation duties. Slade continued after Morrison's death. Slade, *Narrative of the Late Proceedings*, 13–14.

81 On the loss of Morrison as a translator of gazettes, see *Canton Press*, November 28, 1835. See also *Canton Register*, January 5, 1836; *Canton Press*, October 6, 1838, October 20, 1838, February 16, 1839.

82 *Canton Register*, July 12, 1828. The editor of the *Canton Register* responded defensively to the critical stabs made by B. C. D., and continued to print gazette updates as before.

83 *Morning Chronicle*, September 8, 1827; March 3, 1827; April 4, 1827; February 2, 1828; *Times* (London), June 5, 1827. One Havana newspaper published a notice on the end of the insurrection under the heading of "RUSIA." *Noticioso Mercantil*, November 14, 1828.

84 King and Clarke, *China-Coast Newspapers*, 62.

85 John Robert Morrison was the son of missionary John Morrison. Pottinger to Earl of Aberdeen, Hong Kong, July 31, 1843, quoted in Staunton, *Memoirs*, 216.

86 "Wade, Sir Thomas Francis," *Dictionary of National Biography*, 420. For an account of Wade's diplomatic career, see Cooley, *T. F. Wade in China*.

87 Wade, *Note*. See also Wade, *Decree of the Emperor of China*.

88 *North China Herald*, August 24, 1850; "Chinese Gleanings," *Daily News*, September 25, 1850; *Journal des débats*, October 27, 1850.

89 Wade, *Note*, 3–4.

90 Chen, *Chinese Law in Imperial Eyes*, 106.

91 Wade, *Note*, 5–6.

92 Wade, *Note*, 30–39 (quote on 31). Wade's comments on legal cases covered in the gazette suggest that he had read and followed Staunton's discussion of the Qing code.

93 Wade used samples from the gazette to compile his "New Proposals" (*Xin yi lüe lun*), presented to the Qing throne in 1866. Smith, Fairbank, and Bruner, *Robert Hart*, 288–89.

94 TNA, FO 233/58/7, "Peking Gazette," April 4, 1872. The British Library collection was inherited from the Foreign Office. Because the gazettes were understood as "State Papers," they were transferred from the Peking Legation to the British Museum in 1958. Since the British Library also holds the East India Company archives, pre-1834 editions held by the East India Company may have been merged with the Foreign Office holdings. Another hypothesis is that these holdings were associated with the interpreters who transferred from Company to diplomatic service. See Pong, "Kwangtung Provincial Archives," 139–43; Ocko, "British Museum's Peking Gazette," 35–49; and Coates, "Documents in Chinese."

95 Through the twentieth century, Chinese writers always produced the written Chinese versions of dispatches that went out and the archived transcriptions of Chinese documents. They also converted written or oral explanations into documentary language. See Coates, *China Consuls*, 34–35.

96 Translator and diplomat Herbert Giles (1845–1935) wrote in his memoirs, "The future historian, who uses the existing translations from *Peking Gazettes* of by-gone years, may well be warned against accepting them with implicit confidence" due to the frequent inaccuracy of student translations. Aylmer, "Memoirs of H. A. Giles," 28.

97 Porter, *From Belfast to Peking*, 128, 66.

98 SOAS, Correspondence, Papers, and Diaries of Sir Chaloner Alabaster, Diary of 1856.

99 Wilkinson, *English Student-Life at Peking*, 91–92.

100 Meadows, *Desultory Notes*, 17, quoted in Hirth, *Chinese Documentary Style*, 1; Wade, *Yü-yen tzŭ-erh-chi*, iii. Meadows learned Chinese from Karl Neumann. Meadows, *Desultory Notes*, viii.

101 Wade, *Wên-chien tzŭ erh chi*, 3:iii.

102 The Harvard Series began with Fairbank's 1952 *Introductory Syllabus*, and was succeeded by Kuhn's two-part *Introduction to Ch'ing Documents* (1986), of which only the first part was published and circulated.
103 Library of Congress, Caleb Cushing Papers, *Jingchao* (42 volumes, 1842–43) and *Dufu xian yuanbao* (twenty-five single-page issues).
104 Bayly, *Empire and Information*, 56–90.
105 Simpson, "Sketches in China," *Illustrated London News*, March 22, 1873.
106 Simpson, *Meeting the Sun*, vi.
107 Simpson, "Sketches in China," *Illustrated London News*, March 22, 1873; Simpson, *Meeting the Sun*, 269–71.
108 Henry Wadsworth Longfellow Family Papers, Box 13, no.70.
109 New York Public Library, James Legge Collection, OVQ 09-539. See Wilkinson's comments in his memoir of student life. Wilkinson, *English Student-Life at Peking*, 91–98.
110 Michael, *Catalogue of the Exhibit*, 12.
111 *Tizou quangao* (Harvard Yenching Library, XF 09/04/03).
112 "February Meeting," 473. See Peabody, *Memoir of Charles Burroughs*.
113 National Library of Australia, *Dichao zeyao*, http://nla.gov.au/nla.obj-47035802.
114 Wu, "Mary Clabaugh Wright," 134–35.
115 *Jingbao* (Princeton University Library, TZ 03/12/01).
116 Simpson, *Meeting the Sun*, 270.

CHAPTER 6: INFORMATION WARS

1 Mokros, "Documentary Authority."
2 Spence, *God's Chinese Son*; Wooldridge, *City of Virtues*; Kim, *Holy War in China*; Esherick, *The Origins of the Boxer Uprising*.
3 Kuhn, *Rebellion and Its Enemies*; Rankin, *Elite Activism*; Halsey, *Quest for Power*.
4 BL, Peking Gazette Collection, 1854/6.
5 Liu Wenpeng, "Titang kao"; Fairbank and Teng, "Transmission of Ch'ing Documents," 35–39. For a contemporary account, see Milne, "Government Post," *North China Herald*, October 16, 1850.
6 "Peking Gazettes," *North China Herald*, July 9, 1853; August 27, 1853; December 17, 1853; March 24, 1855; March 8, 1856; September 27, 1856; October 25, 1856; April 7, 1860.
7 NPM, JJD, XF 02/11/19, 087570; *QSL-XF*, 76:995b (XF 2/11/19).
8 *QSL-XF*, 119:40b (XF 04/01/22).
9 For a similar document published without protest, see *North China Herald*, September 26–27, 1850.
10 FHA, LFZZ, 03-9677-002 (XF 03/12/19); LFZZ, 03-9677-004 (XF 03/12/20); LFZZ, 03-4578-062 (XF 03/12/22); SYD box 1176, ce 3 (XF 03/12/24); LFZZ, 03-9677-003; 03-9677-006; 03-9677-007; 03-9677-009 (all XF 03/12/26); ZPZZ

04-01-12-0480-115 (XF 04/01/12). BL, Peking Gazette Collection, Boxes 20–23 (XF 3); *North China Herald*, February 18, 1854; February 25, 1854; April 1, 1854.

11 On the use of shrines, gates, and other forms of state-led commemoration to publicize orthodox goals, see Meyer-Fong, *What Remains*, 135–55.

12 On the identification of Taiping sympathizers and spies, see Meyer-Fong, "To Know the Enemy," 405–6.

13 BL, Peking Gazette Collection, 1853/2(1) (XF 03/02/01); 1853/3(1) (XF 03/03/09); 1853/3(1) (XF 03/03/17); 1853/4(1) (XF 03/04/03-04); 1853/4(2) (XF 03/04/15–16), 1853/4(2) (XF 03/04/23–24); 1853/5 (XF 03/05/05); 1853/5 (XF 03/05/20); 1853/6(2) (XF 03/06/10–11).

14 FHA, ZPZZ, 04-01-01-0848-067 (XF 03/12/04). For the court's response, see FHA, Shangyu dang, box 1176, ce 3 (court letter, XF 03/12/26). An abridged version is contained in *QSL-XF*, 126:836b–871a (XF 03/12/26).

15 *QSL-XF*, 119:40b (XF 04/01/22).

16 Based on dates in *Bombay Times* and London *Times*.

17 Medhurst, "Letter to Editor," *North China Herald*, April 5, 1856.

18 Wade, *Note*, 30–38.

19 *North China Herald*, November 10, 1855; *North China Herald*, March 7, 1857.

20 For "bloody and glorious victories," see *North China Herald*, October 11, 1856.

21 *North China Herald*, December 17, 1853.

22 *China Mail*, February 3, 1853; February 14, 1856. King and Clarke, *China-Coast Newspapers*, 22; 51–52.

23 King and Clarke, *China-Coast Newspapers*, 51.

24 TNA, FO 228/154. Medhurst, "Memorandum on the Origin and Progress of the Kwangse Rebellion," March 8, 1853; Medhurst, *Pamphlets Issued by the Chinese Insurgents*.

25 A similar transition in the British valuation of Mughal court diaries happened in nineteenth-century India. See Fisher, "Office of Akhbār Nawīs," 76.

26 Medhurst, "Letter to the Editor," *North China Herald*, April 5, 1856. The comparison to the *Moniteur* also appears in Huc, *L'Empire chinois*, 105–7. Huc's description mainly drew on Contancin's description in the *Lettres édifiantes*, with the addition of his comment about the *Moniteur* and a digression on the political sentiments of the population.

27 Britton, *Chinese Periodical Press*, 8.

28 An 1841 survey of global newspapers referred to official gazettes "read by authority" in England, France, Germany, Belgium, the Netherlands, Switzerland, Russia, Spain, Portugal, Greece, Gibraltar, Turkey, Egypt, the Island of Bourbon [Réunion], Persia, India, Prince of Wales's Island [Malaysia], China, Australia, New Zealand, Canada, Bermuda, the Bahamas, Barbados, St. Kitt's, Trinidad, British Guiana, French Guiana, and Mexico. Simmonds, "Statistics of Newspapers in Various Countries," 113–36. Western press discussions of the gazette echo the language of authority. For example, "The whole contents of the *Pekin Gazette* are composed of documents issued by authority, and 'the

liberty of the press' consists only in being allowed to make copies," in "Newspapers in China," *Glasgow Herald*, February 28, 1866.

29 In colonial India, the British considered items printed in government gazettes to be facts "of a public nature." Syed and Woodroffe, *Law of Evidence Applicable to British India*, 417–18. While the *Qing Code* and legal texts did not articulate this relationship between gazette publication and use as legal evidence, gazette entries were acknowledged in the bureaucracy as valid sources of evidence.

30 For a general narrative, see Platt, *Autumn in the Heavenly Kingdom*, 96–110.

31 Platt, *Autumn in the Heavenly Kingdom*, 28–29.

32 *North China Herald*, February 26, 1859.

33 TNA, FO 233/88, Translation, Nov. 12, 1860.

34 TNA, FO 682/1993/86, Prince Gong to Bruce, Nov. 16, 1860.

35 Imperial Maritime Customs, ed., *Treaties, Conventions, Etc.*, 1:624.

36 Burlingame to Seward, November 6, 1863, in *Foreign Relations of the United States.*

37 Another example comes from Shanghai, where French residents were displeased with official refusals to specifically acknowledge French military assistance in the city's Small Swords Uprising (1853–1855). Roskam, *Improvised City*, 73.

38 Banno, *China and the West.*

39 Bruce to Earl of Malmesbury, *London Gazette*, October 4, 1859.

40 Academia Sinica, Zongli Yamen Archive, 01-02-005-03-022 (XF 08/09/12); 01-02-007-03-077 (XF 08/09/12).

41 Li Ciming, *Yue man tang riji*, 2355 (TZ 2/5/29).

42 Academia Sinica, Zongli Yamen Archive, 01-03-003-01-040 through 01-03-003-01-49.

43 TNA, FO 233/62, Memo of February 22, 1872.

44 Around 1876, in response to provincial requests, the court apparently approved the publication of "abstracts" of an increased number of memorials, as well as lists of military appointments. *North-China Daily News*, January 28, 1876.

45 This strategy was adapted in specific cases, not as a general policy. The Qing court continued to deliberately represent its tributary relations with Chosŏn Korea in the court gazette. Joo, "Remaking a Tributary Relationship," 128–31.

46 1,735 Chinese-language newspapers were founded between 1833 and 1911, about a quarter of them in Shanghai. Shi He, *Zhongguo jindai baokan minglu*. For general histories of the early Chinese press written in the early twentieth century, see Britton, *Chinese Periodical Press* and Ge Gongzhen, *Zhongguo baoxue shi*. For more recent studies, see Fang Hanqi, *Zhongguo xinwen shiye*; Wagner, "Early Chinese Newspapers." On *Shenbao*, see Gentz, "Useful Knowledge," 51–53 and especially Mittler, *Newspaper for China*. On *Shenbao*'s role in organizing national and/or localist political sentiment, see Rankin, "Alarming Crises/Enticing Possibilities," and *Elite Activism*. For debates on the role of the press in the articulation of new public-minded concerns in

the late Qing, see contributions by Rowe, Wakeman, and Rankin, in *Modern China* 19, no.2 (1993).

47 Mittler, *Newspaper for China*, 31–33.

48 Lee and Nathan, "Beginnings of Mass Culture."

49 See Mittler, "Domesticating an Alien Medium," 14–15.

50 "Dibao bie yu xinbao lun," *Shenbao*, July 13, 1872 (see Mittler, "Domesticating an Alien Medium," 16 and 30–1 for a reading of this editorial). Many early editorials were unsigned collaborative efforts between the publisher, Ernest Major, and an editor, Wu Zirang. Gentz, "Useful Knowledge," 51–55. See also Wagner, "Free Flow of Communication," 125–31.

51 Mittler, "Domesticating an Alien Medium," 18, 31.

52 *Jiaohui xinbao* was the predecessor of *Wanguo gongbao*. It received gazettes from Beijing via the missionary translator W. A. P. Martin (1827–1916) and his longtime teacher, the Ningbo native Cao Ziyu. For *Jinhua ribao*'s coverage, see their 1911 application to the Ministry of Civil Affairs in "Wan Qing chuangban baokan shiliao (3)," 70.

53 This continued through the last year of the dynasty, as shown by the applications made by newspapers to the Ministry of Civil Affairs under the new press laws. For applications made between 1908 and 1911, see "Wan Qing chuangban baozhi shiliao (2)," 61–79. Newspapers in Hong Kong printed only selections. Gentz, "Useful Knowledge," 74.

54 "Jingbao," *Shenbao*, May 2, 1872. An undated gazette was also included in *Shenbao*'s first issue on May 30, 1872.

55 "Lun jingbao gui su bu gui chi," *Shenbao*, March 4, 1882.

56 *Shenbao* regularly reprinted provincial gazettes from Liangjiang, Jiangsu, Zhejiang and Jiangxi, and less frequent reports from Fujian, Guangdong, and Hubei.

57 Advertisement for sales at the Hangzhou gazette outlet run by Tao Wenyan ran in *Shenbao* throughout October 1872. In Beijing, *Shenbao* was sold at Juxing Baofang through the summer of 1873. For updated lists of outlets in the 1890s, see "Waibu shou bao chu," *Shenbao*, August 10, 1892, and January 11, 1895.

58 Gentz, "Useful Knowledge," 73.

59 "Lun ribao," *Shenbao*, November 7, 1874.

60 The missionary Timothy Richard suggested in his memoirs that the *Sino-Foreign News* (Zhongwai jiwen) was reprinted in the "Peking Gazette offices" in Beijing. Richard, *Forty-Five Years in China*, 245; Mittler, *Newspaper for China*, 47–48.

61 "Wan Qing chuangban baozhi ziliao," 70–71.

62 *Yuzhe huicun* included a larger selection of memorials than did traditional gazette formats. Fang Hanqi, *Zhongguo xinwen shiye*, 218–19. Xiehua Book Bureau continued to operate through the early Republican era and acted as an agent for Commercial Press publications. See *Shangwu yinshu guan chuban jiaoke shumu*; Huang Zhuoming, *Zhongguo gudai baozhi*, 161–62; Moll

Murata, *State and Crafts*, 233. Part of their facility in Liulichang burned down in 1899. "Jingshi huojing," *Shenbao*, December 16, 1899.

63 Another metallic-type publisher opened in early 1897, promising faster and cheaper official news than traditional formats. "Xin kai baofang," *Hubao*, December 20, 1896.

64 For example, *Dichao zeyao*, published by Tongwen Guan, 1903. Stanford University Library.

65 On the use of steamboat and telegraph transport for official communications with Beijing, see Yoon, "Grand Council," 132–96. The domestic telegraph network was complete in 1897. Thompson, "The Wire," 402.

66 Xu Qi, *Yue xue riji*, juan 1.

67 On the ways that telegraphy rendered state communications networks immaterial (but material upon their breakdown), see Thompson, "The Wire," 407–8.

68 Binchun, *Ge guo riji huibian*, 142:217.

69 Elman, *Cultural History of Civil Examinations*, 578–608.

70 Gentz, "From News," 55–79.

71 "Kuochong baowu yi," *Shenbao*, October 28, 1895.

72 TNA, FO 233/58/18. Mayers, "Memorandum on the 'Peking Gazette,'" April 14, 1874.

73 "Lun huyi dang qing jian Liu Gong zhuanci," *Shenbao*, May 6, 1873.

74 "Li Guangzhao an lüe," *Shenbao*, October 22, 1874. See Mokros, "Reconstructing the Imperial Retreat," 98.

75 See Day, *Qing Travelers*.

76 Zhang Deyi, *Liu shu qi*, 86–106 (GX 23/07/05).

77 Excerpts and translations from foreign newspapers are categorized by topic in the Zongli Yamen archives.

78 Figdor, "Newspapers and Their Regulation," 3–8.

79 *North-China Daily News*, May 20, 1876, 467.

80 This paper was the predecessor of today's *Mainichi shinbun*. Fujiwara, "Fūsetsudome and Political Awareness," 349.

81 Altman, "The Press," 231–40. The Korean court established a gazette the following year. *North China Herald*, January 9, 1884.

82 Huffman, *Creating a Public*, 75–77.

83 TNA, FO 233/58/18. Mayers, "Memorandum on the 'Peking Gazette,'" April 14, 1874.

84 Wook Yoon, "Dashed Expectations," 844–47.

85 For an influential preliminary account of "mass" journalism and fiction, see Lee and Nathan, "Beginnings of Mass Culture," 360.

86 Joo, "Remaking a Tributary Relationship," 131.

87 Christopher Reed, "Re/Collecting the Sources," 163–69. A few *Dianshizhai* articles specifically pointed out gaps and lapses in the gazette coverage. *Dianshizhai Pictorial* had begun sending journalist and artists to the war front during the Sino-French War. Ye, *Dianshizhai Pictorial*, 4–9.

88 *Gazette of the Book Bureau* (*Guan shuju huibao*), an occasional publication of the Books Bureau (Guan Shuju) in Beijing, has been misidentified as an early official gazette (e.g., Li Siyi, "Qingmo 10 nian guanbao huodong gaimao," 128). However, this publication, created and utilized primarily by the Zongli Yamen, contained only digests of translated foreign news and books. See Sun Jia'nai memorial in "Jingbao quanlu," *Shenbao*, August 11, 1898; for an excerpt, see "Lun jiangshi zhi yongming shi hu guo'en zhi houbo," *Shenbao*, April 28, 1898.

89 Yoon, "Literati-Journalists," 48–54.

90 Vittinghoff, "Unity vs. Uniformity," 115, 117–18.

91 Kang Youwei also mentioned this classical practice in his memorial proposing that the *Shiwu bao* be made an official paper. "Qing she Shanghai *Shiwu bao* wei guanbao," in Jiang Yihua and Zhang Ronghua, *Kang Youwei quanji*, 331–32. Rudolf Wagner points out that these classical references were basically tropes by this time. Wagner, "Classic Paving the Way," 89–92.

92 Liang Qichao, "Lun baoguan youyi yu guoshi," *Shiwu bao*, Aug. 1896; "Kai she baoguan," *Quanxue bao* 1, GX 21/11/28 (January 12, 1896).

93 For analysis of Liang's essay, see Judge, *Print and Politics*, 22; Mittler, "Domesticating an Alien Medium," 19–20.

94 Kwong, *Mosaic of the Hundred Days*, 188–99; Yoon, "Literati-Journalists," 71–76. On the breakdown of unity within the *Chinese Progress* establishment, see Vittinghoff, "Unity vs. Uniformity," 97–98. See also Chen Qingnian, *Wuxu yihai*, 87–91, 100–2.

95 "Ben guan jiefeng dian yin," *Shenbao*, Aug. 12, 1898.

96 Harris, *Peking Gazette*, 302; Vittinghoff, "Unity vs. Uniformity," 100; *North China Herald*, October 17, 1898.

97 For documents relating to the establishment of the document bureaus, which originated from a Zongli Yamen system for retrieving and exchanging communications to envoys abroad, see "Qingmo gedi kaishe wenbao ju." In this system, the task of physically transporting documents and mail was given over to private shipping companies and later the Imperial Post Office, a project of the Imperial Customs Service. See Harris, "Post Office and State Formation," 110–15. The establishment of document bureaus also involved the abolition of the position of capital communications liaisons, which had long become a profitable sinecure position. See Mokros, "Spies and Postmen," 42–43.

98 *Beiyang Gazette* was not the first provincial gazette, but it was among the most significant. Japan was an important model for new-style gazettes. In 1905, Sichuan authorities sent a mission to Japan to solicit workers experienced with various types of printing technologies to come to the province to work on gazette publishing as well as the printing of paper money, stock certificates, and other types of documents. "Wan Qing chuangban baokan shiliao (1)," 63.

99 Thompson, "New-Style Gazettes," 82–86.

100 *Beiyang guanbao*, no. 1, preface 1.

101 *Beiyang guanbao*, no. 2, preface 3.

102 *Qiangxue bao*, no. 1 (GX 21/11/28). The journal published three issues. Published in Shanghai, it was associated with the Self-Strengthening Study Society (*Qiangxue hui*), a group sponsored by Zhang Zhidong with branches in Shanghai and Beijing. See Judge, *Print and Politics*, 21.

103 The circulation of most papers was between five thousand and ten thousand copies. This was not small, but was dwarfed by industry leaders like *Shenbao*. Li Siyi, "Qing mo 10 nian guanbao," 136.

104 *Beiyang guanbao* (May 2, 1903), in Jiang Yasha, *Qingmo guanbao huibian*, 1:11.

105 Li Siyi, "Qing mo 10 nian guanbao," 137–38.

106 "Yunnan zongdu Li Shiyi wei *Yunnan guanbao* gailiang faxing qing yun li an shi zhi minzheng bu ziwen," in "Wan Qing chuangban baokan shiliao (3)," 71–72.

107 FHA, LFZZ, 03-5615-038 (GX 24/04/03).

108 Rowe, *China's Last Empire*, 256–60; for a standard overview, see Ichiko, "Political and Institutional Reform," 376–96; for a sample of gazette entries covering the reforms see Harris, *Peking Gazette*, 324–41.

109 This proposal was the origin of the *Guangxu zhengyao* compilation published in 1909. Shen Tongsheng, *Guangxu zhengyao*, 1:1a, 29:12b.

110 Waiwu Bu, 02-015-02-006 (GX 33/05/02).

111 *Xian zheng biancha guan zouding baolü li ce*, item 13; see also Yu Heng, *Da Qing baolü zhi yanjiu*.

112 The Qing court had recently become embroiled in prosecutions of newspapers, including the closure of Wang Kangnian's short-lived newspaper *Jingbao* in Beijing for reputedly impugning Prince Qing as corrupt. *Shenbao*, "Zhuan dian," August 28, 1907, "Jingbao tingzhi chuban zhi ge yuanyin," *Shenbao*, September 3, 1907 and "Baolü zhi jinhua," *Shenbao*, September 19, 1907.

113 FHA, LFZZ, 03-9285-011 (GX 32/10/30?); "Zou she yinshua guanbao ju pian," *Zhongguo jindai chuban shiliao*, 33–34.

114 "Ben guan gongdu," *Zhengzhi guanbao*, GX 32/11/04 (December 19, 1906). This order was apparently not obeyed and was reiterated the next year: "Xianzheng biancha guan wei *Zhengzhi guanbao* chuban riqi bing qing ting tong shi ge baokan shi pian," (GX 33/09/16), in "Wan Qing chuangban baokan shiliao (1)," 69. See also "Neige guanbao faxing zhangcheng shiyao," *Neige guanbao* (XT 03/08/29). Shortly after the establishment of the *Zhengzhi guanbao* in late 1907, the Council of Constitutional Affairs (Xianzheng Biancha Guan) issued an order banning the two most prominent metallic type gazette publishers in Beijing from publishing gazettes.

115 *Jingbao (dibao)*, vols.152–63 and *Dichao*, vols.118–20, both contain gazettes published between 1907 and June 1911. These late gazettes were not printed with wooden movable type. According to Fang Hanqi, Juxing Baofang operated until 1921, although it acted as a distributor for other city papers and did not publish its own gazettes any longer. Fang Hanqi, *Zhongguo xinwen shiye*, 206.

116 "Ben qi fengmian," 1–2; "Yingyin 'Zhengfu gongbao' de shuoming," in *Zhengfu gongbao.*

117 "The Death of the Marquis Tseng," *North China Herald*, May 30, 1890. Zeng died on April 12. The *North China Herald* first reported his death on April 18.

118 See obituary of Zeng Jize in *Times*, April 15, 1890.

119 In addition, many Western newspapers were confused by reports of the court-ordered shuttering of *Jingbao*, a paper of the same title published by the activist intellectual Wang Kangnian. See references in note 112.

120 "The 'Peking Gazette,'" *North China Herald*, August 30, 1907; "Pekin Gazette No More," *The Caucasian*, October 29, 1907; "History Can Now Be Corrected," *New York Times*, October 29, 1907.

121 "History Can Now Be Corrected," *New York Times*, October 29, 1907.

122 Newspapers cited a bevy of dates for the origin of the gazette, including "several thousand years [ago]," "the Tang dynasty," 713, 760, "the 9th century," 911 A.D., 1340, 1361, and other arbitrary dates.

123 "The Esteemed Peking Gazette," *Chicago Daily Tribune*, October 29, 1907.

CONCLUSION. THE TRUE STORY OF THE PEKING GAZETTE

1 Fenster, *Transparency Fix*; Heald, "Varieties of Transparency."

2 Liu, *Communications and National Integration*; Schurmann, *Ideology and Organization*, 62–68; Johnson, "Beneath the Propaganda State." On the twenty-first century, see Stockmann, *Media Commercialization and Authoritarian Rule*; and Repnikova, *Media Politics in China.*

3 On the center, among others, see Bartlett, *Monarchs and Ministers*; and Kuhn, *Soulstealers.* On local administration, see Macauley, *Social Power and Legal Culture*; and Huang, *Civil Justice in China.* On ethnicity, culture, and the frontier, see Crossley, *Transparent Mirror*; Elliott, *Manchu Way*; Perdue, *China Marches West*; and Rawski, *Last Emperors.*

4 Halsey, *Quest for Power*; Wang, *White Lotus Rebels*; see also Rowe, "Significance of the Qianlong-Jiaqing Translation."

5 For scholarship that casts doubt on the depiction of eighteenth-century emperors as literary inquisitors, see Brook, "Censorship," 193–96; and Guy, *Emperor's Four Treasuries.*

6 Ying Zhang, *Confucian Image Politics*; Schneewind, *Shrines to Living Men.*

7 Meyer-Fong, *Building Culture*; Guy, *Emperor's Four Treasuries*; Son, *Writing for Print*; Bian, "Re-Collecting the Glorious Age," 4–5.

8 James Polachek's work anticipated much of the current scholarship. Polachek, *Inner Opium War*; Mosca, *From Frontier Policy*; Han, *After the Prosperous Age*; Rowe, *Speaking of Profit*; Day, *Qing Travelers.*

9 This book focuses on the size and engagement of the audience rather than the quantity and categories of information made available to that audience, as in Mary Elizabeth Berry's important study of "public information" in Tokugawa Japan. In addition, whereas Berry's work interprets the outcome of access to

political information to be the emergence of Japan as a nation, this book focuses on the emergence of modes of critical political consciousness, not the nation as a political entity. See Berry, *Japan in Print*, 34–72; 270.

10 This observation runs contrary to expectations based on the Habermasian model of the public sphere. Nearly thirty years ago, historians of late imperial and modern China lucidly explained the limitations of this European model for application to Chinese society. It seems fitting, therefore, that critical public consciousness would arise via different mechanisms in the Chinese context. See Habermas, *Structural Transformation of the Public Sphere*, 1–56; Rowe, "Public Sphere in Modern China"; Huang, "'Public Sphere'/ 'Civil Society' in China?"

APPENDIX

1 In this book, the term *issue* refers to an individual gazette edition, most commonly bearing a single date. Some publishers released gazettes in two-day increments. Less frequently, gazette issues were dated with longer intervals, most notably the first fifteen days of the year.

2 In addition, reprinted or translated versions of late Qing gazettes can be found in reprint collections and in newspapers like *Shenbao* and in translation in the *North China Herald*. *Dichao*. 120 volumes. Beijing: Beijing Tushuguan Chubanshe, 2004. Volumes 1–7: Xianfeng reign; Volumes 7–22: Tongzhi reign; Volumes 22–120: Guangxu reign (miscellaneous undated items also included in Volume 120); *Jingbao zhaichao,* in *Liu bian Qingdai gao chao ben*. Guangzhou: Guangdong Renmin Chubanshe, 2014. Pts. 283–300; *Jingbao (dibao)*. 163 volumes. Beijing: Quanguo Tushuguan Wenxian Suowei Fuzhi Zhongxin, 2003. Volumes 1–157: Guangxu reign; Volumes 158–163: Xuantong reign. The *North China Herald* also published yearly indexed compilations of translations from the Peking Gazette between 1873 and 1899. See, for example, *Translation of the Peking Gazette for 1876*. Shanghai: *North-China Herald*, 1877.

3 Zhang and Han, *Zhongguo yinshua shu*, 79–80.

4 Xiao, "Xu," in *Yongxian lu*.

5 See the writings of Cyr Contancin in the *Lettres édifiantes* and the transcribed gazettes collected by the Propaganda Fide.

6 Li Zhen, "Xu," in *Benchao tibo gong'an*.

7 BnF, Bréquigny 10.

8 BL, Peking Gazette Collection, 1841/7.

9 Rutgers University Library has a file of gazettes from 1833 in its catalog, but these appear to have been lost.

BIBLIOGRAPHY

ABBREVIATIONS IN NOTES AND BIBLIOGRAPHY

BL	British Library
BL, IOR	British Library, India Office Records
BnF	National Library of France (Bibliothèque nationale)
FHA, LFZZ	First Historical Archives, File Copies of Grand Council Memorials (Lufu Zouzhe)
FHA, ZPZZ	First Historical Archives, Imperially Rescripted Palace Memorials (Zhupi Zouzhe)
KMZZ	Zhongguo Diyi Lishi Dang'an Guan, ed. *Kangxi chao manwen zhupi zouzhe quanyi.* 4 vols. Beijing: Zhongguo Shehui Kexue Chubanshe, 1996.
NGDK	Grand Secretariat Archives (Neige Daku)
NPM, GZD	National Palace Museum, Qing Palace Memorials (Gongzhong Dang)
NPM, JJD	National Palace Museum, Palace Memorial Archive (Junji Dang)
QSL	*Qing Veritable Records* (Qing shilu). Beijing: Zhonghua Shuju, 1986. Cited as *QSL-Reign*, juan: page (date). Reign abbreviations can be found in the Chronology of Major Dynasties and Qing Reign Periods in the front of this book.
SOAS, CWM/LMS	School of Oriental and African Studies, London Missionary Society Archives
TNA, FO	Foreign Office Archives, British National Archives, Kew

ARCHIVAL COLLECTIONS

For a chronologically arranged overview of gazette collections, see the appendix.

Academia Sinica (Taipei)
Grand Secretariat Archive
Ministry of Foreign Affairs (Waiwu Bu) Archive
Zongli Yamen Archive

Bibliothèque nationale (Paris)
Chinese Manuscript Collection
Papers of Louis-Georges de Bréquigny

British Library (London)
India Office Records
Peking Gazette Collection

British National Archives (Kew)
Foreign Office Archives

First Historical Archives (Beijing)
Archive of Edicts and Deliberations (Shangyu Dang)
File Copies of Grand Council Memorials (Lufu Zouzhe)
Imperially Rescripted Palace Memorials (Zhupi Zouzhe)
Register of Documents as They Come to Hand (Suishou dengji)

National Palace Museum (Taipei)
Grand Council Archive (Junji Dang)
Palace Archive (Gongzhong Dang)

University of London School of Oriental and African Studies (London)
London Missionary Society Archive

SELECTED NEWSPAPERS AND JOURNALS

Beiyang Gazette (Beiyang guanbao). Tianjin, 1902–07.
Canton Press and Price Current. Canton, 1835–44.
Canton Register. Canton, 1827–43.
China Mail. Hong Kong, 1845–1911.
Chinese Progress (Shiwu bao). Shanghai, 1896–98.
Chinese Repository. Canton, 1832–51.
Indo-Chinese Gleaner. Malacca, 1817–22.
North China Herald. Shanghai, 1850–1940.
Shenbao. Shanghai, 1872–1949.

PUBLISHED PRIMARY AND SECONDARY SOURCES

Ai Junchuan. "*Tizou shijian* bu shi la ban yinshua pin—jian tan 'Qingdai shiyong la ban yinshua' shuofa yiju bu zu." *Beijing yinshua xueyuan xuebao* no. 6 (2009): 11–13.

Alcock, Rutherford. "The *Peking Gazette*." *Fraser's Magazine* (1873): 245–56.

Altman, Albert A. "The Press." In *Japan in Transition: From Tokugawa to Meiji*, edited by Marius B. Jansen and Gilbert Rozman, 231–47. Princeton, NJ: Princeton University Press, 1988.

Amiot, Jean-Joseph-Marie et al. *Mémoires concernant l'histoire, les sciences, les arts, les moeurs, les usages, etc., des Chinois, par les missionnaires de Pékin*. 15 vols. Paris: Nyon, 1776–91.

Ayao, Hoshi. "Transportation in the Ming Dynasty." *Acta Asiatica* 38 (1980): 1–30.

Aylmer, Charles, ed. "The Memoirs of H. A. Giles." *East Asian History* 13/14 (1997): 1–90.

Banno, Masataka. *China and the West, 1858–1861: The Origins of the Tsungli Yamen*. Cambridge, MA: Harvard University Press, 1964.

Bartlett, Beatrice S. *Monarchs and Ministers: The Grand Council in Mid-Ch'ing China, 1723–1820*. Berkeley: University of California Press, 1991.

Bastid-Bruguière, Marianne. "Currents of Social Change." In *Cambridge History of China*. Vol. 11, Part 2, *Late Ch'ing, 1800–1911*, edited by John K. Fairbank and Kwang-Ching Liu, 535–602. Cambridge, UK: Cambridge University Press, 1980.

Bayly, C. A. *Empire and Information: Intelligence Gathering and Social Communication in India, 1780–1870*. Cambridge, UK: Cambridge University Press, 1999.

Belsky, Richard. *Localities at the Center: Native Place, Space, and Power in Late Imperial Beijing*. Cambridge, MA: Harvard University Asia Center, 2005.

Berg, Maxine. *Luxury and Pleasure in Eighteenth-Century Britain*. Oxford: Oxford University Press, 2005.

Berry, Mary Elizabeth. *Japan in Print: Information and Nation in the Early Modern Period*. Berkeley: University of California Press, 2006.

Bian, He. "Re-collecting the Glorious Age: Yang Fuji and the Disciplining of *Zhaodai Congshu*, 1772–1844." *Late Imperial China* 40, no. 1 (2019): 1–41.

Binchun, comp. *Ge guo riji huibian*. Lidai riji congchao 142. Beijing: Xueyuan Chubanshe, 2006.

Bosmans, Henri, ed. "Les lettres annuelles de la vice-province de la Compagnie de Jésus en Chine, année 1669." *Annales de la Société d'Émulation de Bruges* 62 (1912): 15–61.

Britton, Roswell S. *The Chinese Periodical Press, 1800–1912*. Shanghai: Kelly and Walsh, 1933.

Brokaw, Cynthia J. *Commerce in Culture: The Sibao Book Trade in the Qing and Republican Periods*. Cambridge, MA: Harvard University Asia Center, 2007.

Brokaw, Cynthia J., and Kai-wing Chow. *Printing and Book Culture in Late Imperial China*. Berkeley: University of California Press, 2005.

Brook, Timothy. "Censorship in Eighteenth-Century China: A View from the Book Trade." *Canadian Journal of History* 23, no. 2 (1988): 177–96.

———. "Communications and Commerce." In *The Cambridge History of China*, Vol. 8, edited by Denis C. Twitchett and Frederick W. Mote, 579–707. Cambridge, UK: Cambridge University Press, 1998.

———. *The Confusions of Pleasure: Commerce and Culture in Ming China*. Berkeley: University of California Press, 1998.

———. "Edifying Knowledge: The Building of School Libraries in Ming China." *Late Imperial China* 17, no. 1 (1996): 93–119.

———. *The Troubled Empire: China in the Yuan and Ming Dynasties*. Cambridge, MA: Belknap Press, 2010.

Budgell, Eustace, ed. *The Bee: Or Universal Weekly Pamphlet: Containing Something to Hit Every Man's Taste and Principles*. 9 vols. London: W. Burton, 1733–35.

Cassel, Pär. *Grounds of Judgment: Extraterritoriality and Imperial Power in Nineteenth-Century China and Japan*. Oxford: Oxford University Press, 2012.

Censer, Jack R. *The French Press in the Age of Enlightenment*. New York: Routledge, 1994.

Chang, Michael G. *A Court on Horseback: Imperial Touring and the Construction of Qing Rule, 1680–1785*. Cambridge, MA: Harvard University Asia Center, 2007.

Chang, Te-Ch'ang (see also under Zhang Dechang). "The Economic Role of the Imperial Household in the Ch'ing Dynasty." *Journal of Asian Studies* 31, no. 2 (1972): 243–73.

Chen, Li. *Chinese Law in Imperial Eyes: Sovereignty, Justice, and Transcultural Politics*. New York: Columbia University Press, 2015.

———. "Legal Specialists and Judicial Administration in Late Imperial China, 1651–1911." *Late Imperial China* 33, no. 1 (2012): 1–54.

Chen Guanguo and Li Baotai, comp. *Ganquan xian xu zhi*. 1810. Airusheng Zhongguo Fangzhi Ku Database.

Chen Qingnian. *Wuxu yihai jianwen lu*. In *Qingting wuxu chaobian ji: Wai san zhong*. Edited by Su Jizu. Guilin: Guangxi Shifan Daxue Chubanshe, 2008.

Chia, Lucille. *Printing for Profit: The Commercial Publishers of Jianyang, Fujian (11th–17th Centuries)*. Cambridge, MA: Harvard University Asia Center, 2002.

"China. Edict against Christianity." *Missionary Journal* (January 1813): 18.

Chŏng, Ŭn-suk. *Xiang Yuanbian zhi shu hua shoucang yu yishu*. Taibei: Wen Shi Zhe Chubanshe, 1984.

Chow, Kai-wing. *Publishing, Culture, and Power in Early Modern China*. Stanford: Stanford University Press, 2004.

Ch'ü, T'ung-tsu. *Local Government in China under the Ch'ing*. Cambridge, MA: Harvard University Asia Center, 1962.

Chuang Chi-fa. *Gugong dang'an shuyao*. Taibei: Guoli Gugong Bowuyuan, 1983.

———. *Qingdai zouzhe zhidu*. Taibei: Guoli Gugong Bowuyuan, 1979.

Clossey, Luke. *Salvation and Globalization in the Early Jesuit Missions*. Cambridge, UK: Cambridge University Press, 2008.

Coates, P. D. "Documents in Chinese from the Chinese Secretary's Office, British Legation, Peking, 1861–1939." *Modern Asian Studies* 17, no. 2 (1983): 239–55.

———. *The China Consuls: British Consular Officers, 1843–1943*. Oxford: Oxford University Press, 1988.

Cole, James H. *Shaohsing: Competition and Cooperation in Nineteenth-Century China*. Tucson: University of Arizona Press, 1986.

Cooley, James C., Jr. *T. F. Wade in China: Pioneer in Global Diplomacy, 1842–1882*. Leiden: Brill, 1981.

Courant, Maurice. *Bibliographie coréene: Tableau littéraire de la Corée*. 3 vols. Paris: E. Leroux, 1894–97.

———. *Catalogue des livres chinois, coréens, japonais, etc*. 3 vols. Paris: E. Leroux, 1900–1912.

Crossley, Pamela Kyle. "The *Dayi juemi lu* and the Lost Yongzheng Philosophy of Identity." *Crossroads* 5 (2012): 63–80.

———. *A Translucent Mirror: History and Identity in Qing Imperial Ideology*. Berkeley: University of California Press, 2002.

Da Qing huidian (Guangxu edition). Beijing, 1899. Scripta Sinica Database.

Da Qing huidian (Yongzheng edition). Beijing, 1725. Scripta Sinica Database.

Da Qing huidian shili (Jiaqing edition). Beijing, 1819. Scripta Sinica Database.

Da Qing huidian shili (Guangxu edition). Beijing, 1899. Scripta Sinica Database.

Da Qing huidian zeli (Qianlong edition). Beijing, 1764. Scripta Sinica Database.

Dai, Yingcong. *The Sichuan Frontier and Tibet: Imperial Strategy in the Early Qing*. Seattle: University of Washington Press, 2010.

Dardess, John W. *Blood and History in China: The Donglin Faction and Its Repression, 1620–1627*. Honolulu: University of Hawai'i Press, 2002.

Davis, John Francis. *The Chinese: A General Description of the Empire of China and Its Inhabitants*. 2 vols. London: Knight, 1844.

———. "Extracts from the Peking Gazette for 1824, Being the Fourth Year of Taoukwang." *Transactions of the Royal Asiatic Society of Great Britain and Ireland* 1, no. 2 (1826): 386–412.

Day, Jenny Huangfu. *Qing Travelers to the Far West: Diplomacy and the Information Order in Late Imperial China*. New York: Cambridge University Press, 2018.

De Mailla, Joseph Anne Marie Moyria. *Histoire générale de la Chine, ou annales de cet empire*. 12 vols. Paris, R. D. Pierres, 1777–84.

De Vivo, Filippo. *Information and Communication in Venice: Rethinking Early Modern Politics*. Oxford: Oxford University Press, 2009.

De Weerdt, Hilde. "'Court Gazettes' and 'Short Reports': Official Views and Unofficial Readings of Court News." *Hanxue yanjiu* 27, no. 2 (2009): 167–200.

———. *Information, Territory, and Networks: The Crisis and Maintenance of Empire in Song China*. Cambridge, MA: Harvard University Asia Center, 2015.

Dehergne, Joseph. "Une grande collection: Mémoires concernant les Chinois (1776–1814)." *Bulletin de l'École française d'Extrême-Orient* 72, no. 1 (1983): 267–98.

Delury, John Patrick. "Despotism Above and Below: Gu Yanwu's *Record of Daily Learning* on Power, Money and Mores." PhD diss., Yale University, 2007.

Dennerline, Jerry. *The Chia-ting Loyalists: Confucian Leadership and Social Change in Seventeenth-Century China*. New Haven: Yale University Press, 1981.

Ding Jinjun. "Qing mo gedi kaishe wenbao ju shiliao." *Lishi dang'an* no. 2 (1999): 54–60.

———. "Wan Qing chuangban baozhi shiliao (1–3)." *Lishi dang'an* nos. 2–4 (2000).

Ditmanson, Peter. "Imperial History and Broadening Historical Consciousness in Late Ming China." *Ming Studies* 71 (2015): 23–40.

Dooley, Brendan, ed. *The Dissemination of News and the Emergence of Contemporaneity in Early Modern Europe*. Surrey, UK: Ashgate, 2010.

Dooley, Brendan, and Sabrina A. Baron, eds. *The Politics of Information in Early Modern Europe*. London: Routledge, 2001.

Du Halde, Jean-Baptiste. *Description géographique, historique, chronologique, politique, et physique de l'empire de la Chine et de la Tartarie chinoise*. 4 vols. Paris: P.-G. Le Mercier, 1735.

Du Yu. *Yuanmu riji*. Lidai riji congchao 88. Beijing: Xueyuan Chubanshe, 2006.

Dunstan, Helen. *Conflicting Counsels to Confuse the Age: A Documentary Study of Political Economy in Qing China, 1644–1840*. Ann Arbor: Center for Chinese Studies, University of Michigan, 1996.

Edgren, Sören. "The Weng Family Rare Book Collection." *East Asian Library Journal* 7, no. 2 (1994): 72–132.

Elliott, Mark C. "The Manchu-Language Archives of the Qing Dynasty and the Origins of the Palace Memorial System." *Late Imperial China* 22, no. 1 (2001): 1–70.

———. *The Manchu Way: The Eight Banners and Ethnic Identity in Late Imperial China*. Stanford: Stanford University Press, 2002.

Elman, Benjamin A. *A Cultural History of Civil Examinations in Late Imperial China*. Berkeley: University of California Press, 2000.

Endlicher, Stephen. *Übersicht der chinesischen, mandschouischen, japanischen und koreanischen Bücher der k.k. Hof-Bibliothek in Wien*. Vienna: Beck, 1837.

Esherick, Joseph W. *The Origins of the Boxer Uprising*. Berkeley: University of California Press, 1987.

Fairbank, John King. *Trade and Diplomacy on the China Coast: The Opening of the Treaty Ports, 1842–1854*. Cambridge, MA: Harvard University Press, 1953.

Fairbank, John King, and S. Y. Teng. "On the Transmission of Ch'ing Documents." *Harvard Journal of Asiatic Studies* 4, no. 1 (1939): 12–46.

———. "On the Types and Uses of Ch'ing Documents." *Harvard Journal of Asiatic Studies* 5, no. 1 (1940): 1–71.

Fan, T. C. "Chinese Fables and Anti-Walpole Journalism." *Review of English Studies* 25, no. 98 (1949): 141–51.

Fang Hanqi. "Qingdai Beijing de minjian baofang yu jingbao." *Xinwen xue yanjiu* no. 4 (1990): 205–20.

———. *Zhongguo xinwen shiye tongshi*. 2 vols. Beijing: Zhongguo Renmin Daxue Chubanshe, 1992.

Fang Yurun. *Xinglie riji huiyao*. Lidai riji congchao 57–58. Beijing: Xueyuan Chubanshe, 2006.

Fang Zongcheng. *Wu Zhuru xiansheng nianpu*. Qing ren nianpu xilie 2. Beijing: Beijing Tushuguan Chubanshe, 2006.

"February Meeting." *Proceedings of the Massachusetts Historical Society* 9, no. 3 (March 1867): 469–82.

Feng, Naixi. "Mushroom Cloud over the Northern Capital: Writing the Tianqi Explosion in the Seventeenth Century." *Late Imperial China* 41, no. 1 (2020): 71–112.

Feng Erkang. *Yongzheng zhuan*. Taibei: Taiwan Shangwu, 2014.

Fenster, Mark. *The Transparency Fix: Secrets, Leaks, and Uncontrollable Government Information*. Stanford: Stanford University Press, 2017.

Feyel, Gilles. "Gazette de France." In *Dictionnaire des journaux, 1600–1789*, Vol. 1, edited by Jean Sgard, 443–49. Paris and Oxford: Voltaire Foundation, 1989.

Figdor, Peter. "Newspapers and Their Regulation in Early Meiji Japan, 1868–1883." *Papers on Japan* no. 6 (1972): 1–44.

Fisher, Michael H. "The Office of Akhbār Nawīs: The Transition from Mughal to British Forms." *Modern Asian Studies* 27, no. 1 (1993): 45–82.

Fitzgerald, Devin. "Research Note: Between Paper and Wood, or the Manchu Invention of the *Dang'an*." *Saksaha* 13 (2015): 75–80.

Foreign Relations of the United States. University of Wisconsin Digital Collection. http://digital.library.wisc.edu/1711.dl/FRUS.FRUS1864p1.

Fujiwara, Gideon. "Channeling the Undercurrents: Fūsetsudome, Information Access, and National Political Awareness in Nineteenth-Century Japan." *Journal of Japanese Studies* 43, no. 2 (2017): 319–54.

"Gazette chinoise." *Journal Asiatique* (Series 2) 12 (1833): 567–73.

"Gazette chinoise (suite et fin)." *Journal Asiatique* (Series 2) 13 (1834): 377–79.

"Gazettes de l'empire de la Chine." *Journal Asiatique* (Series 1) 11 (1827): 239–52.

Ge Gongzhen. *Zhongguo baoxue shi*. Beijing: Zhongguo Xinwen Chubanshe, 1926.

Gentz, Natascha. "From News, *Xinwen*, to New Knowledge, *Xinxue*: Newspapers as Sources for Early Modern Chinese Encyclopaedias." In *Chinese Encyclopaedias of New Global Knowledge (1870–1930)*, edited by Milena Doleželová-Velingerová and Rudolf G. Wagner, 55–83. Springer: Berlin, 2014.

———. "Useful Knowledge and Appropriate Communication: The Field of Journalistic Production in Late Nineteenth-Century China." In *Joining the Global Public: Word, Image, and City in Early Chinese Newspapers, 1870–1910*, edited by Rudolf G. Wagner, 47–104. Albany: State University of New York Press, 2007.

Ghobrial, John-Paul A. *The Whispers of Cities: Information Flows in Istanbul, London, and Paris in the Age of William Trumbull*. Oxford: Oxford University Press, 2013.

Goldman, Andrea S. *Opera and the City: The Politics of Culture in Beijing, 1770–1900*. Stanford: Stanford University Press, 2012.

Golvers, Noël. "The Earliest Examples of Chinese Characters Printed in the Southern Low Countries (Leuven, 1672; Antwerp, 1683)." *De Gulden Passer* 94, no. 2 (2016): 319–33.

———. *François de Rougemont, S. J., Missionary in Ch'ang-shu (Chiang-nan): A Study of the Account Book (1674–1676) and the Elogium.* Leuven: Leuven University Press, 1999.

———. *Letters of a Peking Jesuit: The Correspondence of Ferdinand Verbiest SJ (1623–1688), Revised and Expanded.* Leiden: Brill, 2017.

———. *Libraries of Western Learning for China: Circulation of Western Books between Europe and China in the Jesuit Mission (ca. 1650–ca. 1750).* Vol. 1. Leuven: Ferdinand Verbiest Institute, 2012.

Gong Rufu. "Lüe lun Zhongguo gudai guanzhen de zhengzhi zhihui." *Zhongguo Renmin daxue xuebao* 19, no. 1 (2006): 150–55.

Gongwen chengyu. Beijing: Juzhen Tang, 1889.

Goodrich, L. Carrington, and Zhaoying Fang, eds. *Dictionary of Ming Biography, 1368–1644.* 2 vols. New York: Columbia University Press, 1976.

Green, Abigail. "Intervening in the Public Sphere: German Governments and the Press, 1815–1870." *Historical Journal* 44, no. 1 (March 2001): 155–75.

Gu Yanwu. *Tinglin shi wenji.* 4 vols. Shanghai: Shangwu Yinshu Guan, 1922.

Guoli gugong bowoyuan tushu wenxian chu, ed. *Gongzhong dang Yongzheng chao zouzhe.* 75 vols. Taibei: Guoli Gugong Bowuyuan, 1982–1988.

Guy, R. Kent. *The Emperor's Four Treasuries: Scholars and the State in the Late Ch'ien-lung Era.* Cambridge, MA: Harvard University Press, 1987.

———. *Qing Governors and Their Provinces: The Evolution of Territorial Administration in China, 1644–1796.* Seattle: University of Washington Press, 2010.

Habermas, Jürgen. *The Structural Transformation of the Public Sphere: An Inquiry into a Category of Bourgeois Society.* Translated by Thomas Burger. Cambridge, MA: MIT Press, 1991.

Halsey, Stephen R. *Quest for Power: European Imperialism and the Making of Chinese Statecraft.* Cambridge, MA: Harvard University Press, 2015.

Han, Seunghyun. *After the Prosperous Age: State and Elites in Early Nineteenth-Century Suzhou.* Cambridge, MA: Harvard University Asia Center, 2016.

Handover, P. M. *A History of the London Gazette, 1665–1965.* London: H. M. Stationery Office, 1965.

Harris, Bob. *Politics and the Rise of the Press: Britain and France, 1620–1800.* London: Routledge, 1996.

Harris, Lane J. *The Peking Gazette: A Reader in Nineteenth-Century History.* Leiden: Brill, 2018.

———. "The Post Office and State Formation in Modern China, 1896–1949." PhD diss., University of Illinois Urbana-Champaign, 2012.

Harrison, Henrietta. *Interpreters: China's Changing Knowledge of the West from the Macartney Embassy to the Opium War.* Unpublished manuscript.

———. *The Man Awakened from Dreams: One Man's Life in a North China Village, 1857–1942.* Stanford: Stanford University Press, 2005.

———. Newspapers and Nationalism in Rural China 1890–1929." *Past & Present,* no. 166 (2000): 181–204.

Hayes, James. "Specialists and Written Materials in the Village World." In *Popular*

Culture in Late Imperial China, edited by David Johnson, Andrew Nathan, and Evelyn Rawski, 75–111. Berkeley: University of California Press, 1985.

He Changling and Wei Yuan, eds. *Qing jingshi wenbian*. 3 vols. Beijing: Zhonghua Shuju, 1992.

Heald, David. "Varieties of Transparency." In *Transparency: The Key to Better Governance?*, edited by Christopher Hood and David Heald, 25–43. Oxford: Oxford University Press, 2006.

Heijdra, Martin J. "Technology, Culture and Economics: Movable Type versus Woodblock Printing in East Asia." In *Higashi Ajia shuppan bunka kenkyū: "Niwatazumi,"* edited by Akira Isobe, 223–40. Tokyo: Nigensha, 2004.

Hirth, Friedrich. *Notes on the Chinese Documentary Style*. Shanghai: Kelly & Walsh, 1909.

Ho, Ping-ti. *The Ladder of Success in Imperial China: Aspects of Social Mobility, 1868–1911*. New York: Columbia University Press, 1962.

Hong Liangji. *Hong Beijiang quan ji*. Wuchang: Hubei Guan Shuchu, 1889.

Hsia, Florence C. *Sojourners in a Strange Land: Jesuits and Their Scientific Missions in Late Imperial China*. University of Chicago Press, 2009.

Hsia, R. Po-chia. "Jesuit Survival and Restoration in China." In *Jesuit Survival and Restoration: A Global History, 1773–1900*, edited by Robert A. Maryks and Jonathan Wright, 245–61. Leiden: Brill, 2015.

Hu Juqing. *Geng fu riji*. Lidai riji congchao 24–27. Beijing: Xueyuan Chubanshe, 2006.

Huang, Pei. *Autocracy at Work: A Study of the Yung-cheng Period, 1723–1735*. Bloomington: Indiana University Press, 1974.

Huang, Philip C. C. *Civil Justice in China: Representation and Practice in the Qing*. Stanford: Stanford University Press, 1998.

———. "'Public Sphere'/ 'Civil Society' in China?: The Third Realm Between State and Society." *Modern China* 19, no. 2 (1993): 216–40.

Huang Liuhong. *Fuhui quanshu*. Hefei: Huangshan Shushe, 1997.

Huang Qing zouyi. Beijing: Guoshi Guan, Jiaqing reign.

Huang Zhuoming. *Zhongguo gudai baozhi tanyuan*. Beijing: Renmin Ribao Chubanshe, 1983.

Huang Zongxi. *Hongguang shilu chao*. In *Huang Zongxi quanji*. Hangzhou: Zhejiang Guji Chubanshe, 1986.

Huard, Pierre, and Ming Wong. "Les enquêtes françaises sur la science et la technologie chinoises au XVIIIe siècle." *Bulletin de l'École française d'Extrême-Orient* 53, no. 1 (1966): 137–226.

Huc, Évariste-Régis. *L'Empire chinois*. Paris: L'imprimerie impériale, 1854.

Hucker, Charles O. "Governmental Organization of the Ming Dynasty." *Harvard Journal of Asiatic Studies* 21 (1958): 1–66.

Huffman, James L. *Creating a Public: People and Press in Meiji Japan*. University of Hawai'i Press, 1997.

Huizhong, comp. *Qinding taigui*. Beijing: Beijing Chubanshe, 1998.

Hummel, Arthur W., ed. *Eminent Chinese of the Ch'ing Period (1644–1912)*. 2 vols. Washington, DC: US Government Printing Office, 1944.

Hung, Ho-fung. "Orientalist Knowledge and Social Theories: China and the European Conceptions of East-West Differences from 1600 to 1900." *Sociological Theory* 21, no. 3 (2003): 254–80.

Huo Yanfang and Lu Dongqing. "Gong Zizhen dang'an sixiang yanjiu." *Dang'an xue yanjiu* no. 4 (2015): 124–28.

Iakhontov, K. S., and Iu. L. Krol. *Kitaĭskie rukopisi i ksilografy Publichnoĭ biblioteki: sistematicheskiĭ katalog.* St. Petersburg: Russian National Library, 1993.

Ichiko, Chuzo. "Political and Institutional Reform, 1901–11." In *Cambridge History of China,* Vol. 11, Part 2, edited by John K. Fairbank and K. C. Liu, 375–415. Cambridge, UK: Cambridge University Press, 1980.

Imbault-Huart, Camille. "Le Journal et le Journalisme en Chine." *Bulletin de la société de géographie commerciale de Paris* 15 (1892–93): 37–65.

Imperial Maritime Customs, ed. *Treaties, Conventions, etc., between China and Foreign States.* 2 vols. Shanghai: Inspectorate General of Customs, 1908.

Infelise, Mario. "News Networks between Italy and Europe." In *The Dissemination of News and the Emergence of Contemporaneity in Early Modern Europe*, edited by Brendan Dooley, 51–68. Burlington, VT: Ashgate, 2010.

Irwin, Richard Gregg. "Notes on the Source of de Mailla, Histoire Generale de la Chine." *Journal of the Hong Kong Branch of the Royal Asiatic Society* 14 (1974): 92–100.

Ji Yun, et al. *Qinding lidai zhiguan biao.* Wenyuan ge siku quanshu 601–2. Taipei: Taiwan Shangwu, 1986.

Ji Zengyun. *Zhejiang tongzhi.* 1735. Airusheng Zhongguo Fangzhi Ku Database.

Jiang Yasha, ed. *Qingmo guanbao huibian.* 78 vols. Beijing: Xinhua Shudian, 2006.

Jiang Yihua and Zhang Ronghua, eds. *Kang Youwei quanji.* 12 vols. Beijing: Zhongguo Renmin Daxue Chubanshe, 2007.

Jingbao (dibao). 163 vols. Beijing: Quanguo Tushuguan Wenxian Suowei Fuzhi Zhongxin, 2003.

Johnson, Matthew D. "Beneath the Propaganda State: Official and Unofficial Cultural Landscapes in Shanghai, 1949–1965." In *Maoism at the Grassroots: Everyday Life in China's Era of High Socialism*, edited by Jeremy Brown and Matthew D. Johnson, 199–229. Cambridge, MA: Harvard University Press, 2015.

Jones, Susan Mann, and Philip A. Kuhn. "Dynastic Decline and the Roots of Rebellion." In *The Cambridge History of China*, Vol. 10, edited by John K. Fairbank, 107–62. Cambridge, UK: Cambridge University Press, 1978.

Joo, Hyun-ho. "Remaking a Tributary Relationship: The Representation of Chosŏn Korea in the *Jingbao.*" *Journal of Asian History* 45, no. 1/2 (2011): 119–33.

Judge, Joan. *Print and Politics: "Shibao" and the Culture of Reform in Late Qing China.* Stanford: Stanford University Press, 1997.

Karasawa, Yasuhiko. "From Oral Testimony to Written Records in Qing Legal Cases." In *Thinking with Cases: Specialist Knowledge in Chinese Cultural History*, edited by Charlotte Furth, Judith T. Zeitlin, and Ping-chen Hsiung, 101–24. Honolulu: University of Hawai'i Press, 2007.

Kaske, Elisabeth. "Fundraising Wars: Office Selling and Interprovincial Finance in Nineteenth-Century China." *Harvard Journal of Asiatic Studies* 71, no. 1 (2011): 69–141.

———. "Metropolitan Clerks and Venality in Qing China: The Great 1830 Forgery Case." *T'oung Pao* 98, no. 1 (2012): 217–69.

———. "The Price of an Office: Venality, the Individual, and the State in 19th Century China." In *Metals Monies, and Markets in Early Modern Societies: East Asian and Global Perspectives*, edited by Thomas Hirzel and Nanny Kim, 279–304. Berlin: LIT Verlag, 2008.

Kelly, Thomas Edward. "The Anti-Christian Persecution of 1616–1617 in Nanking." PhD diss., Columbia University, 1971.

Kim, Ho-dong. *Holy War in China: The Muslim Rebellion and State in Chinese Central Asia, 1864–1877*. Stanford: Stanford University Press, 2004.

King, Frank H. H., and Prescott Clarke. *A Research Guide to China-Coast Newspapers, 1822–1911*. Cambridge MA: Harvard University Press, 1965.

Kishimoto Mio. *Min-Shin kōtai to Kōnan shakai: 17-seiki Chūgoku no chitsujo mondai*. Tokyo: Tokyo Daigaku Shuppankai, 1999.

———. "'Rekineki' ni miru Shinsho chihō shakai no seikatsu." *Shigaku zasshi* 95, no. 6 (1986): 53–77.

Kong Xiangji. *Qing ren riji yanjiu*. Guangzhou: Guangdong Renmin Chubanshe, 2008.

Kong Zhengyi. "Qingdai dibao yanjiu." Master's thesis, Zhongguo Renmin Daxue, 2011.

Koopmans, Joop W., ed. *News and Politics in Early Modern Europe (1500–1800)*. Leuven: Peeters, 2005.

Kuhn, Philip A. *Rebellion and Its Enemies in Late Imperial China: Militarization and Social Structure, 1796–1864*. Cambridge, MA: Harvard University Press, 1970.

———. *Soulstealers: The Chinese Sorcery Scare of 1768*. Cambridge, MA: Harvard University Press, 1990.

Kwong, Luke S. K. *A Mosaic of the Hundred Days: Personalities, Politics, and Ideas of 1898*. Cambridge, MA: Harvard University Press, 1984.

Kyle, Chris R. "Monarch and Marketplace: Proclamations as News in Early Modern England." *Huntington Library Quarterly* 78, no. 4 (2015): 771–87.

Landry-Deron, Isabelle. *La preuve par la Chine: La "Description" de J.-B. Du Halde, Jésuite, 1735*. Paris: Editions de l'Ecole des hautes études en sciences sociales, 2002.

Le Gobien, Charles, et al. *Lettres édifiantes et curieuses, écrites des missions étrangères*. 34 vols. Paris: N. Leclerc, 1707–1776.

———. *Lettres édifiantes et curieuses, écrites des missions étrangères, Nouvelle édition*. 26 vols. Paris: J.G. Merigot, 1780–1783.

Lee, Leo Ou-fan, and Andrew Nathan. "The Beginnings of Mass Culture: Journalism and Fiction in the Late Ch'ing and Beyond." In *Popular Culture in Late Imperial China*, edited by David Johnson, Andrew Nathan, and Evelyn Rawski, 360–95. Berkeley: University of California Press, 1985.

Li, Han. "News, Public Opinions, and History: Fiction on Current Events in Seventeenth-Century China." PhD diss., University of California, Irvine, 2009.

Li Bin. *Tangdai wenming yu xinwen chuanbo*. Beijing: Zhongguo Renmin Daxue Chubanshe, 2014.

Li Boyuan. *Officialdom Unmasked*. Translated by T. L. Yang. Hong Kong: Hong Kong University Press, 2001.

Li Ciming. *Yue man tang riji*. 18 vols. Yangzhou: Guangling Shushe, 2004.

———. *Yue man tang riji bubian*. 4 vols. Taipei: Wenguang Tushu Gongsi, 1965.

Li Lüyuan. *Qilu deng*. Beijing: Zhonghua Shuju, 2004.

Li Siyi. "Qingmo 10 nian guanbao huodong gaimao." *Xinwen yanjiu ziliao*, no. 3 (1991): 127–44.

Li Zhen. *Benchao tibo gong'an*. Beijing: Rongjin Tang, 1720.

———. *Dingli quanbian*. Beijing: Rongjin Tang, 1715.

Li Zhifang. *Li Wenxiang gong zouyi*. 1702.

Lin, Manhoung. *China Upside Down: Currency, Society, and Ideologies, 1808–1856*. Cambridge, MA: Harvard University Asia Center, 2006.

Lin Yuanqi. *Dibao zhi yanjiu*. Taibei: Hanlin Chubanshe, 1977.

Lin, Yutang. *History of the Press and Public Opinion in China*. Chicago: University of Chicago Press, 1936.

Lin Zexu. Li Yuandu, comp. *Lin Wenzhong gong zheng shu*. Preface dated 1851.

Liu, Alan P. *Communications and National Integration in Communist China*. Berkeley: University of California Press, 1971.

Liu, Kwang-ching. "Education for Its Own Sake: Notes on Tseng Kuo-fan's Family Letters." In *Education and Society in Late Imperial China, 1600–1900*, edited by Benjamin A. Elman and Alexander Woodside, 76–108. Berkeley: University of California Press, 1994.

Liu Guilin. "Qingdai neige silun bu." *Wenwu* no. 1 (1990): 60–65.

Liu Wenhua. "Jiaqing ershisi nian wang gong dachen tanting guan shi an dang'an." *Lishi dang'an* no. 2 (2016): 40–54.

Liu Wenpeng. "Titang kao." *Qingshi yanjiu* no. 4 (2007): 87–91.

Liu Yongqiang. "Ming-Qing dibao yu wenxue zhi guanxi." In *Beijing daxue bai nian guoxue wencui, wenxue juan*, edited by Xie Maosong, 558–71. Beijing: Beijing Daxue Chubanshe, 1998.

Liubu chengyu. Beijing: Wensheng Tang, 1751.

Lu Dunji. *Panghuang qilu: Wan Qing mingshi Li Ciming*. Beijing: Shehui Kexue Wenxian Chubanshe, 2012.

Lü Xiaoxian. "You guan Qingdai dichao de sange wenti." *Qingshi yanjiu* no. 1 (2000): 91–96.

Lui, Adam Yuen-chung. "Censor, Regent and Emperor in the Early Manchu Period (1644–1660)." *Papers on Far Eastern History* 17 (1978): 81–102.

Macauley, Melissa A. *Social Power and Legal Culture: Litigation Masters in Late Imperial China*. Stanford: Stanford University Press, 1998.

Magone, Rui. "Once Every Three Years: People and Papers at the Metropolitan Examination of 1685." PhD diss., Freien Universität Berlin, 2001.

Man mingchen zhuan. 6 vols. Taipei: Mingwen Shuju, 1985.

Mann, Susan. *Local Merchants and the Chinese Bureaucracy, 1750–1950*. Stanford: Stanford University Press, 1987.

Marat, Jean-Paul. *Plan de Législation sur les Matieres Criminelles.* Amsterdam: Chez Barthelemiulam, 1779.

McDermott, Joseph. "The Ascendance of the Imprint in China." In *Printing and Book Culture in Late Imperial China*, edited by Cynthia J. Brokaw and Kai-wing Chow, 55–104. Berkeley: University of California Press, 2005.

McMahon, Daniel. "Dynastic Decline, Heshen, and the Ideology of the Xianyu Reforms." *Tsing Hua Journal of Chinese Studies* 38, no. 2 (2008): 231–55.

McNicholas, Mark. *Forgery and Impersonation in Imperial China: Popular Deceptions and the High Qing State*. Seattle: University of Washington Press, 2016.

Meadows, Thomas Taylor. *Desultory Notes on the Government and People of China, and on the Chinese Language.* London: Allen, 1847.

Medhurst, W. H. *Pamphlets Issued by the Chinese Insurgents at Nan-king; to Which is Added a History of the Kwang-se Rebellion [. . .].* Shanghai: Offices of the *North China Herald*, 1853.

Menegon, Eugenio. "Interlopers at the Fringes of Empire: The Procurators of the Propaganda Fide Papal Congregation in Canton and Macao, 1700–1823." *Cross-Currents: East Asian History and Culture Review* 7, no. 1 (2018): 26–62.

———. "*Surinama Tragoedia,* Religious and Political Martyrdom in the Yongzheng Period." Paper presented at Symposium on the History of Christianity in China, Hong Kong, October, 1996.

Metzger, Thomas A. *The Internal Organization of Chʻing Bureaucracy: Legal, Normative, and Communication Aspects.* Cambridge, MA: Harvard University Press, 1973.

Meyer-Fong, Tobie. *Building Culture in Early Qing Yangzhou*. Stanford: Stanford University Press, 2003.

———. "To Know the Enemy: The *Zei qing huizuan,* Military Intelligence, and the Taiping Civil War." *T'oung Pao* 104 (2018): 384–423.

———. *What Remains: Coming to Terms with Civil War in 19th Century China.* Stanford: Stanford University Press, 2013.

Michael, William Henry. *A Catalogue of the Exhibit of the Department of State at the Pan-American Exposition, Buffalo, 1901.* Washington, DC: Government Printing Office, 1901.

Millstone, Noah. *Manuscript Circulation and the Invention of Politics in Early Stuart England.* Cambridge, UK: Cambridge University Press, 2016.

Millward, James A., Ruth W. Dunnell, Mark C. Elliott, and Philippe Forêt, eds. *New Qing Imperial History: The Making of Inner Asian Empire at Qing Chengde.* New York: Routledge, 2004.

Milne, William. *A Retrospect of the First Ten Years of the Protestant Mission to China.* Malacca: Anglo-Chinese Press, 1820.

Mittler, Barbara. "Domesticating an Alien Medium: Incorporating the Western-Style Newspaper into the Chinese Public Sphere." In *Joining the Global Public:*

Word, Image, and City in Early Chinese Newspapers, 1870–1910, edited by Rudolf G. Wagner, 13–46. Albany: State University of New York Press, 2007.

———. *A Newspaper for China? Power, Identity, and Change in Shanghai's News Media, 1872–1912*. Cambridge, MA: Harvard University Asia Center, 2004.

Mokros, Emily. "Communication, Empire, and Authority in the Qing Gazette." PhD diss., Johns Hopkins University, 2016.

———. "Documentary Authority." In *Information: A Historical Companion*, edited by Ann Blair, Paul Duguid, Anja-Silvia Goeing, and Anthony Grafton, 413–16. Princeton, NJ: Princeton University Press, 2021.

———. "Reading the Guides, Directories, Manuals, and Anthologies of Liulichang." *East Asian Publishing and Society* 7, no. 2 (2017): 127–66.

———. "Reconstructing the Imperial Retreat: Politics, Communications, and the Yuanming Yuan under the Tongzhi Emperor, 1873–4." *Late Imperial China* 33, no. 2 (2012): 76–118.

———. "Spies and Postmen: Communications Liaisons and the Evolution of the Qing Bureaucracy." *Frontiers of History in China* 14, no. 1 (2019): 19–50.

Moll Murata, Christine. *State and Crafts in the Qing Dynasty (1644–1911)*. Amsterdam: Amsterdam University Press, 2018.

Mosca, Matthew. *From Frontier Policy to Foreign Policy: The Question of India and the Transformation of Geopolitics in Qing China*. Stanford: Stanford University Press, 2013.

Mossman, Samuel. "The Peking Gazette." *Leisure Hour* (1865): 119–22.

Muffat, Karl August. *Die königliche Hof- und Staats-Bibliothek in München*. Munich: 1832.

Mungello, David E. *The Great Encounter of China and the West, 1500–1800*. Lanham, MD: Rowman & Littlefield, 2009.

Mustonen, Juha. *The World's First Freedom of Information Act: Anders Chydenius' Legacy Today*. Kokkola, Finland: Anders Chydenius Foundation, 2006.

Na Silu. *Qingdai zhongyang sifa shenpan zhidu*. Taibei: Wenshizhe Chubanshe, 1992.

Naquin, Susan. *Peking: Temples and City Life, 1400–1900*. Berkeley: University of California Press, 2000.

Needham, Joseph, and Tsien Tsuen-Hsuin. *Science and Civilisation in China*. Vol. 5, *Chemistry and Chemical Technology*. Part 1, *Paper and Printing*. Cambridge, UK: Cambridge University Press, 1985.

Ocko, Jonathan. "The British Museum's Peking Gazette." *Ch'ing-shih wen-t'i* 2, no. 9 (1973): 35–49.

"Official Reports from Different Parts of the Chinese Empire." Canton: Printed by Order of the Select Committee, 1815.

Ōki Yasushi. *Minmatsu Kōnan no shuppan bunka*. Tokyo: Kenbun Shuppan, 2004.

Ono Kazuko. "*Banri teishō* to *Banri soshō*." *Tōyōshi kenkyu* 39, no. 4 (1981): 667–86.

Osawa Akahiro. "Sūēden ōritsu toshokan no kanseki ni tsuite." *Gengō, Bunka, Shakai* 2 (2004): 161–201.

Osterhammel, Jürgen. Robert Savage, trans. *Unfabling the East: The Enlightenment's Encounter with Asia*. Princeton, NJ: Princeton University Press, 2018.

Pan Tianzhen. "Qianlong, Jiaqing jian suo yin ribao 'Tizou shijian' de faxian." *Wenwu* (1992): 82–91.

Pan Xianmo. "Qingchu de yulun yu chaobao." *Xinwen yanjiu ziliao* (1981): 245–62.

Park, Nancy E. "Corruption in Eighteenth-Century China." *Journal of Asian Studies* 56, no. 4 (1997): 967–1005.

Patterson, Don D. "The Journalism of China." *University of Missouri Bulletin* 23, no. 34 (1922): 3–89.

Peabody, Andrew P. *Memoir of Charles Burroughs, D. D.* Cambridge: MA: Press of J. Wilson and Son, 1871.

Peacey, Jason. *Print and Public Politics in the English Revolution.* Cambridge, UK: Cambridge University Press, 2013.

Percy, Thomas. *Hao Kiou Choaan, or The Pleasing History.* London: R. and J. Dodsley, 1761.

Perdue, Peter C. *China Marches West: The Qing Conquest of Central Eurasia.* Cambridge, MA: Belknap Press, 2005.

Peterson, Willard J. "The Life of Ku Yen-Wu (1613–1682)." *Harvard Journal of Asiatic Studies* 28 (1968): 114–56.

———. "The Life of Ku Yen-Wu (1613–1682)." *Harvard Journal of Asiatic Studies* 29 (1969): 201–47.

Pettegree, Andrew. *The Invention of News: How the World Came to Know about Itself.* New Haven: Yale University Press, 2014.

Platt, Stephen R. *Autumn in the Heavenly Kingdom: China, the West, and the Epic Story of the Taiping Civil War.* New York: Alfred A. Knopf, 2012.

———. *Provincial Patriots: The Hunanese and Modern China.* Cambridge, MA: Harvard University Press, 2007.

Polachek, James M. *The Inner Opium War.* Cambridge, MA: Harvard University Asia Center, 1992.

Pong, David. "The Kwangtung Provincial Archives at the Public Record Office of London: A Progress Report." *Journal of Asian Studies* 28 (1968): 139–43.

Popkin, Jeremy D. *News and Politics in the Age of Revolution: Jean Luzac's "Gazette de Leyde."* Ithaca, NY: Cornell University Press, 1989.

Porter, David. *The Chinese Taste in Eighteenth-Century England.* Cambridge, UK: Cambridge University Press, 2010.

Porter, Francis Knowles, and J. L. McCracken. *From Belfast to Peking, 1866–1869: A Young Irishman in China.* Dublin: Irish Academic Press, 1996.

Porter, Jonathan. *Tsêng Kuo-Fan's Private Bureaucracy.* Berkeley: Center for Chinese Studies, University of California, 1972.

"Proceedings of the Royal Asiatic Society of Great Britain and Ireland." *Asiatic Journal* (January 1826): 67.

"Proceedings of the Royal Asiatic Society of Great Britain and Ireland." *Asiatic Journal* (February 1826): 223.

"Proceedings of the Royal Asiatic Society of Great Britain and Ireland." *Asiatic Journal* (December 1826): 691.

"Professor Neumanns Sammlungen aus China." *Bayerische Blätter für Geschichte, Statistik, Literatur und Kunst*, April 7, 1832.

Qian Huilu. *Xian gong Tianjian fu jun nianpu*. Qing chu mingru nianpu 4. Beijing: Beijing Tushuguan Chubanshe, 2006.

Qian Yiji, comp. *Bei zhuan ji*. 9 vols. Taipei: Mingwen Shuju, 1985.

———. *Qian Wenduan gong (Chenqun) nianpu*. Taipei: Wenhai Chubanshe, 1973.

Qing wu chao jiancha yushi jishizhong deng tiaochen mizou. Beijing: Quanguo Tushuguan Wenxian Suowei Zhongxin, 2010.

Qingdai wenzi yu dang. Shanghai: Shanghai Shudian, 1986.

Qiu Runxi and Liu Guangsheng, eds. *Zhongguo youyi shiliao*. Beijing: Beijing Hangkong Hangtian Daxue Chubanshe, 1999.

Quesnay, François. *Œuvres économiques et philosophiques*. Paris: Peelman, 1888.

Rankin, Mary Backus. "Alarming Crises/Enticing Possibilities: Political and Cultural Changes in Late Nineteenth-Century China." *Late Imperial China* 29, no. 1S (2008): 40–63.

———. *Elite Activism and Political Transformation in China: Zhejiang Province, 1865–1911*. Stanford: Stanford University Press, 1986.

———. "Some Observations on a Chinese Public Sphere." *Modern China* 19, no. 2 (April 1993): 158–82.

Rawski, Evelyn S. *Early Modern China and Northeast Asia: Cross-Border Perspectives*. Cambridge, UK: Cambridge University Press, 2015.

———. *The Last Emperors: A Social History of Qing Imperial Institutions*. Berkeley: University of California Press, 1998.

Raymond, Joad. *The Invention of the Newspaper: English Newsbooks, 1641–1649*. Oxford: Clarendon Press, 1996.

Reed, Bradly W. *Talons and Teeth: County Clerks and Runners in the Qing Dynasty*. Stanford: Stanford University Press, 2000.

Reed, Christopher A. "Re/Collecting the Sources: Shanghai's *Dianshizhai Pictorial* and Its Place in Historical Memories, 1884–1949." *Modern Chinese Literature and Culture* 12, no. 2 (2000): 44–71.

Rennie, D. F. *Peking and the Pekingese*. Vol. 1. London: John Murray, 1865.

Repnikova, Maria. *Media Politics in China: Improvising Power Under Authoritarianism*. Cambridge, UK: Cambridge University Press, 2017.

Richard, Timothy. *Forty-Five Years in China*. New York: Frederick A. Stokes, 1916.

Roskam, Cole. *Improvised City: Architecture and Governance in Shanghai, 1843–1937*. Seattle: University of Washington Press, 2019.

Rowe, William T. *China's Last Empire: The Great Qing*. Cambridge, MA: Belknap Press, 2009.

———. "Introduction: The Significance of the Qianlong-Jiaqing Transition in Qing History." *Late Imperial China* 32, no. 2 (2011): 74–88.

———. "The Public Sphere in Modern China." *Modern China* 16, no. 3 (1990): 309–29.

———. *Saving the World: Chen Hongmou and Elite Consciousness in Eighteenth-Century China*. Stanford: Stanford University Press, 2001.

———. *Speaking of Profit: Bao Shichen and Reform in Nineteenth-Century China.* Cambridge, MA: Harvard University Asia Center, 2018.

Rydholm, Lena. "China and the World's First Freedom of Information Act: The Swedish Freedom of the Press Act of 1766." *Javnost—The Public* 20, no. 4 (2013): 45–63.

Schäfer, Dagmar. *The Crafting of the 10,000 Things: Knowledge and Technology in Seventeenth-Century China.* Chicago: University of Chicago Press, 2011.

Schimmelpenninck van der Oye, David. *Russian Orientalism: Asia in the Russian Mind from Peter the Great to the Emigration.* New Haven: Yale University Press, 2011.

Schneewind, Sarah. *Shrines to Living Men in the Ming Political Cosmos.* Cambridge, MA: Harvard University Asia Center, 2018.

Schurmann, Franz. *Ideology and Organization in Communist China.* Berkeley: University of California Press, 1977.

Shangwu yinshu guan chuban jiaoke shumu. Shanghai: Commercial Press, 1905.

Shaw, Shiow-jyu Lu. *The Imperial Printing of Early Ch'ing China.* San Francisco: Chinese Materials Center, 1983.

Shen Qiliang. *Da Qing quanshu.* Beijing: Wanyu zhai, 1683. In Digital Collection of Staatsbibliothek zu Berlin. http://resolver.staatsbibliothek-berlin.de/SBB0000317A00000000.

Shen Tongsheng, comp. *Guangxu zhengyao.* Shanghai: Chongyi Tang, 1909.

Shi He, et al, comp. *Zhongguo jindai baokan minglu.* Fuzhou: Fujian Renmin Chubanshe, 1991.

Shi Xiaofeng, ed. *Yun Yuding cheng zhai riji.* 2 vols. Hangzhou: Zhejiang Guji Chubanshe, 2004.

Shi Yuanyuan. *Qingdai qianzhongqi xinwen chuanbo shi.* Fuzhou: Fujian Renmin Chubanshe, 2008.

Shizong xian huangdi shangyu neige. Yingyin wenyuan ge siku quanshu 414–15. Taipei: Taiwan Shangwu Yinshua Guan, 1983.

Shizong xian huangdi yuzhi wenji. Yingyin wenyuan ge siku quanshu 1300. Taipei: Taiwan Shangwu Yinshua Guan, 1983.

Shuck, J. Lewis. *Portfolio Chinensis: Or a Collection of Authentic Chinese State Papers Illustrative of the History of the Present Position of Affairs in China.* F. F. de Cruz: Macao, 1840.

Si, Jia. "Breaking through the 'Jargon' Barrier: Early 19th Century Missionaries' Response on Communication Conflicts in China." *Frontiers of History in China* 4, no. 3 (2009): 340–57.

Silvestre de Sacy, Jacques. *Henri Bertin, dans le sillage de la Chine (1720–1792).* Paris: Éditions Cathasia, 1970.

Simmonds, P. L. "Statistics of Newspapers in Various Countries." *Journal of the Statistical Society of London* 4, no. 2 (1841): 111–36.

Simpson, William. *Meeting the Sun: A Journey All Round the World through Egypt, China, Japan, and California.* London: Longmans, 1874.

Sirén, Osvald. *The Walls and Gates of Peking: Researches and Impressions*. London: John Lane, 1924.

Skinner, G. William. "Introduction: Urban Social Structure in Ch'ing China." In *The City in Late Imperial China*, edited by G. William Skinner, 521–54. Stanford: Stanford University Press, 1977.

Slade, John. *Narrative of the Late Proceedings and Events in China*. Canton: Canton Register, 1839.

Slauter, William. "The Paragraph as Information Technology: How News Traveled in the Eighteenth-Century Atlantic World." *Annales HSS* 67, no. 2 (2012): 253–78.

———. "Periodicals and the Commercialization of Information in the Early Modern Era." In *Information: A Historical Companion*, edited by Ann Blair, Paul Duguid, Anja Goeing, and Anthony Grafton, 128–51. Princeton, NJ: Princeton University Press, 2021.

Smith, Richard J., John K. Fairbank, and Katherine F. Bruner, eds. *Robert Hart and China's Modernization: His Journals, 1863–1866*. Cambridge, MA: Harvard University Asia Center, 1991.

Söderblom Saarela, Mårten. "Manchu and the Study of Language in China (1607–1911)." PhD diss., Princeton University, 2015.

Son, Suyoung. *Writing for Print: Publishing and the Making of Textual Authority in Late Imperial China*. Cambridge, MA: Harvard University Asia Center, 2018.

Soong Chien-cheng. "Zhongyang zhengfu gongbao de qiyuan ji xingzhi." *Jiaoyu ziliao kexue* 18, no. 2 (1980): 99–108.

Spence, Jonathan D. *God's Chinese Son: The Taiping Heavenly Kingdom of Hong Xiuquan*. New York: Norton, 1996.

———. *Treason by the Book*. New York: Penguin Books, 2002.

———. *Ts'ao Yin and the K'ang-Hsi Emperor: Bondservant and Master*. New Haven: Yale University Press, 1966.

Standaert, Nicolas. "Jean-François Foucquet's Contribution to the Establishment of Chinese Book Collections in European Libraries: Circulation of Chinese Books." *Monumenta Serica* 63, no. 2 (2015): 361–424.

Staunton, George Thomas. *Memoirs of the Chief Incidents of the Public Life of Sir George Thomas Staunton*. London: L. Booth, 1856.

———. *Narrative of the Chinese Embassy to the Khan of the Tourgouth Tartars*. London: John Murray, 1821.

Stifler, Susan Reed. "The Language Students of the East India Company's Canton Factory." *Journal of the North-China Branch of the Royal Asiatic Society* 69 (1938): 46–82.

Stockmann, Daniela. *Media Commercialization and Authoritarian Rule in China*. Cambridge, UK: Cambridge University Press, 2014.

Struve, Lynn A. "Chinese Memory Makes a Martyr: The Case of Huang Chunyao (1605–1645)." *History and Memory* 25, no. 2 (2013): 5–31.

———. *The Dreaming Mind and the End of the Ming World*. Honolulu: University of Hawai'i Press, 2019.

———. "The Hsü Brothers and Semiofficial Patronage of Scholars in the K'ang-hsi Period." *Harvard Journal of Asiatic Studies* 42, no. 1 (1982): 231–66.

———. *The Ming-Qing Conflict, 1619–1683: A Historiography and Source Guide.* Ann Arbor, MI: Association for Asian Studies, 1998.

Su, Ching. "The Printing Presses of the London Missionary Society among the Chinese." PhD diss., University of London, 1996.

Su Jiasi and Tan Shaoyuan, comp. *Changsha fu zhi.* 1685. Airusheng Zhongguo Fangzhi Ku Database.

Sun Guangsi. *Sun Guangsi ji.* Jinan: Qilu Shushe, 2014.

Syed, Ameer Ali, and George Woodroffe. *The Law of Evidence Applicable to British India.* 3rd Edition. Calcutta: Thacker, Spink, & Co., 1905.

Taylor, Charles. *Modern Social Imaginaries.* Durham, NC: Duke University Press, 2004.

Thompson, Roger. "New-Style Gazettes and Provincial Reports in Post-Boxer China: An Introduction and Assessment." *Late Imperial China* 8, no. 2 (1987): 80–101.

———. "The Wire: Progress, Paradox, and Disaster in the Strategic Networking of China, 1881–1901." *Frontiers of History in China* 10, no. 3 (2015): 395–427.

Tianbian dichao. Zhihai congshu. Shanghai: Shanghai Datong Shuju, 1935.

Timkovskii, E. F. *Travels of the Russian Mission through Mongolia to China and Residence in Peking in the Years 1820–1821.* 2 vols. London: Longman, 1827.

Todd, Christopher. *Political Bias, Censorship and the Dissolution of the "Official" Press in Eighteenth-Century France.* Lewiston, ME: Mellen Press, 1991.

Translations from the Original Chinese; With Notes. Canton: The Honorable East India Company's Press, 1815.

"Translations from the Original Chinese; with Notes." *Quarterly Review* 13, no. 26 (1815): 409–18.

Tung, Yung-chang. "Confronting the Job Shortage: The Commercialization of Personnel Information in Song China." *Journal of Song-Yuan Studies* 48 (2019): 57–98.

Tuo Xiaotang. *Changshu Weng shi cangshu tulu.* Shanghai: Shanghai Kexue Jishu Wenxian Chubanshe, 2000.

Vittinghoff, Natascha. "Unity vs. Uniformity: Liang Qichao and the Invention of a 'New Journalism' for China." *Late Imperial China* 23, no. 1 (2002): 91–143.

Voltaire. *Essai sur les moeurs et l'esprit des nations.* 2 vols. Paris: Garnier frères, 1963.

Wade, Thomas Francis, trans. *Decree of the Emperor of China: Asking for Counsel, and the Replies of the Administration, 1850–1851, With Other Papers.* London: Harrison, 1878.

———. *Note on the Conditions and Government of the Chinese Empire in 1849.* Hong Kong: China Mail Office, 1850.

———. *Wên-chien tzŭ-erh chi, a Series of Papers Selected as Specimens of Documentary Chinese, Designed to Assist Students of the Language as Written by the Officials of China, In Sixteen Parts, with Key.* 2 vols. London: Trübner, 1867.

———. *Yü-yen tzŭ-erh chi, A Progressive Course Designed to Assist the Student of Colloquial Chinese, As Spoken in the Capital and the Metropolitan Department: In Eight Parts, with Key, Syllabary, and Writing Exercises.* London: Trübner, 1867.

Wagner, Rudolf G. "A Classic Paving the Way to Modernity: The *Ritual of Zhou* in the Chinese Reform Debate since the Taiping Civil War." In *Modernity's Classics*, edited by S. C. Humphreys and R. G. Wagner, 77–99. Springer: Berlin, 2013.

———. "The Early Chinese Newspapers and the Chinese Public Sphere." *European Journal of East Asian Studies* 1, no. 1 (2002): 1–33.

———. "The Free Flow of Communication Between High and Low: The *Shenbao* as Platform for Yangwu Discussions on Political Reform, 1872–1895." *T'oung Pao* 104, no. 1–3 (2018): 116–88.

Wakeman, Frederic E. "The Civil Society and Public Sphere Debate: Western Reflections on Chinese Political Culture." *Modern China* 19, no. 2 (April 1993): 108–38.

———. *The Great Enterprise: The Manchu Reconstruction of Imperial Order in Seventeenth-Century China.* 2 vols. Berkeley: University of California Press, 1985.

Walter, Xavier. *La Troisième Mort des Missions de Chine.* Paris: François-Xavier de Guibert, 2008.

Wang, Chelsea Zi. "Dilemmas of Empire: Movement, Communication, and Information Management in Ming China, 1368–1644." PhD diss., Columbia University, 2017.

———. "More Haste, Less Speed: Sources of Friction in the Ming Postal System." *Late Imperial China* 40, no. 2 (2019): 89–140.

Wang, Hung-tai. "Information Media, Social Imagination, and Public Society during the Ming and Qing Dynasties." *Frontiers of History in China* 5, no. 2 (2010): 169–216.

Wang, Juan. *Merry Laughter and Angry Curses: The Shanghai Tabloid Press, 1897–1911.* Vancouver: University of British Columbia Press, 2012.

Wang, Wensheng. *White Lotus Rebels and South China Pirates: Crisis and Reform in the Qing Empire.* Cambridge, MA: Harvard University Press, 2014.

Wang Bin and Xu Xiushan, eds. *Beijing diming dian.* Beijing: Zhongguo Wenlian Chubanshe, 2008.

Wang Fuzhi. *Chuanshan quanshu.* Changsha: Yuelu Shushe, 2011.

Wang Huizu. *Menghen yulu.* Qingdai minguo cangshujia nianpu 1–2. Beijing: Beijing Tushuguan Chubanshe, 2004.

———. *Shuangjie tang yongxun.* In *Wang Longzhuang xiansheng yishu.* Vol. 6. Shandong Shuju: 1886.

Wang Qingyun. *Jinghua guan riji.* 2 vols. Beijing: Shangwu Yinshu Guan, 2015.

Wang Wensi. *Wang Anfu nianpu.* Beijing tushuguan cang zhenben nianpu congkan 171. Beijing: Beijing Tushuguan Chubanshe, 1999.

Wang Yuanchong. "Qingdai shixian shu yu Zhongguo xiandai tongyi duo minzu guojia de xingcheng." *Zhongguo shehui kexue* no. 5 (2018): 185–203.

Wang Zengfang and Cheng Guan. *Jinan fu zhi*. 1840. Airusheng Zhongguo Fangzhi Ku Database.

Wang Zhonghan, comp. *Qing shi lie zhuan*. Beijing: Zhonghua Shuju, 1987.

Wang Zhonglin. *Wang Zhonglin riji*. Lidai riji congchao 59–60. Beijing: Xueyuan Chubanshe, 2006.

Wanli dichao. 3 vols. Yangzhou: Jiangsu Guangling Guji Keyinshe, 1991.

Watt, John R. *The District Magistrate in Late Imperial China*. New York: Columbia University Press, 1972.

Wen Qing, et al., comp. *Chouban yiwu shimo*. Scripta Sinica Database.

Weng Lianxi, ed. *Qing neifu keshu dang'an shiliao huibian*. 2 vols. Yangzhou: Guangling Shushe, 2007.

Weng Tonghe. *Weng Tonghe riji*. Edited by Chen Yijie. 6 vols. Beijing: Zhonghua Shuju, 1989.

Wenxian congbian. 2 vols. Taibei: Guofeng Chubanshe, 1964.

Wilkinson, W. H. *"Where Chinese Drive": English Student-Life at Peking*. London: W. H. Allen, 1885.

Will, Pierre-Étienne. *Bureaucracy and Famine in Eighteenth-Century China*. Stanford: Stanford University Press, 1990.

———. "Coming of Age in Shanghai during the Ming-Qing Transition." *Gujin lunheng* 4 (2000): 15–39.

———. *Handbooks and Anthologies for Officials in Imperial China: A Descriptive and Critical Bibliography*. 2 vols. Leiden: Brill, 2020.

———. "La paperasse au secours de l'homme: Communication et militantisme, 1600–1850." *Études chinoises* 13, no. 1–2 (1994): 65–108.

———. Review of *Monarchs and Ministers: The Grand Council in Mid-Ch'ing China, 1723–1820*, by Beatrice S. Bartlett. *Harvard Journal of Asiatic Studies* 54, no. 1 (1994): 313–37.

———. "Views of the Realm in Crisis: Testimonies on Imperial Audiences in the Nineteenth Century." *Late Imperial China* 29, no. 1S (2008): 125–59.

Williams, John R. "Fraud and Inquest in Jiangnan: The Politics of Examinations in Early Qing China." PhD diss., University of California Berkeley, 2005.

Williams, Samuel Wells. *The Middle Kingdom*. 2 vols. New York: C. Scribner's Sons, 1883.

Woodside, Alexander. *Lost Modernities: China, Vietnam, Korea, and the Hazards of World History*. Cambridge, MA: Harvard University Press, 2006.

Wooldridge, Chuck. *City of Virtues: Nanjing in an Age of Utopian Visions*. Seattle: University of Washington Press, 2015.

Wright, Mary Clabaugh. *The Last Stand of Chinese Conservatism: The T'ung-Chih Restoration, 1862–1874*. Stanford: Stanford University Press, 1957.

Wu, Eugene. "Mary Clabaugh Wright: A Memorial." *China Quarterly* 43 (1970): 134–35.

Wu, Silas H. L. *Communication and Imperial Control in China: Evolution of the Palace Memorial System, 1693–1735*. Cambridge, MA: Harvard University Press, 1970.

———. "The Memorials System of the Ch'ing Dynasty (1644–1911)." *Harvard Journal of Asiatic Studies* 27 (1967): 7–75.

———. *Passage to Power: K'ang-hsi and His Heir Apparent, 1661–1722*. Cambridge, MA: Harvard University Press, 1979.

Wu, Yulian. *Luxurious Networks: Salt Merchants, Status, and Statecraft in Eighteenth-Century China*. Stanford: Stanford University Press, 2017.

Wu Changyuan. *Chenyuan shilüe*. 1788.

Wu Jing. *Wu Songpu fu jun ziding nianpu*. Beijing tushuguan cang zhenben nianpu congkan 117. Beijing: Beijng Tushuguan Chubanshe, 1999.

Wu Jingzi. *The Scholars*. Translated by Gladys Yang. New York: Columbia University Press, 1993.

Wu Yue. *Zhongguo de juanna zhidu yu shehui*. Nanjing: Jiangsu Renmin Chubanshe, 2013.

Xianzheng biancha guan zouding baolü li ce. Guangzhou: Guangdong Guangya Shuju, 1910.

Xiao Shi. *Yongxian lu*. Beijing: Zhonghua Shuju, 1997.

Xu Ke. *Qing bai leichao*. 13 vols. Beijing: Zhonghua Shuju, 1984.

Xu Daling. *Qingdai juanna zhidu*. Taipei: Wenhai Chubanshe, 1977.

Xu Qi. *Yue xue riji*. Lidai riji congchao 136. Beijing: Xueyuan Chubanshe, 2006.

Xu Zonggan. *Si wei xin zhai zhuren ziding nianpu*. Beijing tushuguan cang zhenben nianpu congkan 148. Beijing: Beijing Tushuguan Chubanshe, 1999.

Yan, Zinan. "Routine Production: Publishing Qianlong's Poetry Collections." *T'oung Pao* 103, no. 1–3 (2017): 206–45.

Yanchang. *Nian shi jilüe*. Beijing tushuguan cang zhenben nianpu congkan 173. Beijing: Beijing Tushuguan Chubanshe, 1999.

Yang Guozhen. *Yang Guozhen Hailiang shi zi xu nianpu*. Beijing tushuguan cang zhenben nianpu congkan 137–38. Beijing: Beijing Tushuguan Chubanshe, 1999.

Yang Jingting. *Dumen jilüe*. Zhongguo fengtu zhi congkan 14. Yangzhou: Guangling Shushe, 2003.

Yang Lili. *Tianlai chuan han: Mingdai Jiaxing Xiang Yuanbian jiazu de jiancang yu yishu*. Taibei: Shitou Chuban Gufen Youxian Gongsi, 2012.

Yang Yuliang. "Qingdai zhongyang guanzuan tushu faxing qianxi." *Gugong bowuyuan yuankan* no. 4 (1993): 88–92.

Yao Fushen. "You guan dibao jige wenti de tansuo." *Xinwen yanjiu ziliao* (1981): 107–24.

Yao Tinglin. *Linian ji*. In *Qingdai riji huichao*, 1:39–173. Shanghai: Shanghai Renmin Chubanshe, 1982.

———. *Shang pu jingli biji*. Beijing tushuguan cang zhenben nianpu congkan 79. Beijing: Beijing Tushuguan Chubanshe, 1999.

Yao Yanfu. *Guangxu Linqu xian zhi*. 1884. Airusheng Zhongguo Fangzhi Ku Database.

Ye, Xiaoqing. *The Dianshizhai Pictorial: Shanghai Urban Life, 1884–1898*. Ann Arbor: Center for Chinese Studies, University of Michigan, 2003.

Yin Huiyi. *Yin taifu ren nianpu*. Beijing tushuguan cang zhenben nianpu congkan 89. Beijing: Beijing Tushuguan Chubanshe, 1999.

Yin Yungong. *Zhongguo Mingdai xinwen chuanbo shi*. Chongqing: Zhongqing Chubanshe, 1990.

Yoon, Seungjoo. "Literati-Journalists of the *Chinese Progress* (*Shiwu bao*) in Discord, 1896–1898." In *Rethinking the 1898 Reform Period: Political and Cultural Change in Late Qing China*, edited by Rebecca E. Karl and Peter Zarrow, 48–76. Cambridge, MA: Harvard University Asia Center, 2002.

Yoon, Wook. "Dashed Expectations: Limitations of the Telegraphic Service in the Late Qing." *Modern Asian Studies* 49, no. 3 (2015): 832–57.

———. "The Grand Council and the Communication Systems in the Late Qing." PhD diss., Yale University, 2008.

———. "Prosperity with the Help of 'Villains,' 1776–1799: A Review of the Heshen Clique and Its Era." *T'oung Pao* 98, no. 4/5 (2012): 479–527.

Yu Heng. *Da Qing baolü zhi yanjiu*. Taibei: Taiwan Zhonghua Shuju, 1985.

Yuan Dong. *Shuyin congshuo*. Xuxiu siku quanshu 1137. Shanghai: Shanghai Guji Chubanshe, 2002.

Yuan Shouding. *Tumin lu*. Hefei: Huangshan Shushe, 1997.

Zelin, Madeleine. *The Magistrate's Tael: Rationalizing Fiscal Reform in Eighteenth-Century Ch'ing China*. Berkeley: University of California Press, 1984.

Zeng Guofan. *Qiu que zhai riji leichao*. Xuxiu siku quanshu 559. Shanghai: Shanghai Guji Chubanshe, 1995.

Zhang, Lawrence. "A Legacy of Success: Office Purchase and State-Elite Relations in Qing China." *Harvard Journal of Asiatic Studies* 73, no. 2 (2013): 259–97.

Zhang, Ting. "Buying and Selling Law Books in Qing Beijing." *East Asian Publishing and Society* 7, no. 2 (2017): 94–126.

———. *Circulating the Code: Print Media and Legal Knowledge in Qing China*. Seattle: University of Washington Press, 2020.

Zhang, Ying. *Confucian Image Politics: Masculine Morality in Seventeenth-Century China*. Seattle: University of Washington Press, 2016.

Zhang Chen. *Richu riji*. Lidai riji congchao 105. Beijing: Xueyuan Chubanshe, 2006.

Zhang Dechang. *Qingji yige jingguan de shenghuo*. Hong Kong: Zhongwen Daxue, 1970.

Zhang Deyi. *Liu shu qi: Fu Qi shu qi weicheng gao*. Changsha: Yuelu Shushe, 2016.

Zhang Jinglu. *Zhongguo jindai chuban shiliao, er bian*. Beijing: Zhonghua Shuju, 1957.

Zhang Xiumin and Han Qi. *Zhongguo yinshua shu de faming ji qi yingxiang*. Shanghai: Shanghai Renmin Chubanshe, [1958] 2009.

Zhao Chunying. "Qingdai 'la ban yinshua' shizheng zongshu." *Yinshua shi yanjiu* no. 7 (2013): 98–101.

Zhao Erxun, et al. *Qing shi gao*. Taibei: Dingwen, 1981.

Zhao Ying. "19 shiji xi ren dui jingbao de yijie chuanbo yu Zhong-Ying guanxi." PhD diss., Fudan University, 2015.

Zhongguo di'er lishi dang'an guan, ed. *Zhengfu gongbao*. Shanghai: Shanghai Shudian, 1988.

Zhongguo diyi lishi dang'an guan, ed. *Kangxi qijuzhu*. 3 vols. Beijing: Zhonghua Shuju, 1984.

———. *Qianlong chao junjichu suishou dengji dang*. 46 vols. Guilin: Guangxi Shifan Daxue Chubanshe, 2000.

———. *Qianlong chao shangyu dang*. 18 vols. Guilin: Guangxi Shifan Daxue Chubanshe, 2008.

———. "Qianlong nianjian wei Sun Jiagan zougao an shiliao (1–8)." *Lishi dang'an* (1998–99).

———. *Yongzheng chao hanwen zhupi zouzhe huibian*. 10 vols. Nanjing: Jiangsu Guji Chubanshe, 1989.

———. *Yongzheng chao manwen zhupi zouzhe quanyi*. 2 vols. Hefei: Huangshan Shushe, 1998.

———. *Yongzheng chao neige liu ke shi shu – li ke*. 83 vols. Guilin: Guangxi Shifan Daxue Chubanshe, 2002.

Zhongyang yanjiu yuan jindai shi yanjiusuo, ed. *Daoguang Xianfeng liang chao chouban yiwu shimo buyi*. Taibei: Zhongyang Yanjiuyuan Jindaishi Yanjiusuo, 1966.

Zhu Chuanyu, ed. *Li Ciming zhuanji ziliao*. 2 vols. Taibei: Tianyi Chubanshe, 1979.

———. *Songdai xinwen shi*. Taibei: Zhongguo Xueshu Zhuzuo Jiangzhu Weiyuan Hui, 1967.

———. *Xian Qin Tang Song Ming Qing chuanbo shiye lunji*. Taipei: Taiwan Shangwu Yinshuguan, 1988.

Zhu Qingqi and Bao Shuyun. *Xing'an huilan*. Taibei: Chengwen Chubanshe, 1968.

Zhu Saihong. "Qing wanqi Wuyingdian xiushu chu 'xiu shu' yu 'fei xiu shu' zhineng de xiaozhang—ji yu Qing gong dang'an de kaocha." *Zhongguo chuban shi yanjiu* no. 2 (2015): 137–55.

INDEX

Locators in italics refer to figures and maps.

CPSIA information can be obtained
at www.ICGtesting.com
Printed in the USA
BVHW082237130321
602452BV00004B/6

9 780295 748795